BERLIN

INSIGHT *City* GUIDES

Edited by Wieland Giebel
Designed by Hans Höfer and V. Barl
Translated by Jane-Michael Rushmer and Wendy Reed

APA
PUBLICATIONS

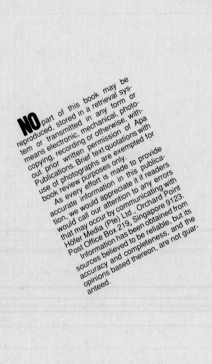
BERLIN

Third Edition
© **1992 APA PUBLICATIONS (HK) LTD**
All Rights Reserved
Printed in Singapore by Höfer Press Pte. Ltd

ABOUT THIS BOOK

The Wall has gone; once again Berlin is the capital of Germany and one of the world's most important international metropolises. At last the frontier-town feeling has disappeared, and the era in which West Berlin was just a walled community without a hinterland has ended. Everything is changing. Politicians and administrators are now faced with the huge task of coming to terms with the colossus, with its 3.2 million inhabitants and surrounding countryside.

As the Wall fell and the world celebrated, Apa Publications, which maintains an editorial office in Germany, was well-placed to respond with a guidebook that would be bang up to date. You are holding the result: this volume is a totally revised *Insight Cityguide: Berlin*, completely rewritten to take account of the city's new horizons in the 1990s. As reunification proceeded apace, its editors had to assess lasting effects in a time of change, pose the latest questions and simultaneously supply the basic information which readers expect from an Insight Guide.

The Writers

The task of finding suitable writers in both Eastern and Western sectors of the city, and of drawing the threads together, was undertaken by **Wieland Giebel**. As a baby, Giebel got stuck in Berlin – literally; as his family was fleeing from East to West, his pram became jammed in the doors of the underground train. Helpful Berliners dragged it into the carriage as the train pulled away, whilst his mother remained screaming on the platform. Many years later Giebel entered publishing, founding his own publishing company in 1973. By the end of the 1980s he was working in the editorial team of the daily newspaper *taz* before joining Apa's Munich office. Giebel is also the editor of the Insight Guides to *New Germany* and *Dresden*.

Nobody in Berlin has their finger on the city's pulse more closely than the editorial team of the Berlin magazine *Zitty*, not to mention the journalists working for *taz* and for local radio. They all made valuable contributions to this book.

Arnold Seul of *Zitty*, who has lived in Kreuzberg for many years, describes the southeast. He is a lecturer at the Berlin Free University, as is **Ute Frings**, whose editorial work at *Zitty* has led her to specialise in day-to-day politics. At the Free University she lectures in post-war history – her subject in this book.

Petra Dubilski of *taz* took over the task of revising much of the historical material in the book, researching in both East and West to do so. A native of Berlin, she has worked continuously, since the Wall fell, on subjects linked to her city. **André Beck** studied for five years in Moscow, becoming an editor with ADN in East Berlin before joining the news department of *taz* in 1990. **Hans-Martin Tillack** is the editor in charge of environmental themes; for many years he has studied the pollution content of the air above Berlin.

Michael Bienert, a Germanicist, philosopher and writer, has studied developments in what is at present the liveliest quarter of the city, the Prenzlauer Berg. As a leader of city guided tours, he knows Berlin like the back of his hand. Bienert was also one of the writers involved in producing the Insight Guides to Germany and Dresden.

Eva Schweitzer, a specialist on houses

Giebel

Dubilski

Tillack

Bienert

and housing, knows the scandal behind every historic building in the city. As a travel editor **Günter Ermlich** is caught up in a perpetual dilemma: should he give away his secret tips about Berlin, or keep quiet for the sake of the environment? He has solved the conflict by preaching the art of gentle tourism.

Annette Leo comes from East Berlin. As a historian, she has been involved in a study of the history of the GDR (40 years is a manageable period!). She is press correspondent of the Bündnis 90 party in the "Red" Town Hall. Finally, **Christoph Busch**, a freelance who works for *taz* and for television, wrote "The People's Dream Factory", about the DEFA, the German Film Company.

Many Berliners know the name of **Hellmut Kotschenreuther** from the literary supplement of the *Tagesspiegel*, the daily newspaper. He has worked as a music and drama critic since 1951.

Michael Ellsässer, a native of Swabia who has made his home on the Spree, writes for the cultural and educational broadcasting department of the SFB. He has observed Berliners with Swabian detachment for many years. Using principles of democratic fairness and historical accuracy, **Anne Worst** has allocated equal importance to the city's twin centres – the Kurfürstendamm and Unter den Linden. She works for various radio programmes. Microphone at the ready, **Sigrid Hoff** regularly undertakes journeys across Berlin for a television series produced by SFB. For this book she travelled through Charlottenburg, Spandau, Wedding and Zehlendorf. **Barry Graves** introduces pop music broadcasts and published the *Dictionary of Rock*.

Two other contributors also have colourful biographies. **Michael Stone** writes on the fall of the Nazi dictatorship. Born in 1922, he grew up in a Jewish family in Berlin before fleeing to England; after a visit to Berlin at the end of the 1960s, he stayed on as a drama critic. **Michael S. Cullen** is a New Yorker who since 1964 has lived and worked as an art dealer in Berlin, where he owns a gallery. Since 1971 he has acted on behalf of Christo, the packaging artist, who hopes to be permitted to wrap up the Reichstag.

The Photographers

As always with Apa guides, great attention has been paid to picking the most stunning photographs of the destination. The majority of the images of the western part of the city were taken by **Günter Schneider**, who, having worked there for many years, knows every nook and cranny of the city. **Erhard Pansegrau** has been a freelance photographer since the end of the 1970s. His work has appeared in many Insight Guides, including *China, Germany* and *The Rhine*.

Virtually all the other photographers are Berlin residents: **David Baltzer,** his American colleague **Michael Hughes** who works for the Sequenz agency, **Sabine** and **Karl-Heinz Kraemer** from Alpha Press, **Harald Hauswald** and **Thomas Sandberg** from Ostkreuz, **Christine Engel, Benno Kraehahn, Kai Ulrich Müller** and **Stefan Maria Rother**.

The book was assembled in Apa's Munich editorial office, under the direction of **Dieter Vogel**. It was translated into English by **Jane-Michael-Rushmer**, **Wendy Reed** and **Susan Sting**, under the direction of **Tony Halliday**, copy-edited by **Marcus Brooke**, and proofread and indexed by **Mary Morton**.

Schweitzer

Hoff

Pansegrau

Vogel

History and People

Places

Maps

TRAVEL TIPS

A Modern Myth

More history and more shock waves have reverberated through the world from Berlin than from virtually any other European metropolis. Ever since its foundation, and more especially since the beginning of this century, Berlin has existed in a permanent state of transition: the seat of an Imperial dynasty became a hotbed of revolution; the arena of the Roaring Twenties gave way to the headquarters of National Socialism; the scene of the greatest devastation in the German Reich was succeeded by a divided city dominated by two dialectically opposed hostile systems. West Berlin was a capitalist oasis, attached to an artificial life-support system and surrounded by a sea of socialism; East Berlin was the show capital, the shop window of socialist achievement. And Berlin itself served as the turn-table between East and West.

It can hardly be claimed that some of the city's shock waves served to enrich the rest of the world. During this century alone, Berlin became the capital from which two world wars were initiated and here, too, the extermination of the Jewish race was planned. Berlin was also the the starting point for the wave of student protest which spread across the West during the 1960s – whilst, across the Wall, mammoth parades were held with red flags waving in celebration of a senile Politburo which had lost its sense of reality.

Berlin is a myth: those who visit often forget that Berlin is actually nothing more than a conglomeration of villages amalgamated into a city in relatively recent times. Berlin can be described as an accumulation of Prussian conservatism whose significance has been artificially imposed.

In the eastern sector of the city, during the SED regime, politicians were wont to make much of Berlin's "Prussian heritage". Most of the buildings from that glorious epoch were only rebuilt in recent years – constructed, like the Palais Ephraim, of concrete behind a pseudo-rococo facade.

Another facet of the Berlin myth is that history and legends are made here almost casually. The only people who find significance in such events are the politicians and those who will not or cannot accept that they are merely a part of everyday life. For the citizens of Berlin, history is only relevant at the moment of crisis; once that is over, they rapidly return to their daily routine. The destruction of the Wall? After a few weeks of jubilation, picnickers could be seen on what until recently had been a barrier of death.

Perhaps herein lies the true attraction of the city: in its ability to fuse historic events with everyday happenings, in its trivialisation of the momentous. As the true Berliner maintains, it is all simply "nothing out of the ordinary."

Preceding pages: fragments of history; the bustle of the Kurfürstendamm; witness to a golden past – Charlottenburg Palace; Alexanderplatz is dominated by the TV tower; an enduring form of transport. Left, a hurdy-gurdy man.

Since 1990, Berlin has no longer been a divided city. After 28 years of separation through Wall and politics, at last "that which belongs together can grow together", as ex-mayor Willy Brandt declared. A few months after the Wall was opened, severed roads and underground lines were relinked. Berliners quickly readjusted to the big-city atmosphere. To meet someone at the Alexanderplatz no longer involves a circuitous route for a resident of Steglitz; people living in Treptow now think nothing of shopping in the Karl-Marx-Strasse in Neukölln, in Berlin's "West End".

And yet East and West Berlin are, in many ways, still two different cities. Barriers continue to exist even though the physical symbol of separation, the Wall, has long since disappeared. The architecture is different: in the West, historic buildings have been largely restored; in the East, functional but ugly concrete blocks predominate, even in the ancient Nikolai Quarter.

And then there is the contrast in the amount of greenness: in the West, there is hardly a street without trees, or at least a few tubs of flowers, whilst in the East the broad avenues which have been laid out with cars in mind are completely lacking in vegetation of any description, quite apart from the acres of soulless car-parks.

The infrastructure of the East grows daily more and more like that of the West. Since the currency reform, its cafés, shops and snack bars not only offer the same goods, but are to be found in the same numbers as on the Kurfürstendamm. However, the rapprochement between Berliners from both sides of the Wall is proving less straightforward. Their roots in two different social systems are evident in the most basic everyday events. Turns of phrase often have different connotations, and misunderstandings are (still) commonplace. Here it is still a case of "them" and "us".

Left, the day the wall came down. **Above**, an interesting mural in Neukölln.

On the periphery: On the map you will find Berlin to the east of the Elbe in the Brandenburg Marches, on about the same latitude as London and the same longitude as Naples. Before Germany was divided at the end of World War II, the capital also lay at the geographical centre of the German Empire founded in 1871. During the post-war years Berlin served as a focal point in another respect: here the world superpowers, Russia and the United States, confronted each other more directly than anywhere else on earth.

A city of parks: Approaching Berlin, the traveller will be surprised to discover how green the city is. The woods and open spaces give way to the sea of houses characteristic of any big city, but no less than 40 percent of the built-up area consists of parks and stretches of water. Even the surroundings are liberally sprinkled with woods and lakes – mostly groundwater reservoirs – which have become once again favourite excursion destinations for the city's residents. The water is sadly polluted. Berlin's three main lakes –

the Tegeler See, the Wannsee and the Müggelsee – are linked by the Spree, which divides into several arms within the metropolitan area, and the Havel, which widens out to form a lake beyond Potsdam.

Since the very beginnings of the city's history both these rivers have played a vital role as highways. They are linked within the city boundaries by a system of canals and also provide access, via other waterways, to all the principal rivers of Europe.

Berlin's area, covering 883 sq. km (340 sq. miles), makes it the largest city in Germany. Its north-south axis measures some 38 km (24 miles), and the east-west axis approxi-

ceased, West Berlin became dependent on settlers from elsewhere. Executives from the Federal Republic were lured to the city by a large number of privileges; guest workers from the poorer countries of Europe were also welcomed – although without these advantages. In East Berlin, which by this time had been transformed into a relatively well-equipped capital city, immigrants from other countries within the "socialist brotherhood", such as Vietnam and Mozambique, were employed as cheap labour. Executives were produced at home through active membership of the SED.

In view of its location far from all sources

mately 45 km (28 miles). Its present population totals some 3.2 million.

West Berlin's former isolated position and the succession of political crises – the Blockade in 1948, the Khrushchev Ultimatum of 1958 and the construction of the Wall in 1961 – have produced very different effects in the two halves of the city.

The labour market: Before the construction of the Wall, East Berlin lost considerable numbers of its citizens, who emigrated to the western half of the city or used it as a stepping stone to the Federal Republic. Since 1961, when the flow of refugees suddenly

of raw materials, Berlin could not develop primary or heavy industries. Instead, processing and refining industries were established in both sectors of the city. The range of products varied, from cigarettes to light bulbs, and from furniture and tools to complicated production machinery. The principal employer, however, was the civil service. This is a sphere which will expand still further as Berlin grows into its role as capital of a reunited Germany.

Living in the inner city: In spite of the heavy bomb damage, the streets of the former working class districts – Wedding, the

Prenzlauer Berg and Kreuzberg – are still characterized by their old 19th-century tenement houses – usually five-storey buildings with dismal backyards, inadequate sanitation and no comfort. But this, too, is a characteristic of Berlin.

Towns within the borders of the Federal Republic were able to expand beyond their original boundaries, but West Berlin during the era of the Wall had to be particularly sparing in its allocation of building land. Although the environs of East Berlin are dotted with *dachas* – weekend cottages – when it came to providing living accommodation within the city, the socialist town

spite of their landscaping, and full of social tensions. The catchword today is "city repair", as the town planners abandon the futuristic euphoria of the 1960s in an attempt to save the old street layouts and to breathe new life into blighted districts.

Housing shortage: Wrong decisions in the approach to rehabilitation and demolition and omissions in the modernisation of old buildings in the inner city led, during the 1970s, to protest action, occupation of derelict houses and conflict. The Senate of West Berlin immediately undertook a programme designed to renovate unoccupied flats, and supported self-help groups. This resulted in

planners preferred ugly prefabricated units. Most Berliners therefore continue to live in rented accommodation, usually in relatively old buildings.

Of course, some parts of the city are very modern. These include Gropius district in the south, the Märkisches Viertel in the north, the Falkenhagener Feld in the west and Marzahn and Hellersdorf in the east. These dormitory suburbs are faceless concrete jungles, utterly lacking in atmosphere in

Left, a view of the River Havel from the Grunewald Tower. **Above**, soon in the country.

an easing of the short-term situation within the housing market. In East Berlin, before the Wall was demolished, the renovation of old houses was not even considered. Entire districts were in danger of degenerating into housing slums.

Here, too, empty houses, and particularly apartments, were occasionally subject to occupation. People simply took over uninhabited flats and carried out necessary repairs as far as possible, certain that the general indifference of the communal housing administration would ensure that they were left in peace. Once the Wall had gone, young people made a point of demonstratively occupying entire apartment houses. They did so not only in order to acquire a longed-for place of their own, but also – as had already happened in West Berlin – in order to experiment with alternative living arrangements. Funds are still lacking for the restoration of the dilapidated housing areas on the Prenzlauer Berg. The problem is to be tackled with the assistance of the Senate of West Berlin. Exactly how, given the size of the task and the costs involved, remains to be resolved.

A metropolis full of village churches: Berlin's individual districts are much older than the city itself. In its present form, the metropolis

has only existed since 1 October 1920. On that date a "Law governing the creation of a new city community in Berlin" came into force. The state of Prussia welded together seven towns, 59 rural communities and 27 estates, to form a single administrative unit, the city of Berlin. The rural communities and estates had always been effectively part of the metropolitan area.

This move provided the basis for the city's rise to a metropolis of international stature. Six communities formed the heart of the original city: Mitte, Tiergarten, Wedding, Prenzlauer Berg, Friedrichshain and Hallesches Tor, now known as Kreuzberg. After unification Charlottenburg, Köpenick, Lichtenberg, Neukölln, Schöneberg, Spandau and Wilmersdorf, all independent towns until then, retained their names and their imposing town halls.

Other rural communities and estates were united to form a further seven administrative districts, each bearing the name of the most populous village lying within its boundaries: these were Pankow, Reinickendorf, Steglitz, Tempelhof, Treptow, Weissensee and Zehlendorf.

The land reforms of 1920 made Berlin the second-largest city in Europe. During the following years it experienced a short-lived Golden Age as a cultural and intellectual world metropolis, a period which has already acquired the status of a legend. In spite of, or perhaps as a result of the way it grew up, Berlin's districts have retained much of their original small-town characteristics. Witness to these rural origins are the former village churches, many of them dating from the 13th century.

Two centres: Berlin has one further unique feature. The division of the city has resulted in the development of two centres. The traditional heart of the city was the island on the Spree and the magnificent avenue "Unter den Linden" (an avenue of lime trees), which contains most of the monuments from the reign of the Kings of Prussia.

The second centre, the "new West" around the Kurfürstendamm, arose later, during the Empire. The Ku'damm became the metropolitan boulevard par excellence during the 1920s and, after World War II, the heart of the city of West Berlin. It was separated from the original city centre by the Tiergarten and the Wall.

In Berlin, many landmarks occur in duplicate: two Town Halls – the "Red" one and the Schöneberger Rathaus; two favourite meeting places – Alexanderplatz and Breitscheidplatz; and two zoos. And now, one by one, they are to be reduced to a single specimen. But in fact, there is much to be said for this dual existence – in Berlin, whatever happens, one has a choice.

The freight terminal in Moabit.

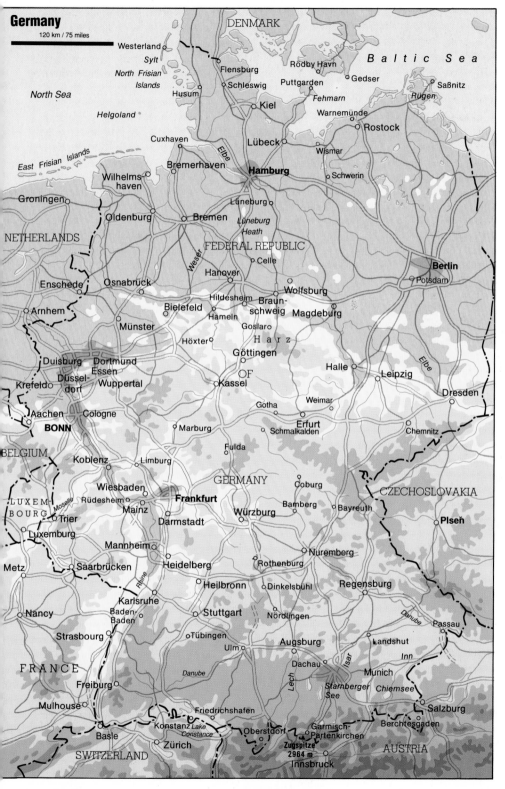

Germany

120 km / 75 miles

DENMARK

Baltic Sea

North Sea

Westerland
Sylt
North Frisian Islands
Flensburg
Rödby Havn
Gedser
Saßnitz
Husum
Schleswig
Puttgarden
Rügen
Helgoland
Kiel
Fehmarn
Warnemünde
Rostock

Cuxhaven
Lübeck
Wismar
East Frisian Islands
Bremerhaven
Schwerin
Wilhelms-haven
Hamburg

Groningen
Oldenburg
Bremen
Lüneburg
Schwerin

NETHERLANDS
Lüneburg Heath

Weser
FEDERAL REPUBLIC
Celle
Berlin
Enschede
Osnabrück
Hanover
Potsdam

Arnhem
Bielefeld
Hildesheim
Braun-schweig
Wolfsburg
Magdeburg

Münster
Hameln
Goslaro
Höxter
H a r z
Göttingen
OF
Halle
Leipzig
Duisburg
Dortmund
Essen
Kassel
Elbe
Krefeld
Düssel-dorf
Wuppertal
Weimar
Dresden
Aachen
Cologne
Gotha
Erfurt
BONN
Marburg
Schmalkalden
Chemnitz

BELGIUM
Fulda
Koblenz
Limburg
GERMANY
Coburg
CZECHOSLOVAKIA
LUXEM-BOURG
Wiesbaden
Rüdesheim
Moselle
Mainz
Frankfurt
Würzburg
Bamberg
Bayreuth
Trier
Darmstadt
Plzeň
Luxemburg
Mannheim
Heidelberg
Rothenburg
Nuremberg
Metz
Saarbrücken
Rhine
Heilbronn
Dinkelsbühl
Regensburg
Karlsruhe
Nancy
Baden-Baden
Stuttgart
Nördlingen
Danube
Passau
Strasbourg
Tübingen
Augsburg
Landshut
Ulm
Inn
F R A N C E
Danube
Dachau
Isar
Munich
Freiburg
Lech
Starnberger See
Chiemsee
Mulhouse
Friedrichshafen
Salzburg
Berchtesgaden
Konstanz *Lake Constance*
Oberstdorf
Garmisch-Partenkirchen
Basle
Zürich
Zugspitze 2964 m
AUSTRIA
SWITZERLAND
Innsbruck

THE TOWN ON THE SPREE

Berlin's 750-year history begins with two separate towns. Lying on adjacent islands in the Spree, the twin settlements of Berlin and Cölln were already closely linked by common economic interests when, at the start of the 14th century, they banded together under a joint municipal administration.

The first settlers probably made their homes on the islands during the last third of the 12th century. Cölln is mentioned in contemporary records for the first time in 1237, with Berlin appearing seven years later. Both received town charters in 1230.

After the unification of the Germanic tribes in the 10th century, Otto the Great extended his empire east of the Elbe as far as the Oder. It was only after a revolt by Slavic tribes, however, that a second military invasion enabled him to bring under permanent German rule the regions east of the Elbe. The region was given the name of the Brandenburg Marches after Brennabor on the Havel, the first Slavic town to be conquered. By 1157 the Imperial Counts of the Ascanian dynasty, who had received the Marches in fief, had taken possession of the Fortress of Spandau and by the middle of the 13th century the entire area occupied by the present-day city of Berlin lay under their sway. Shortly after this, their power extended northwards as far as Pomerania, and in the east into lands beyond the Oder.

Trade and shipping: In those days the Havel-Spree region was an inhospitable, sparsely populated area. Some places were very sandy whilst others were densely forested, broken up by a network of lakes, watercourses and low-lying marshes. The inhabitants of the little Slavic villages grazed their cattle and scratched out a meagre living in their fields in the clearings. Only after the invention of the wheeled plough and iron ploughshare were they able to cultivate the clay soils, a development which played a significant role in the growth and prosperity of Cölln and Berlin. Throughout the entire Middle Ages, other than wood, linen and woollen cloth, rye from the Marches remained the principal trading commodity. Vassal noblemen and knights Templar summoned by the Ascanians built a defensive network of castles across the land and founded new villages. Peasants, craftsmen and merchants were recruited from the Lower Rhine, Flanders and the foothills of the Northern Harz, the original home of the Ascanians.

Unlike Spandau and Köpenick, the two other medieval towns lying within the area occupied by Germany's present capital, the twin cities of Berlin and Cölln, owed their existence to trade. For miles around the ford linking the Spree islands provided the easiest way for carts to cross the river. In addition, their situation gave them control over river traffic. Soon the merchants and boatmen of Berlin had a monopoly not only of the supply of goods to the immediate hinterland, but also of long-distance trade on behalf of the Brandenburg Marches.

With trade came wealth and increasing demands on the part of the aristocracy and merchants. Art and crafts flourished. More permanent housing gradually replaced the thatched-roofed wattle and daub houses; churches and monasteries were built. Magistrates and noblemen acquired land, or entire villages, throughout the neighbourhood.

Compared with the well-established German trading centres on the Rhine and the Danube, Berlin's prosperity at this time must have seemed quite modest. During the Middle Ages the city played virtually no part in the cultural and economic life of Germany. Thus, when the Ascanian dynasty died out, its demise precipitated the collapse of the power of the margraves and consequently of law and order in the province. The Marches, terrorised by highwaymen and bands of robbers, appealed in vain to the emperor. He, however, was beset by problems concerning his own crown and was caught up in a feud with the Pope. Under the leadership of Ber-

Preceding pages: the elegance of Unter den Linden around 1770. **Left**, the Elector Joachim II of Brandenburg (an oil painting from 1562).

lin, the towns decided to take the matter into their own hands. They organised a local militia; there were battles in which first one side and then the other was victorious. There would be no peace until 1411, when Burgrave Frederick of Nuremberg, a member of the Hohenzollern family, became governor and subsequently Elector of the Marches.

The first castle: The arrival of the Hohenzollerns in Brandenburg marks the end of the medieval power struggle among towns, knights and princes within the kingdom of Germania. During the reign of the second Hohenzollern elector a dispute arose in Berlin between the high-handed patrician town

had prevailed until this time. An attempt by the citizens of Berlin to regain their lost civil rights through rebellion ended in failure.

The prince had a city fortress built at Cölln and half a century later, Berlin and Cölln would become royal seats. Knights, officials, merchants and courtiers travelled from the Hohenzollerns' Franconian possessions to take up residence on the Spree.

During the course of the Reformation of 1539 the clergy had their *latifundia* confiscated by the ruler of the day. The city fortress was rebuilt in the Renaissance style; two castles in Grunewald and Köpenick served as hunting lodges. The beginnings of a courtly

council and the burghers, who demanded the right to determine their own affairs. The common people called upon their ruler for assistance, but he took advantage of the opportunity to increase his own authority over the town. Far-reaching decrees interfering with the constitution of the community meant that from this point onwards the administrative council was subject to the will of the prince, who had the right to approve the appointment of councillors and who took over the jurisdiction once more, preventing alliances with other towns and annulling the joint administration of the twin towns which

culture can be seen in the founding of a *cappella*, a royal choir, and in the acquisition of a number of pictures by Lukas Cranach for the royal chapel.

Amongst the bourgeoisie, too, culture and education were making great strides. New schools were being built, a printer's workshop and a chemist were established, and there is the first record of a theatrical performance. In 1617 Berlin's first weekly newspaper made its debut.

Domestic sanitary conditions left much to be desired. There was no municipal refuse collection scheme and in 1576, 4,000 citizens fell victim to the plague. Not until the beginning of the Thirty Years' War did the population reach its old level of 12,000.

The three decades of war between 1618 and 1648 marked a time of great privation for the city, although the actual battles were fought elsewhere. Berlin's wealth was swallowed up by war contributions, general inflation as well as a trade slump and plundering by Swedish and Imperial troops. Thousands of citizens became homeless when one of the Emperor's ministers, fearing an attack by Sweden, had the city suburbs burned to the ground. A magistrates' report dating from this period registers a rising suicide rate.

Berlin had become larger – it now had a polulation of 20,000 – and more beautiful. However, it remained a provincial backwater by comparison with Paris or even with Vienna, which was seven times as big.

The arrival of the Huguenots: A series of shrewd ordinances by the elector brought about a revival of the ruined economy. A tax reform reactivated trade and business, and the construction of the canal linking the Oder with the Spree provided a waterway between Breslau and Hamburg.

The Great Elector's adroit policy of offering asylum to Jews and persecuted French Protestants had a highly favourable effect on

Many Berliners were forced to emigrate. All told, the population dwindled by 6,000 after the beginning of the war.

Friedrich Wilhelm of Brandenburg, later known as the Great Elector, instigated an extensive rebuilding programme for his capital, adding fortifications to protect it against possible attack. Towards the end of his reign, which stretched over almost half a century, a transformation had taken place.

Left, Frederick William, the Great Elector, receives refugees from France. **Above**, Berlin-Cölln in 1729 (an engraving by Peter von der Aa).

economic and cultural development. He gave letters of protection and virtually unrestricted trading rights to 50 wealthy Jewish families who had been expelled from Austria. Their capital, experience and international contacts soon made them a more or less indispensable part of the economic scene. This fact protected them to some extent from envy and growing animosity on the part of their Christian competitors. Inroads were gradually made into the privileges enjoyed by the Jews, who were forbidden initially to built a synagogue. A special taxation system ensured that they were victimised financially, and restrictive regulations passed during in the 18th century resulted in all but the very richest Jews fleeing the country.

Money and economic experience were also brought to Berlin by approximately 5,000 French Huguenots, who found refuge following the revocation of the Edict of Nantes in 1685. Berlin profited from their skills as technicians and craftsmen, acquiring simultaneously a touch of the more sophisticated lifestyle they brought with them from France. The Huguenots founded a number of new industries – silk weaving, and paper and glass manufacture – as well as introducing tobacco as a crop within the Marches.

Academy of Arts was founded in 1696, followed a few years later by the Academy of Sciences, whose first president was the philosopher Gottfried Wilhelm Leibniz.

By cunning, force, marriage and inheritance the Hohenzollerns increased their possessions; and with the acquisition of the Polish duchy of Prussia, their sway extended as far as the Russian frontier. In 1701 the Great Elector's successor demonstrated this new self-confidence by having himself crowned King of Prussia. Berlin became a royal residence.

The master builders Schlüter, Nering and Eosander were responsible for the construc-

Further groups of persecuted Protestants – from the Palatinate, Switzerland, Bohemia and the Salzburg region – were soon flocking to Berlin in considerable numbers. This cosmopolitan atmosphere helped to form the characteristic tolerance and open-mindedness for which Berlin's citizens were once famed.

The city's economic upsurge during the last third of the 17th century had a favourable effect on culture and science. A daily newspaper already existed; a medical college supervised practitioners, and the alchemist Johann Kunckel discovered a procedure for the manufacture of ruby-coloured glass. The

tion of some fine examples of baroque architecture. However, the vast remodelling of the city palace, and the building of the residences of Charlottenburg and Monbijou, as well as the Arsenal, the Academy and the two cathedrals on the Gendarmenmarkt drove the nation to the point of bankruptcy.

Military drill and economy measures: When Friedrich Wilhelm I ascended the throne in 1713, there was no room for further royal extravagance. "Army and Economy" were the twin overriding interests of the "King-Sergeant". He slashed four-fifths of the court maintenance budget. The palace gardens at

Charlottenburg were planted with cabbages, and the pleasure garden was turned into a drill ground. The king regarded art and science (apart from medicine) as unnecessary; the foundation of the *Charité*, which he ordained, was an innovation by virtue of its dual function as research institute and hospital. Furthermore, it was to the "Father of militarism" that Prussia owed the introduction of compulsory education.

In order to be able to finance his well-trained army the king was also concerned about the economic development of his country. At the beginning Berlin suffered considerably under the universal conscription law. Over a period of two years there was a mass exodus of 17,000 people – half of them skilled workers – despite the death penalty which they were thereby risking. The city was eventually excluded from the regulation. From this point new manufacturing industries, mostly suppliers of military equipment, attracted new recruits for the workforce.

Under Friedrich II, who succeeded the "King-Sergeant" in 1740, there was a renaissance of courtly culture and pleasures. An opera house was built at this time, and once again the city was the scene of celebrations, music and plays. The militarism remained, however. Friedrich's wars earned him the nickname "the Great" as well as considerably increasing the size of his kingdom and Prussia became a major European power.

The centre of the Enlightenment: A policy of subvention resulted in the introduction of new industries; the city's population grew by a half over the next two decades. The restructuring of the city centre by Knobelsdorff, Gontard and others began before the war

with the building of the Opera House, the Cathedral and the Roman Catholic Cathedral of St Hedwige. It was now continued in the Gendarmenmarkt complex and reached its apogee in the remodelling of the Lindenallee to form a monumental avenue. Under Friedrich's successor the latter received its magnificent conclusion in the form of the classicist Brandenburg Gate.

At this time, great thinkers like Lessing, Nikolai and Mendelssohn were making their contribution to the literary criticism of the Enlightenment. It was because of them that Berlin acquired its reputation as the German

Left, Frederick the Great inspects the 1st Battalion. Above, the Berlin-Potsdam railway around 1850.

intellectual capital. A century after the first Jew acquired full civil rights in Prussia, Jewish salons became the centres of "witty Berlin". The Romantic era began. Based on French models, nobility and the *haute bourgeoisie* cultivated a new kind of liberal democratic society.

In 1806, during the Napoleonic Wars, both the army and national sovereignty suffered defeat at the battles of Jena and Auerstadt. The French emperor and his troops marched victoriously through the Brandenburg Gate. Two years of occupation followed, giving way to many years of French supremacy. Meanwhile, intense feelings of patriotism were fermenting. Friedrich Jahn, the father of physical education, trained the male youth of Berlin in preparation for the struggle against the oppressors; between 1813 and 1815 their fight for liberation was to be rewarded with victory.

The sentiments of freedom expressed during the French Revolution found an echo in Prussia. The absolute rulers were forced to make concessions. But as the forces of restoration started to regain ground, there came a time of increased repression, denunciations and police terror. In resignation the bourgeoisie retreated into the safety of business and private pleasures.

From 1810 Berlin had been the seat of a university. A succession of important scholars, including Wilhelm von Humboldt, Fichte, Schelling and Hegel, ensured its rapidly growing reputation. After only a few decades its students numbered over 2,000, making it the largest seat of learning in the country.

The first tenement houses: Socially and economically the long reign of Friedrich Wilhelm III (1797–1840) marked the emancipation of the bourgeoisie and the beginning of industrialisation, accompanied by increasing impoverishment of the masses and the emergence of the working class. Whilst Langhans and Schinkel were adorning the royal seat with neo-classical churches and palaces, the age of the tenement house and the backyard had begun in the suburbs. A few years before Friedrich Wilhelm III ascended the throne the first steam engine was commissioned in the Royal Porcelain Factory in Dresden. Two decades later, the first steam-powered boat was sailing on the Spree. Towards the end of the monarch's reign you could even travel by train from Berlin to Potsdam.

Initially, the accession of Friedrich Wilhelm IV aroused great hopes. But social reforms linked to a new constitution did not occur. A loosening of censorship did little to alleviate the situation. The king drew up extravagant plans for the embellishment of his capital, and spent large sums of money persuading aging cultural celebrities to come to Berlin. They included the poets Rückert and Tieck, the philosopher Schelling, and the painter Cornelius. The brothers Grimm, exiled from Göttingen, were offered asylum and a position. Meyerbeer took over the direction of the Opera House. In 1844 Germany's first zoo was inaugurated.

In the meantime, there was no respite from the growing misery of the impoverished masses. Half of Berlin's 400,000 inhabitants was classified as belonging to the lower class. In 1847 the city was obliged to devote 40 percent of its annual budget to charity. On several occasions there was unrest in Prussia, the most violent being the Silesian weavers' riots. When, in the spring of 1848, revolution broke out in Paris and then in Vienna, the middle and working classes of Berlin also took to the streets. The ensuing bloody battles claimed 200 victims, but the revolutionaries were victorious. The king was forced to pay his respects to the corpses as they lay in state on the Schloßplatz.

The dreams of a better future lasted for over six months. They were discussed in democratic clubs and in 150 (!) new newspapers (freedom of the press as well as freedom of assembly had been guaranteed). But nationalists and democrats blocked each other with paralysing political disputes, and in 1848 General Wrangel occupied Berlin at the head of the royal troops. A further period of repression began. The constitution, when eventually approved, made only modest concessions to the liberals whilst cementing the autocratic position of the ruling dynasty.

Right, Wilhelm I, the first German emperor, holds a reception in the "White Hall" of the Berlin palace (painting by A. von Menzel, 1897).

BECOMING A METROPOLIS

During the second half of the 19th century, Berlin became the largest industrial city in Europe after Paris. As early as 1859, Karl Marx, who had studied on the Spree two decades previously, remarked: "People who saw Berlin 10 years ago would not recognise it today. In those days it was a sterile parade ground; now it is the bustling centre of German engineering." The leading concern was the factory of Borsig, the king of steam locomotives. Subsequently to the opening, in 1847, of the "Telegraphic Construction Company" of Siemens and Halske, new avenues were being opened up in the field of electrotechnology. The invention of the dynamo in particular was to prove a significant factor in the city's economic development.

The workers' movement established itself as a counterbalance to the world of capitalist enterprise. Despite a 16-hour working day the proletariat was barely able to eke out an existence in the drab tenement houses. Socialist views found increasing numbers of supporters in the slums to the north and east of the city. In 1863 Ferdinand Lassalle founded the first social democratic workers' organisation, the General Association of German Workers. Berlin became the centre of the trades union movement and increasingly the bastion of the social democratic movement, checked only by Bismarck's persecution of the socialists. In 1875 the General Association of German Workers was amalgamated with the Social Democratic Workers' Party, founded in Eisenach in 1869 by Wilhelm Liebknecht and August Bebel.

Germany's first capital: In the meantime, Prussia had increased its territorial possessions through wars with Denmark and Austria. North of the Main, it now ruled most of Germany between the French frontier to the west and the Russian to the east. With the dissolution of the German Alliance in 1866, Austria stepped out of the political power

struggle within Germany which it had waged for more than a century. Prussia had won the upper hand; the dream of Frederick the Great had come true. In the same year, Berlin became the capital of the North German Alliance which, linked to the southern German states by treaties, represented the last stage on the road to the unification of a Germany not including Austria.

Five years later, the German princes offered the Imperial Crown to the King of Prussia in

the wake of their successful war against France (1870–71) – not out of pure inclination, but because in doing so they were bowing to the gravitational forces of politics and economics, which required a unified nation state. On 18 January 1871, immediately following the victory over France, the Second German Empire was proclaimed in the Hall of Mirrors at Versailles. King Wilhelm I of Prussia (1797–1888) was elected Emperor of Germany. The first Imperial Chancellor was Otto von Bismarck (1815–98), the real force behind the political union. During his period of office (1871–90) he was

Left, lunchtime at the Borsig factory (painting by Hans Baluschek, 1912). **Right,** wretched living conditions in Prenzlauer Berg.

to play an important role in the shaping of European politics from Berlin. Thus the former residential city of the Prussian-Brandenburg monarchy became the capital of Imperial Germany.

The years of expansion: With its 826,000 inhabitants, the nation's new capital was by far the largest city in Germany. Nonetheless, compared with Paris – which was twice the size – or with cosmopolitan London, it still retained a provincial air. After the foundation of the Empire in 1871, however, Germany's economic and industrial expansion was no longer held back by small-state politics. Fuelled by French reparation funds, the

many of the newly established joint-stock companies had no sound basis, or were even fraudulent. Crashes and financial scandals were commonplace in the building and land speculation markets. As it expanded, industry was searching for sites for new factories, whilst the prosperous bourgeoisie wanted plots of land on which to build villas and country houses. A steady stream of new labour converged on Berlin from all corners of the empire. They needed somewhere to live. Mass production tenement houses were built cheaply and quickly. In the rural communities on the edge of the city, land prices rose to 50 times their prewar levels; the

country rapidly made up for lost time. Between 1871 and 1873 Germany experienced the boom years of the *Gründerzeit*, during which the German Empire, having arrived on the scene almost too late, was caught up in the gargantuan economic and technical process of modernisation. Because the links which were forged between the blossoming sciences and the Industrial Revolution took place later than elsewhere on the continent they occurred extremely rapidly. National contracts and the repayment of war loans resulted in large sums of money becoming available on the industrial front. However,

farmers of Wilmersdorf, Schöneberg and Tempelhof were able to retire on their newly acquired wealth.

Land speculation continued to be a profitable business even after the stock market crash of 1873, which was followed by years of depression. There was a chronic housing shortage and building continued apace. The industrial suburbs, the villages and the villa colonies grew ever closer to each other between the Havel and the Spree. Greater Berlin became a reality even before 1920, when the many urban and rural communities, with a population which in the meantime had almost reached the four million mark, were finally joined together as a political and administrative unit.

The rapid transformation of Berlin into the first modern metropolis in Germany at the end of the 19th century reflected the economic prosperity and, for better or for worse, the rise of the German Reich to its new position as a world power. It is an impressive record. The construction of a drainage system lowered the risk of infectious disease, whilst a covered market and a central slaughterhouse improved food supplies. Even traffic problems caused by the rapid expansion were solved by encircling railway and suburban

street lamps and a telephone network with about 50 subscribers. At the turn of the century, horseless carriages and buses began slowly to supersede horse-drawn vehicles. The opening of the first over- and underground railway line in Berlin between the Warschauer Brücke and the Zoological Gardens was celebrated in 1902.

The Wilhelminian Era: Kaiser Wilhelm I died of old age on 18 January 1888. He had allowed his "Iron Chancellor", Bismarck, a fairly free hand in the formation of the new German Empire. And so began what came to be known as the "year of the three Emperors": his successor, Friedrich III, followed

trains, by the construction of wide streets and by a network of horse-drawn trams. In 1879, the year in which the Technical High School (now the Technical University) was founded, Siemens and Halske demonstrated the first electric railway. Only two years later it became part of the public transport system in Lichterfelde.

By this time there were already electric

Left, a parade in front of Emperor Wilhelm II to celebrate the inauguration of the National Monument. **Above**, women demonstrate for the right to vote, 1912.

him to his grave only 99 days later. The next in line was his ambitious and profoundly "Prussian" son, Wilhelm II, who saw a strong chancellor such as Bismarck as an obstacle to his own aims. And so, in March 1890, amidst much bitterness, the latter was forced to resign. The "pilot of German politics" was obliged to leave the ship of state, and the Wilhelminian Era began. It was a period which saw the completion of the transition of Germany from an agricultural to a modern industrial state, with Berlin as the economic and political centre of one of the world's leading imperialistic nations.

The city's rapid economic development and its equally rapid population growth produced a spirit of dynamism and modernity which was to characterise the next decades in spite of the underlying conservatism of the Wilhelminians. The literary scene was revived by an influx of youth and new ideas. Poets, radical thinkers and "cultural gypsies" dreamed of recreating the world through art. The premières of Gerhard Hauptmann's naturalistic plays marked the beginning of a new chapter of German theatrical history. Berlin became a melting pot for all that was new and modern and the list of men and women of letters who lived and worked in the city at least at some stage after the 1890s reads like a litany of modern German literary history. Virtually no name is missing, from Hauptmann and Heinrich Mann to Frank Wedekind, Rainer Maria Rilke, Stefan George and Robert Musil, not to mention the poets of the Expressionist generation – Else Lasker-Schüler, Georg Heym and Gottfried Benn. Even Strindberg spent a longish period in Berlin, as did the Norwegian artist Edvard Munch. The scandal caused by an exhibition of his paintings led, shortly before the turn of the century, to the foundation of the Secessionist Group of artists. Its members, especially Max Liebermann, created an impressionist-realistic form of expression, in opposition to the official school of painting patronised by state and court. A good 10 years later, following the arrival of Dresden's "Brücke" – Kirchner, Heckel, Pechstein etc. – Berlin also became the centre of Expressionist art.

From the turn of the century, the Imperial capital led the rest of the country in virtually every sphere. Berlin's press and its critics set the tone for the Empire. The theatre, under the direction of Max Reinhardt, led the nation. Richard Strauß was engaged as composer and conductor at the National Court Opera; Hans Pfitzner directed the privately-owned "Theater des Westens". The Berlin Philharmonic had already won international fame under first Hans von Bülow and then Arthur Nikisch.

A long list of names, including those of Theodor Mommsen, Rudolf Virchow, Paul Ehrlich, Robert Koch, Max Planck and Albert Einstein, testifies to the significance of Wilhelminian Berlin as a centre of research and teaching in the humanities and, increasingly, in the natural sciences. At the turn of the century, half-a-dozen future Nobel laureates lived in Berlin.

The Kaiser abdicates: The tensions in Europe became more acute during the early years of the 20th century. International confidence dwindled as each country became drawn into the arms race. In 1914 the crisis reached its climax. On 28 June the heir to the Austrian throne was assassinated in Sarajevo. Six weeks later, most of Europe was at war. In a burst of patriotism, German youth left for the front. The military leaders were talking of a six-month fight before victory was theirs. Their estimates were completely wrong. A sea blockade was erected around Germany and soon the world was embroiled in war. Its consequences became increasingly evident in civilian life. Prices rose and a black market developed. In 1915 food was rationed and some items disappeared completely from the shops. During the winter of 1917–18, following a poor potato harvest, famine was rife. Bakers' and butchers' shops in Berlin were raided.

Meanwhile, under the leadership of Karl Liebknecht and Rosa Luxemburg, a group who opposed the war had broken away from the SPD and was agitating for peace. The success of the Russian revolution in 1917 aroused hopes that here, too, the old order could be overturned. Workers and sections of the bourgeoisie continued to press for a negotiated peace. In January 1918, 300,000 workers came out on strike. Military intervention put a brutal end to the rebellion.

During the war years, the fronts of the Central Powers collapsed progressively. In November 1918 there was a naval mutiny in Wilhelmshaven and Kiel, which rapidly spread to other places. A committee of workers and sailors called for a general strike in Berlin; the Kaiser abdicated. On 9 November Philipp Scheidemann, the Social Democrat, proclaimed the first German Republic from the window of the Reichstag.

Right, reading out the mobilisation order, Unter den Linden 31 July 1914.

The events of November 1918 started as a revolution, but were in fact unworthy of the name. "The Kaiser went, but the generals stayed" was Theodor Plivier's oblique explanation of the root of the problem as he described the Kiel mutiny in his novel of personal experience bearing the same title.

Initially, however, the entire country was swept along in a mood of revolutionary ardour. The old order was on the verge of being toppled. Throughout the empire, workers and soldiers formed committees. In many places the red flag fluttered in the breeze above town halls and barracks. A "People's Naval Division" of 3,000 mutinying sailors from Kiel arrived in Berlin. They occupied the imperial palace and the royal stables. Some of the locally garrisoned troops espoused their comrades' cause. The people, tired of war, marched through the streets shouting "Peace, freedom, bread!"

In the face of the popular revolution, the Imperial Chancellor, Prince Max of Baden, handed over the reins of government to Friedrich Ebert, the leader of the SPD. The Social Democrats had the majority of votes in parliament. The socialist workers' movement became the strongest element in what was otherwise a political vacuum. But divisions within the party meant that it was not prepared for this sudden rise to power. The Socialists under Ebert and Heinrich Scheidemann decided to go the way of parliamentary democracy, whilst a splinter group of Independent Socialists campaigned for a reform of the state along revolutionary principles. On the extreme left, the militant Spartacus League believed that the hour had come for a soviet government along the lines of the Russian October Revolution.

Scarcely had Scheidemann announced the birth of the "German Republic" before the cheering crowds in front of the Reichstag building, Karl Liebknecht, the leader of the Spartacists, proclaimed the "Free Socialist Republic of Germany" from a balcony of the Palace. Thus, even on 9 November 1918, it was clear that the split in the German Left was irreconcilable. It was this schism which, 14 years later, was to sound the death knell of the Weimar Republic.

Barricades in the press district: But to return to the beginning. When he fled into exile, the empire that the Kaiser left behind him was chaos. In the centres of industry, demonstrations by starving workers blocked the streets. Wildcat strikes were paralysing the economy. Some two million soldiers came back from the front with the Western Army; many of them lounged around the barracks in disillusionment. One such was an unsuccessful artist and lance-corporal by the name of Adolf Hitler.

Civil war was in the air. The provisional government in Berlin saw the necessity for draconian measures in order to re-establish their authority. For this they turned to troops from the old army, as some units had reformed as so-called volunteer corps following demobilisation.

During the winter of 1918, Berlin's historic city centre resembled a revolutionary army camp. Sailors of the "People's Naval Division" and Red Workers' brigades patrolled the streets. At the end of December Gustav Noske, the Minister of Defence, had the palace forcibly cleared by government troops. There were 67 fatalities. Bloody skirmishes finally escalated into an open power struggle when, on 5 January 1919, a mass demonstration protested against the dismissal of the revolutionary chief of police. The Spartacus League, which in the meantime had been re-christened the German Communist Party (KPD), called for a general strike. Armed Red Front fighters erected barricades by the Brandenburg Gate: the press district, near what later became Checkpoint Charlie, was transformed into a stronghold. Some 3,000 government troops drove the Spartacists out of their bases; the revolution collapsed.

Karl Liebknecht and Rosa Luxemburg,

Left, November Revolution 1918 – mutinous sailors from Kiel have taken over the palace.

the two leaders of the November revolution, went into hiding. On 15 January they were discovered in a flat in Wilmersdorf and brought to the Hotel Eden, the headquarters of the Infantry Division. After interrogation they were assaulted by their guards during their transfer to the Moabit Criminal Court, and subsequently murdered in the Tiergarten park. Rosa Luxemburg's body was thrown into the Landwehr Canal; the killers got off scot-free.

General strike versus military coup: The elections for the National Assembly were held that week. The Social Democrats gained the most votes. The members of parliament re-

spread the lie that in 1919 the front-line forces had only had to cede victory because of treachery from within their ranks. The "stab in the back" legend poisoned the political atmosphere, and in view of the unacceptable terms of the treaty, agitation from the Right fell on fertile soil when it came to those responsible for setting the tone: the civil service, the law, and business and academic circles.

The republic could not rely on public opinion, a fact demonstrated by the "Kapp Putsch" of 13 March 1920. The freedom fighters of the Erhard Brigade returned from their camp at Döberitz to the city; this time they paraded

tired from the restless capital to Weimar. There, on 11 August 1919, they approved the Weimar Constitution. Friedrich Ebert became the President of Germany.

Meanwhile, faced with an ultimatum, the German negotiators acquiesced to the peace terms contained in the Treaty of Versailles. It is difficult to imagine a worse debt of guilt than that placed by the victorious allies on the new republic. The extremists of the Right protested loudly against the "shameful decree"; monarchists and the military were reluctant to admit their own failure. With the words "unconquered on the battlefield" they

behind the black, white and red battle standard and wore swastikas on their steel helmets. The 6,000 soldiers occupied the government district and other strategic points.

Baron Walter von Lüttwitz had been the instigator of the military putsch which declared the constitutional government to be null and void. His man was Wolfgang Kapp, provincial director and arch-conservative official from Eastern Prussia. He was virtually unknown in Berlin.

It was not only the army, but also the workers who saved the republic. The government and the trades unions announced a general strike. Berlin was without water, gas, electricity and telephone. Post offices and banks remained closed. After only four days the spectre of military dictatorship had vanished.

A series of political assassination attempts was attributed to right-wing fanatics from the volunteer corps, including that on the life of Walter Rathenau, the Foreign Minister. He was shot on 24 June 1922 in a street near his villa in Grunewald.

The "Golden Twenties": was the name given, particularly in Berlin, to the years leading up to the great Wall Street Crash of 25 October 1929. In point of fact, the start of the decade

black marketeers and speculators flourished. Only the introduction of the rentenmark in 1923 brought about a period of economic stability.

The Berlin of the Weimar Republic was a city of stark contrasts. The former imperial capital blossomed into a metropolis whose name was mentioned in the same breath as London, Paris and New York. Its population grew between the wars from 3.8 million to 4.3 million. The immediate cause of this rapid expansion was the controversial territorial reform of October 1920, which by a single act increased the city's area thirteenfold. Industry expanded into the outer dis-

was anything but auspicious. The payment of war reparations led to a rapid currency devaluation. The cost of living was exorbitant.

The US dollar, with a 1914 value of 4.20 marks, was worth 7,500 reichsmarks in 1922. One year later, when inflation had reached its peak, the exchange rate had rocketed to 4.2 billion. During the years of mass poverty,

Left, the "Golden Twenties" – a show in the **Admiralspalast** at **Friedrichstrasse Station**. **Above**, the airship *Graf Zeppelin* hovers over **Berlin in 1928**.

tricts. The citizens left the bleak tenements for the green belt communities on the periphery. Public utility companies created model suburban estates such as the Hufeisen settlement in Britz.

During this period, Berlin can lay claim to a number of exemplary achievements in the realm of local government politics. Thanks to the tireless endeavours of Ernst Reuter, the Director of Transport, the Berlin Public Transport Company (BVG) was founded on 1 January 1929. It was responsible for 92 tram routes, 30 bus routes and four underground railway lines. For a fixed price of 20 pfennigs anyone could cross the city in all directions.

The Weimar years gave Berlin its trades fair centre and Tempelhof Airport – the "air crossroads of Europe". The suburban railway was electrified, and the city's countenance was enriched by the architecture of the Bauhaus.

A modern Babylon: Republican Berlin was marked by a previously unknown freedom and cosmopolitanism, as well as by a series of crass social contrasts. Increased awareness brought about by political tensions heightened the senses and consciousness in every aspect of life. Against this background Berlin became the focal point of the arts scene for the entire continent. It was a latter-day Babylon to which flocked men of letters, artists, architects, musicians, film makers and journalists from all over Europe. For them, the "Golden Twenties" was a reality. It was the age of the Charleston and the Shimmy, of jazz, cabaret and spectacular revues.

The new "West End" around the Kur–fürstendamm became the centre of the city's nightlife, the meeting place of high society and *bohémiens* alike. The streets were lined with cinemas, bars with dancing and artists' hangouts. As Günter Birkenfeld remarked, the Romanisches Café near the Gedächtniskirche was the rendezvous of "everyone from Reykjavik to Tahiti who could claim some sort of relationship, whether professional or amorous, with the Muses and the Graces".

The biggest film studios in Europe were built in Babelsberg, just outside the city limits, by Universum Film AG (UFA). World-famous films were produced here, from Robert Wiene's *The Cabinet of Dr. Cagliari* and Friedrich Murnau's *Nosferatu* to Fritz Lang's *Metropolis*. The Polish actress Pola Negri became the star of German silent films. Producers of world calibre – G.W. Papst, Ernst Lubitsch and Erich Pommer – worked in Berlin. Billy Wilder was here as a reporter. Greta Garbo and Marlene Dietrich used the city as a stepping stone to Hollywood. Werner Krauss, Emil Jannings, Conrad Veidt and Peter Lorre ("M") found fame as the first character actors of sound films.

In the theatrical world, Berlin experienced an unexpected Golden Age thanks to productions by Max Reinhardt, Erwin Piscator, Leopold Jessner and Jürgen Fehling. Max "The Wizard" Reinhardt staged the first Berlin productions of G. B. Shaw's plays. In 1927, Piscator's political revue *Hurrah! We're alive* had its première in the Theater am Nollendorfplatz – now called the "Metropol". His pioneering approach enriched the art of live drama with such innovations as the dubbing of films and, as in *The Brave Soldier Schweijk*, the use of dual action.

During the period between the wars Berlin

also became an important centre of press and publishing, under the aegis of such great names as Ullstein, Scherl and Mosse. Almost 150 daily and weekly newspapers reported on politics, culture and other events from every conceivable angle. Of the 19 German Nobel laureates of the Weimar years, 10 – including Max Planck and Albert Einstein – lived in Berlin.

A "strange man": Initially, there were few signs of Nazi activity in a city of such magnitude. Hitler's planned march on Berlin in November 1923 collapsed ignominiously along with his putsch in the Bürgerbräukeller in Munich. In 1927, at a closed party meeting in the capital, he could claim 680 supporters. In 1928 he spoke for the first time in the Palace of Sports. As the newspapers reported, most of his audience consisted of "curious observers who have come to see this strange man".

There seems little doubt that it was difficult for the Nazis to establish themselves in Berlin. For Hitler, this hectic, sharp-tongued metropolis was anathema. And so he set up his headquarters in Munich, where he was respected. On the other hand, he was well aware that the road to power must lead through the capital. At the end of 1926 he sent his best

agitator to the Spree as gauleiter. Joseph Goebbels organised his "fight for Berlin" under the precept that whoever controls the streets will rule the city. Whenever possible, he transferred his propaganda campaigns to the "red" working-class districts of Wedding, Kreuzberg and Neukölln. Brown-shirted raiding parties ambushed their political opponents and Nazi troops provoked

Left, Communists demonstrate in front of the cathedral in 1932. **Above**, the Nazi Minister of Propaganda Josef Goebbels addresses the masses in 1931.

bloody fights at party meetings. During the elections for the town council in November 1929, Hitler's supporters gained only 13 out of a total of 225 seats. Meanwhile, however, "Black Friday" on the New York Stock Exchange had precipitated a worldwide recession and a whole chain of other events.

Hitler's rise to power: The social consequences of the lost war and subsequent inflation can be studied in the literature of the Weimar Republic. Dramatists such as Carl Sternheim and Ödön von Horvath described in their plays the moral eclipse of a broad spectrum of the middle classes and the *petite bourgeoisie*. A similar theme was treated by Erich Kästner in his novel *Fabian*, and above all by Alfred Döblin in *Berlin Alexanderplatz*.

George Grosz commented on the spirit of the times in his bitterly satirical drawings depicting the brutality and rapaciousness of the ruling classes. Heinrich Zille ("Henry Paintbrush") portrayed the city's working classes in their tenement dwellings and back yards; Käthe Kollwitz wrote frank descriptions of the misery of the poor. The prevailing climate was one of hopelessness, which made the man-in-the-street susceptible to both nationalist and anti-Semitic propaganda.

By the end of 1929, Germany's unemployed totalled 2.8 million. The following year, in the Reichstag elections, no fewer than 6.38 million voters placed their faith in Adolf Hitler, the man they saw as their saviour. In Berlin the Communist Party gained the majority of seats. Early in 1932 the number of jobless had risen to six million, 600,000 of whom lived in the industrial capital, Berlin. In the Reichstag itself, a radicalisation of Right and Left resulted in the parliamentary Centre being unable to function. In accordance with Paragraph 48 of the so-called Emergency Decree, a Presidial Cabinet assumed responsibility for day-to-day government.

After a rapid succession of chancellors – Brüning, von Papen and von Schleicher – Adolf Hitler eventually emerged as the leader of the strongest party in the Reichstag. The President of Germany, Paul von Hindenburg, gave him the task of forming a "Cabinet of National Concentration" with the German Nationalist Party. He was nominated Chancellor of the German Reich on 30 January 1933. That same evening, a mammoth torchlight procession wound its way through the Brandenburg Gate, past the balcony of the Chancellery building and along the Wilhelmstrasse. Because no photographers were present the entire performance was repeated the next day for the media.

The road to dictatorship: New elections for the Reichstag were planned for 5 March 1933. One week before, the parliamentary building on the Spree was engulfed in flames. Were the Nazis responsible for the fire or was it the work of a solitary anarchist by the name of van der Lubbe? The question remains unanswered to this day. Whatever the explanation, the burning of the Reichstag provided the National Socialists with an ideal excuse for embarking on a wave of brutal terrorism of their left-wing opponents.

The Communist Party was banned. Its leader, Ernst Thälmann, was arrested, sent to concentration camp and murdered there shortly before the end of the war. Although the Nazis had been waging a massive campaign of intimidation and already controlled virtually the entire media, especially radio, they failed to gain an absolute majority in the elections. They were only able to achieve this result by declaring the 81 Communist mandates to be null and void. The SPD was the last party to oppose the so-called Enabling Act by means of which Hitler annulled the constitution on 23 March 1933, thereby arrogating dictatorial powers for himself.

It became evident what this meant on 1 April 1933, when SA and SS troops marched through the streets of Berlin in support of a boycott of Jewish businesses. On 1 May there was a mass demonstration on the airfield at Tempelhof to mark "National Labour Day" and the next day, SA commandos stormed the trades union buildings.

On 22 July 1933 the SPD was banned,

while the civic parties disbanded of their own accord. The Nazis set up concentration camps in the Columbiahaus in Tempelhof and in Oranienburg, outside Berlin. During his first year in office, Hitler had 150,000 people arrested on political grounds and sent to the 100 concentration camps which had been built.

Many opponents of the Nazi regime, including prominent artists and intellectuals, were forced to flee the country. As a result of this exodus of its German-Jewish cultural elite, Berlin lost its international appeal. More than 20,000 books by "Un-German" authors such as Heinrich Heine, Thomas Mann and Kurt Tucholsky, were burnt on the square in front of Berlin University. This act was to be the opening move in the process of bringing all public artistic and intellectual life into line with Nazi doctrine. Supervising the *gleichschaltung* was the Minister of Public Enlightenment and Propaganda, Joseph Goebbels.

The Third Reich: Those who believed that the police terror, the book burning and the first persecutions of Jews would prove to be short-lived excesses were taught the error of their ways by the Nuremberg Decrees of September 1935. Jews were now isolated

During the Olympic summer of 1936 the city's nightlife was resurrected – even jazz was allowed. "No entry for Jews" signs and the anti-Semitic newspaper *Der Stürmer* disappeared for a few weeks.

On 9 November 1938 Goebbels unleashed an orgy of anti-Semitic destruction after a young Jew from Hanover shot a German diplomat in Paris. During the Crystal Night, SA and SS mobs laid waste Jewish shops, flats and synagogues. In Berlin, the two main synagogues in the Fasanenstrasse and the Oranienburger Strasse were set alight. The Kurfürstendamm and the Tauentzien were a sea of broken glass.

from "Teutonic-blooded Aryans" and as members of a lesser race were the object of discrimination and deprived of their rights.

The following year, the youth of the world converged on a festive Berlin for the XI Olympic Summer Games. The Nazis hoped to impress favourably the rest of the world by perfect organisation and brilliant spectacles.

<u>Left</u>, the Brandenburg Gate was the focal point of the Nazi torchlight parade of 30 January 1933. <u>Above</u>, the first boycott of Jewish businesses came in 1933 – SA men in the streets of Berlin with their slogan "Germans defend yourselves".

Plans dating from the 1930s show Hitler's scheme for making Berlin the capital of his "Thousand-Year Empire". Entire districts were to be razed to the ground to make way for new party buildings. The focal point was to be a magnificent boulevard, 7 km (4 miles) long, with a triumphal arch. At the end, occupying more or less the site of the present-day Platz der Republik, would stand a domed hall housing 180,000. Of all these grandiose schemes, Hitler's Inspector General of Works, Albert Speer, was to complete only one – the New Chancellery in the Vossstrasse. World War II would end the Führer's dream of "Germania", as he intended to name the capital of his imperium.

World War II: This time, in contrast to the jubilant crowds who thronged the city streets of Europe in 1914, there was no cheering - not even in Berlin. "I can only say that the mood was one of extreme depression and gloom", wrote Neville Henderson, the British ambassador who handed over the British ultimatum at the German Foreign Ministry on 3 September 1939.

A series of quick victories in Poland, Scandinavia and in the West restored the optimism of the populace as well as making any resistance to Hitler and his regime seem difficult if not hopeless.

On the morning of 22 June 1941 the citizens of Berlin were roused from their Sunday relaxation by a fanfare on the radio. Normal broadcasts were interrupted and a statement by the Führer announced that the invasion of the Soviet Union was under way.

As early as the summer of 1940, in the midst of the Battle of Britain, the Royal Air Force had started its night bombing raids on Berlin. In 1942 they began to bombard all major cities in Germany. During the winter of 1943–44 it was the turn of the capital. A series of 16 devastating attacks followed. The Americans also participated in the closing phases of the Battle of Berlin. The air offensive escalated into a non-stop campaign; until mid-April 1945 scarcely a day went by without an air raid warning.

After the military debacle of Stalingrad, Goebbels incited the masses in the Palace of Sports on 18 February 1943 to support his calls for "total war". All men between the ages of 16 and 65, and all women between 17 and 45, were called up for war service.

At night, transport trains left the railway station at Grunewald. In January 1942, during the Wannsee Conference, the SS delegates had decided on the "Final solution of the European Jewish question". This meant the annihilation of all Jews on the continent. In June 1933 there were some 130,000 Jews living in Berlin. By 1942 there were 60,000, who were now systematically deported to extermination camps and murdered.

At the end of January 1945, Soviet troops reached the Oder near Küstrin. They set up a bridgehead on the west bank; their advance tanks were then only 70 km (44 miles) from the city boundary. That year, Berlin experienced a spring full of foreboding in the shadow of the Red Army.

During January and February the capital suffered the worst air raids of the war. American bombers reduced almost the entire city centre to rubble. Theatres and entertainment had closed, victims of the "total war". Only a few cinemas remained open. The film they were showing was Veit Harlan's *Kolberg*. It was an oblique exhortation to hold out, portraying the defence of the fortress of Kolberg against Napoleon: now Berlin, too, was to be defended "to the last man and the last bullet".

On the morning of 16 April the window panes on the east side of the city shook. On the Oder front, almost 20,000 gunners began the main Soviet offensive with an artillery salvo. Ten days later, they closed the ring around Berlin. On 29 April the Russians launched a massive three-pronged attack on the inner defences of the "Citadel". Their main targets behind the fortifications were the Führer's bunker and the Chancellery building. On 30 April Hitler committed suicide with his mistress Eva Braun.

One week later, Field Marshal Wilhelm Keitel, the head of German Supreme Command, arrived in Berlin. In the Russian headquarters, as the prisoner of the Allies, he signed the document of unconditional surrender on behalf of the German Reich.

During the course of the war, the Allied planes had dropped some 45,000 tonnes of bombs on Berlin. During the last offensive the Russian artillery had fired over 1.1 million shells at the city. Berlin, which a megalomaniac dictator and his henchmen had planned to transform into the seat of power of a world empire, had been reduced to a pile of rubble.

Harry Hopkins, the American presidential advisor, gazed down on the endless devastation as he flew over the Spree on 25 May 1945 on his way to Moscow. The capital of Germany had become, he said, "a second Carthage".

Right, May 1945 – troops of the Red Army fire their victory salute atop the Brandenburg Gate.

The Battle of Berlin raged for 12 days. In their fanatical attempts to avoid defeat the Nazis even forced children and old people to defend the city with bazookas. Thousands were killed during the air raids and street fighting; others fell foul of mobile courts martial as SS patrols carried out a last-minute hunt for so-called deserters. Victims were executed on the spot and hung from street lamps.

The balance sheet for Berlin during the Nazi dictatorship reveals 80,000 dead and 75 million cubic metres of rubble, one-seventh of the total for the entire country. The city centre was littered with corpses and burnt-out tanks. Of the capital's 4.3 million inhabitants not more than 2.8 million – possibly, according to some sources, as few as two million – still lived there. Most of them were women, children and old people who eked out a miserable existence in the city's ruined buildings and cellars.

Experts seriously considered the possibility of leaving the devastation to decay, and rebuilding the city elsewhere from scratch. Of a total of 245,000 buildings 50,000 had been completely destroyed and 23,000 badly damaged. There was no electricity, no gas, and running water only in the outer districts. One-third of all underground railway tunnels were flooded; half the city's road bridges were unusable. The collapse of hygiene led to dysentery and other illnesses. Famine seemed inevitable.

Official food distribution satisfied no more than half the daily calorie requirements. Those determined to survive were forced to resort to barter, to make foraging trips to the country, or to buy goods on the black market. Not only food, but practically every other commodity, was the subject of haggling.

The prime occupation of most Berliners, and one which took up most of their waking hours, came to be known as "organising". This involved the acquisition of food supplies, repair materials and equipment and other items in short supply. Everything was in short supply and winter was approaching fast. It was a fight for survival. The legendary *Trümmerfrauen*, the women who cleared away the rubble, were the first to make an impression. They broke up stones – 125 per hour, 1,000 per day, for a weekly wage of 28 marks and a ration card. During these early days, few Berliners exhibited more than a passing interest in politics. They were powerless anyway.

The four-sector city: As far as the three western sectors of Berlin were concerned, the Red Army was a temporary caretaker of the city. This did not apply to the conquest of large tracts of Central Germany by General Eisenhower's troops. During April 1945 they advanced as far as the Wismar-Magdeburg-Leipzig line, well beyond the predetermined boundary of the west-east zone. At the end of June the Anglo-American forces withdrew from Mecklenburg, Saxony and Thuringia, taking over their sectors in Berlin at the beginning of July. The French followed in August; Churchill had ceded them the districts of Wedding and Reinickendorf, originally part of the British sector. Three months after the surrender at Karlshorst, the former imperial capital had become the four-sector city of Berlin.

The London Protocol of 12 September 1944 was the basis for the exchange of troops between East and West. In this document the Big Three powers agreed on the division of Germany and the occupation status of Greater Berlin. By means of secured approach roads the Western Allies had thus moved onto a bomb site which lay over 100 km (63 miles) east of the Elbe, in the middle of the Soviet-occupied zone.

During the summer of 1945, Harry Truman, Josef Stalin and Winston Churchill – succeeded during the course of the negotiations by Clement Attlee – discussed the future of Germany within the framework of the Potsdam Conference. They agreed that the country should be completely demilitarised

Left, the war reduced Berlin to 75 million cubic metres of rubble.

and de-Nazified, as well as deciding on reparations and the creation of a new administration along democratic principles. The unity of the country as a whole, with Berlin as the capital, was not questioned by the three superpowers in the Potsdam Agreement of 2 August 1945.

From this point onwards, Berlin was ruled jointly by the four victorious powers. The Allied Command consisted of the supreme commanders of the armies in question. Policy decisions depended upon unanimity. They were passed on to the politically neutral mayor, Dr. Arthur Werner, who had been appointed to the city's first postwar munici-

the Christian Democratic Union (CDU), the Liberal Democrats (LPD) and the new Social Unity Party (SED), an amalgamation of Social Democrats and Communists; the latter was vehemently disowned by the SPD in the Western sectors of the city. The SPD gained the overall majority; barely 20 percent of the electorate voted for the SED, which was favoured by the Soviets. The elections were regarded as being a sort of referendum, reflecting the proportions of Berliners favouring the West and the East.

Regardless of the election results, the Soviets continued with the erection of a popular democratic society in their sector. A reap-

pal authority by Berlin's first Soviet commandant, General Bersarin, before the Western Allies even reached the city. The boundaries between the various sectors were of no significance in the everyday lives of the populace. Food rationing was the same everywhere, and there was freedom of movement within the city.

Berlin goes to the polls: The first, and what would prove to be the last post-war town council elections for many years, took place under the supervision of the Allies on 10 October 1946. Four parties campaigned for power: the German Socialist Party (SPD),

pointment of public posts, which the Russians had filled before the elections with trustworthy German communists, did not take place. In June 1947, the Soviet city commandant vetoed the election of Ernst Reuter (SPD) as the city's new mayor. At this juncture Louise Schröder, Reuter's courageous deputy, took on the job – the first woman to head a Berlin town council.

Stalin's hunger blockade: The opposing interests of the victorious allies became increasingly clear. Things came to a head in February 1948 when, following the London Conference, the Western Allies agreed on a policy for the economic rehabilitation of Germany within their three zones. Moscow saw this move as a breach of the Four-Power agreement and withdrew under protest its cooperation within the Allied Control Council. Marshal Solokovski's departure on 20 March marked the end of the joint administration of Germany. The inclusion of the three western sectors in the West German currency reform provided an excuse for the Berlin Blockade. On 24 June 1948 the Soviet military authorities closed all roads, waterways and railway lines to the West.

Two-and-a-half million Berliners were imprisoned in the city, without electricity, and

with food for 36 days and coal for 45 days. The American military governor, Lucius D. Clay, described the situation as "one of the more brutal attempts in modern Russian history to use mass starvation as a means of exerting political pressure."

Clay took up the challenge. He found an ally in the mayor, Ernst Reuter, who was certain that the Berliners themselves would

Left, the Berlin Airlift – US transport planes at Tempelhof airport. **Above**, Berlin's Mayor Ernst Reuter addresses a demonstration for freedom in front of Reichstag.

"stand up for their freedom". With utmost speed an air bridge was set up; the first American transport plane, a Douglas Dakota bearing three tonnes of freight, landed at Tempelhof airport on 25 June. During the following 11 months the American and British were to make 277, 264 flights to Berlin. They brought the city a total of 1.8 million tonnes of essential supplies. For almost a year the local citizens lived without fruit and vegetables. Milk and eggs were available only in powdered form. Electricity was supplied for only a few hours each day. In the autumn the Russians offered the besieged West Berliners food ration cards in the Eastern sector. Only 100,000 accepted.

Following secret diplomatic talks in New York, the USSR lifted the blockade on 12 May 1949. Stalin had failed to achieve his aim of forcing the Allies to abandon Berlin. This marked a moment of victory for the city's population, but doubtless another stage along the road to partition. The democratically elected Town Council had transferred its seat to West Berlin in September 1948; only the SED faction remained in the Eastern sector. The latter called an "extraordinary town council meeting", and appointed a municipal council in accordance with the wishes of the Soviet authorities. As a countermove the Western half of the city set up its own municipal council – which later became a senate – under the leadership of Ernst Reuter, the first Mayor of West Berlin.

On 7 September 1949, the split between Germany and Berlin was widened by the birth of the Federal Republic of Germany with Bonn as its provisional capital – an arrangement originally intended as a temporary measure. Two months later, the German Democratic Republic was formed in East Berlin. The law of the Federal Republic declared Berlin to be one of its constituent *Länder* with the Allied restriction that the city was not to be "governed by the Federal Government". The supreme command was to remain in the hands of the forces of occupation. The Soviet authorities made no formal attempt to encroach upon the city's status, challenging it in practice only by their choice of Berlin (East) as the seat of government of the GDR.

The showcase of the Western world: Initially, the economic development of West Berlin proceeded slowly. The uncertain political situation, the blockade, its isolated location and the correspondingly long haulage distances all proved to be inhibiting factors. In order to compensate for the city's geographical disadvantages, and above all in order to create as rapidly as possible a representative "showcase for western democracy" in this exposed position, enormous sums of money were invested by the United States and increasingly, as time went by, by West Germany itself. As the political and economic links with the Federal Republic grew stronger, and stores were a major attraction in West Berlin. The building industry was booming, and factory chimneys were once more belching out smoke. In East Berlin, on the other hand, there was a shortage of practically everything – a situation exacerbated by the high level of war reparation due to the Soviet Union in the shape of goods. There was universal discontent at the living conditions in the so-called Workers' and Peasants' State.

Matters finally came to a head in the popular revolt of 17 June 1953. The catalyst was a decree by the SED government that the average work rate should be increased without a corresponding increase in wages. Next

West Berlin became progressively more isolated from the eastern half of the city and the surrounding GDR.

In May 1952 the SED authorities cut the telephone lines; in January 1953 they severed the tram and bus routes within the city limits. West Berliners now required official permission to visit the surrounding GDR. The remaining passenger services (underground and suburban railway lines) within the city limits were not affected. Some 500,000 people continued to cross the sector boundaries daily in both directions.

Since currency reform, well-stocked shops

day, in the Stalin-Allee, 5,000 building workers downed tools in protest. They were involved in the construction of the "first socialist avenue in Germany", which was to be lined with houses in the wedding-cake monumental style of the Stalinist era. Abandoning their work, they marched together to the ministry offices in the Leipziger Strasse and demanded that the decree be rescinded. On the morning of 17 June the unpremeditated rebellion spread to other towns within East Germany. The workers took to the streets, demonstrating for higher wages, for the removal of the frontiers between the zones and for free elections. They stormed the SED offices in East Berlin, and plundered official shops. Demonstrators lowered the red flag flying above the Brandenburg Gate. At 1 p.m. the Soviet commandant declared a state of emergency. Police closed the border crossings to the Western sector. Russian T34 tanks rolled through the streets, crushing the revolt and thereby killing – according to official East German sources – 23 people. From this date until reunification in 1990, 17 June was marked in the Federal Republic and West Berlin as the "Day of German Unity".

Bolt hole Berlin: The authorities employed tanks to crush the protests within the Soviet

of bleeding to death, because most who left were young and employable, and in some cases highly qualified.

The Soviet prime minister Nikita Khrushchev came to the assistance of the GDR with his Berlin Offensive. In November 1958 he sent a memo to the three Western allied powers terminating the Four-Power agreement. He demanded in an ultimatum the withdrawal of the Western forces within six months, and the transformation of Berlin into a "free, de-militarised city". Otherwise he would negotiate with East Germany a separate pact of non-aggression and would transfer Russian sovereignty over the Berlin

sector of Berlin. They were unable, however, to remove the thorn in their flesh – the other half of the city, to which the inhabitants of the Eastern sector continued to enjoy unrestricted access. Attracted by the West's Economic Miracle and the freer life it offered, during the 1950s the citizens of East Berlin migrated in increasing droves in a westerly direction. The GDR was in danger

air corridors to the Ulbricht government. The Western powers refused to agree to his terms. Talks held in Geneva by the Great Powers between May and September 1959 ended in stalemate. The crisis deepened. By mid-1961 one in every nine GDR citizens had fled the country.

The Wall: The tension grew after Khrushchev and US President John F. Kennedy had parted as implacable opponents following their summit meeting in Vienna in mid-June 1961. The American answer to Khrushchev's threats of war was to increase its defence budget by US$ 3.2 billion. When the *Tages-*

Left, 17 June 1953 on Potsdamer Platz – Soviet tanks crush the uprising. **Above**, the Kurfürstendamm in 1968 – demonstration against the Vietnam war.

spiegel, the West Berlin newspaper, reported large-scale air and land manoeuvres in Carolina on 10 August, the citizens of the divided city knew for which emergency the troops were rehearsing.

Khrushchev summoned Ulbricht, the Secretary General of the SED, and other Party chiefs of the Warsaw Pact countries to a secret conference in Moscow on 3 August. He proposed that the sector boundary within the Berlin city limits should be turned into an East German frontier, in order to "guarantee constant surveillance and effective controls". Ten days later the SED leadership put his plan into practice. On 13 August 1961 the

perts and ambitious professionals packed their bags. Berlin seemed in danger of slipping into provincial obscurity in every sphere.

On the other side of the border, the authorities were at pains to develop the capital of East Germany into a "spiritual and cultural centre" as well as a worthy seat of the national government. Taking stock of the city's cultural heritage, the SED leaders were not content with merely rebuilding the historic city centre: in some cases they redesigned it along lines in keeping with their socialist illusions of grandeur. Compared with the other towns within the GDR, East Berlin was relatively well supplied with consumer goods

news agency UPI reported: "On Sunday night, large contingents of Communist People's Police sealed off the border between the eastern and western sectors."

In the cold light of morning the Wall proved a heavy burden for the crowded metropolis. With the banishing of all dreams of a united Germany came an increased awareness of the lack of security, of the precarious nature of the city's access routes and its insular overcrowding. The rag trade moved to Munich and Düsseldorf: the film studios became silent. Many firms transferred their headquarters to the Federal Republic. Ex-

– a fact which made it a popular place of residence amongst the country's citizens. Many of the nationally owned companies were either rebuilt or newly established. Ambitious town-planning programmes were carried out at the expense of other parts of the country. The intention was to provide the city's flashy Western counterpart with a socialist alternative.

Youth rebels: All over the world, 1967-68 was characterised by a young people's rebellion. This was the period of turbulent general meetings and sit-ins at the Free University and anti-Vietnam demonstrations and water cannon on the Kurfürstendamm. Students' unrest brought Berlin into the public eye from a completely different angle. It became the capital of the anti-authoritarian movement which fought for the new freedoms and the new social order of the 1970s. The alternative scene became a glittering kaleidoscope of unconventional groups, projects and initiatives. Once again, Berlin had become a forum for new ideas.

Towards the end of the 1960s a wind of political change blew through the world international situation surrounding Berlin. There was a relaxation of the tensions between the two superpowers; in Bonn, the

socialist-liberal coalition government under Federal Chancellor Willy Brandt introduced its new Ostpolitik, based on non-aggression and an acceptance of the territorial changes which had taken place at the end of World War II. This involved recognition of East Germany. It was obvious that the relaxation of tensions within Europe as a whole would not go unnoticed in Berlin. On 27 February 1969, President Richard Nixon of the United States challenged the Soviet Union to join him at the negotiating table, adding that the

The Allies parade along the "Street of 17 June".

two countries should abandon the notion of Berlin as a bone of contention. On 10 July, Moscow announced through its Foreign Minister Andrei Gromyko that it would be prepared to agree to an exchange of views as to "how we can avoid complications over Berlin now and in the future". The talks began on 26 March 1970 at the former Allied Command Control headquarters. On 3 September 1971 the ambassadors of the four powers initialled the results. The new Berlin Agreement came into force on 3 June 1972. It introduced no new regulations, but merely confirmed the status quo from 13 August 1961.

For West Berliners, the practical inter-German agreements under the aegis of the Four-Power Agreement assumed vital importance. These included in particular the improvement of the transit routes, along which the East German authorities now agreed to abandon their luggage and vehicle checks. It became possible once more to telephone from one half of the city to the other. There were also humanitarian improvements in the form of a formal laisser-passer. Henceforth West Berliners were permitted to visit East Berlin or the GDR for periods of up to 45 days. An exchange of permanent representatives led to a maintenance of normal relations between the governments of the two Germanies.

Berlin's future: After many years during which the citizens of Berlin had become accustomed to living in a divided city, the breaking down of the Wall on 9 November 1989 came as a surprise. The stunned delight of the first weeks soon gave way to the necessary pragmatism. For the second time, the reconstruction of Berlin was tackled with unparalleled energy. Today, what remains of the Wall serves merely as a memorial. Since currency union and the removal of the frontiers on 1 July 1990, the two halves of the city are slowly returning to normality. Following the first municipal elections in the GDR in May 1990, East Berlin had a Social Democratic mayor like its western counterpart. In the joint elections for the Berlin Senate on 2 December 1990, the Christian Democratic Union emerged as the strongest party. Berlin is once more the capital of a united Germany.

Deutschland umarmt sich

Einigkeit und Recht und Freiheit

Samstag, 11. November 1989 · 50 Pf
Nr. 264/A5 · Druck in Essen-Kettwig · C 8756 A · M

Bild
UNABHÄNGIG · ÜBERPARTEILICH

Jede Entscheidung in und über Berlin ist eine Entscheidung für ganz Deutschland
Axel Springer

Von PETER BARTELS und
HANS-HERMANN TIEDJE

Berlin gestern, kurz vor 13 Uhr. Im Turm der Kaiser-Wilhelm-Gedächtniskirche ertönen die Glocken. Plötzlich bleiben auf dem Kurfürstendamm die Menschen stehen. Sie falten die Hände. Mitten auf der Straße fangen sie an zu beten. Bürger aus Ost- und West-Berlin – viele weinen. Einige schlagen die Hände vor das Gesicht, andere knien sich hin.

Das war vielleicht der ergreifendste Augenblick in der Geschichte dieser Stadt. In der Geschichte unseres Landes.

Und es war der friedvollste, der hoffnungsvollste.

Was sich in der Nacht zuvor, gestern den ganzen Tag und in der heutigen Nacht in der geteilten Stadt, im geteilten Deutschland abspielte, war herzzerreißend. Menschen aus Ost und West stürmten Mauer und Grenze, sanken sich weinend und lachend in die Arme. Es war, als würde sich ganz Deutschland umarmen. Und die Polizei Ost und die Polizei West sah schmunzelnd zu, tauschten Stullen aus. Nachdem das DDR-Fernsehen Donnerstag abend verkündet hatte, daß „ab sofort" Reisefreiheit herrsche, hielt es die Menschen in Ost und West nicht mehr zurück. Brandenburger Tor, Kurfürstendamm, Alexanderplatz – das war der Tag der Wiedervereinigung, der Tag der Deutschen, das machtvolle Bekenntnis zu Einigkeit und Recht und Freiheit. Am Abend dann brausender Jubel, als Willy Brandt, der ehemalige Bürgermeister von Berlin vor dem Schöneberger Rathaus den Tausenden zurief: „Ich habe im Sommer geschrieben, Berlin wird leben und die Mauer wird fallen – Berlin lebt, die Mauer ist gefallen."

Was immer jetzt geschehen mag – diesen Tag wird uns keiner mehr nehmen. Es war ein Tag für Deutschland.

Helmut Schmidt bei BILD
Schickt Pakete, feiert mit ihnen Weihnachten

Hamburg – „Wir sollten die Reformbewegung im Osten Europas nicht allein unterstützen, sondern auf jeden Fall gemeinsam mit den europäischen Verbündeten. Besonders geeignet dafür ist der nächste Pariser EG-Gipfel unter der Führung von François Mitterrand." Das sagte Ex-Bundeskanzler Helmut Schmidt über Hilfe für den Osten bei einem Besuch der BILD-Chefredaktion in Hamburg. **Weiter Seite 6**

Das Unvorstellbare ist Wirklichkeit geworden – Berliner aus Ost und West haben die Mauer vor dem Brandenburger Tor erklommen, verharren ergriffen, viele mit Tränen in den Augen. Das Brandenburger Tor, 28 Jahre lang Symbol der Teilung ist wieder das, was es immer war – Symbol der Einheit.

The red-letter day of 9 November 1989 began with an exceptionally boring press conference in East Berlin. The world-shattering events of the past weeks seemed doomed to premature death under the suffocating rigidity of the SED Politburo. Following the mass exodus from Hungary and the Monday demonstrations in the towns of East Germany, everyone was still waiting for the "change of heart" within the Central Committee.

At 6.57 p.m., at the end of the press conference, one of the journalists present posed a question. Günter Schabowski, the Politburo spokesman for Information and the Media, produced from his jacket pocket a folded sheet of paper which had previously been passed to him by Erich Honecker's successor, Egon Krenz. Schabowski hesitated as he read its contents. It was evident to observers that even he was surprised at what it contained. He realised that there was something wrong with the note, but he was too inexperienced to conceal his personal amazement.

That scene was repeated a dozen times during the television news bulletins that evening. Schabowski declared that "the Council of Ministers of the German Democratic Republic has decided that, until a permanent regulation approved by the People's Chamber is brought into force, the temporary regulation governing exit rights, i.e. the right to leave the country, shall be lifted". Incomprehensible? Totally. When asked whether the new rules were to apply to Berlin as well, Schabowski had to refer to his memo once more. He confirmed that they also applied to Berlin. Schabowski's statement meant, in plain language, that the border was open. Driving home after the press conference, Schabowski learned by telephone of the mass march to the Wall. The citizens of Berlin, and with them the entire world, had reacted more quickly than he did.

They had no intention of waiting to apply

Preceding pages: the zone of death; the "Trabbi" breaks through the Wall. Left, the *Bild Zeitung* was also there when the Wall collapsed.

for a visa the next day. Hesitantly at first, for the situation seemed somewhat unreal, the masses approached the Wall on foot and by car. The frontier guards still stood impassively at their control posts and the fear and the memories of years lived in its shadow still outweighed the desire to cross the border. But then the *sekt* corks started popping and the growing crowd of East Berliners gradually surged westwards. Nothing happened. Despite the latent fears that the guards might even now prevent them crossing, nothing happened.

Then there was jubilation, there were tears and shouts of joy as those present embraced and kissed each other, echoing again and again the cry which has since acquired a proverbial irony: *Wahnsinn*! – Lunacy! The Wall was breached and attacked with picks as the entire area was transformed into a scene of untrammelled celebration and exuberant joy.

13 August 1961: *Wahnsinn*. More than 28 years previously, the citizens had been unable to find words to describe the senseless reality. Berlin, divided into four sectors after World War II, was until this day still a single city. Its inhabitants commuted between East and West with very few restrictions. Trade between the Soviet and Western sectors flourished; for friends and relatives it was largely irrelevant who lived in which part of the city. But the crisis between the superpowers of the Eastern and Western blocs was becoming steadily more acute.

The 13 August 1961 was a warm summer's day. As on virtually every other day, another 2,662 refugees from all regions of East Germany had made their way to the emergency reception camp at Marienfelde in West Berlin – people who were no longer prepared to suffer the pressure of the one-party state on every aspect of their lives, or who were attracted by the affluence of the West. The flood of emigrants had increased dramatically since June. East Germany, which in any case suffered from a chronic shortage of qualified workers, was in danger of bleeding to death as a result of the many who were choosing to vote with their feet. The frontier crossers and refugees were costing East Germany upwards of three billion marks per year – a disaster for any country with a shortage of hard currency. The "Danger on the Western Front" was not military, but the lure of affluence and freedom.

Nikita Khrushchev, the Soviet leader, finally intervened. He informed the Western allied powers that he would revoke Berlin's four-power status and that the city should become a demilitarised zone. Failing that, he would sign a pact of non-aggression with East Germany and transfer to the SED re-

of the SED regime there were three possible solutions to the Berlin problem. Two of them – a sealing off of the whole of Berlin from East Germany or the closing of the air corridors – were rejected. The third remained – to build a wall through the middle of Berlin.

During the night of 13 August 1961, military transport vehicles rolled through the Eastern sector; the sleeping city was awakened by the rumbling of armoured cars. Machine guns at the ready, soldiers of the People's Army and members of the armed factory reserve groups took up their positions along the line of the border between eastern and western sectors of the city. Barbed

gime Russia's sovereign rights over the Berlin air corridors. The ultimatum was an unmistakable, albeit oblique, threat of war. Nonetheless, the allies turned it down. The mood was tense, pregnant. What would happen to Berlin, that capitalist island in the midst of a sea of socialism?

"Nobody has any intention of building a wall", maintained Walther Ulbricht, the SED leader, at an international press conference on 15 June 1961. The decision was, in fact, taken at the beginning of August. The party chiefs of the Warsaw Pact countries met in Moscow. Taking into account the standpoint

wire fences were unrolled and chevaux-de-frise (portable barricades) were erected.

The next morning the barrier was complete. A few last-minute refugees dared to leap over the barbed wire, but most observers gazed in dismay at the new frontier, constructed overnight and severing every link between the two halves of the city. During the weeks which followed, closely guarded teams of building workers erected the "Anti-Fascist Protective Wall", as the Wall was officially known. It was claimed that it afforded protection from possible attack. In reality, the sole purpose of the Wall's existence was to prevent the citizens of East Berlin from defecting.

On that Sunday, every Berliner was filled with impotent rage. Like a dissecting knife the Wall had cut the lively metropolis in half; in some places it ran down the middle of the road. Neighbours who were accustomed to being able to look through each other's windows and to see what was cooking, suddenly found themselves separated by a stone barrier and guards with orders to shoot. Overnight, East Berlin commuters with jobs in the West were no longer able to reach their place of work. The suburban and underground lines between the two sectors were cut off –

night an artist swung himself hand over hand across the border along a high-tension wire. But each year, as the security measures surrounding the Wall became more sophisticated, fewer and fewer people managed to escape. Some escapes went badly wrong and on one occasion a digging team lost its way and instead of surfacing in the West, emerged on a major thoroughfare in East Berlin to find themselves facing a platoon of GDR border guards.

With German thoroughness the authorities extended their "Ring around Berlin (West)" to form a border security system with alarms and obstacles. The first-genera-

even cemeteries were cut in two.

The deadly frontier: Many East Berliners made desperate attempts to escape incarceration behind the Wall. They dug tunnels, highjacked boats, waded through the sewers, which were sealed off by underground gratings, and even deceived the border guards at Checkpoint Charlie by disguising themselves in fake Russian uniforms. Young men burst through the Wall in heavy lorries or dived into the Spree. One freezing winter's

Left, August 1961 – the Wall takes shape. **Above**, a tourist attraction.

tion Wall was a hastily erected makeshift affair, but the "fourth-generation" barrier (after 1976 in the city centre) had grown to a height of 5 metres (15 ft). A circular pipe mounted on top, with a diameter of 35–40 cm (1 ft), prevented all attempts to climb over. The Wall around West Berlin was 165 km (103 miles) long. On the Eastern side, the area of No Man's Land, which was up to 50 metres (160 ft) wide in places, was demarcated by an alarm fence 1.5–2 metres high and constructed of electrically charged copper or barbed wire.

Immediately in front of the Wall was a 15-

metre (50-ft) wide strip of raked sand designed to retain all footprints and other evidence. This was the notorious "Death Strip". In accordance with their standing orders, border guards were required to aim at and to shoot without warning any person attempting to "violate the frontier". Within the No Man's Land were situated additional security complexes such as observation towers, earth bunkers or guard dog patrols. The entire Wall was under constant surveillance by six regiments of East German border guards with a total of 13,000 soldiers.

National boundary and garden fence: As the years passed, the Berliners who were free to

From that date West Berliners and West Germans were able to visit East Berlin once more, albeit with an interminable period of formalities. Acquiring a one-day visa usually took about three days; if, for some inexplicable reason, one's name appeared on the dreaded list of *personae non gratae*, a visa was refused.

The DM25 per day which visitors were compelled to change into East German currency, and the DM5 visa fee, came to be known as the "entrance fee to the socialist zoo". Tourists arriving in East Berlin walked through the city as through an exotic land with foreign inhabitants. The contrast be-

leave the city at any time – those in the West – learned to live with the everyday threat posed by the Wall. The inner-city section became an open-air art gallery. Spray paint artists and graffiti experts embellished the endless expanse of concrete with surrealist pop art, silly comments, declarations of love and political statements. The Wall became West Berlin's most famous sight, an attraction for tourists from all over the world.

Ostpolitik: In 1971 Willy Brandt, former Mayor of West Berlin and later Chancellor of the Federal Republic, negotiated an easing of travel restrictions with East Germany.

tween the grey drabness of socialist reality and the multi-coloured glitter of West Berlin made some of them shudder. West Berliners visited East Berlin in order to visit their relatives; they filled their pockets beforehand with "real coffee", tropical fruits, cosmetics and jeans.

Telephone contact between the two halves of the city remained difficult. Soon after the Wall was built the SED government had most of the telephone lines cut – a circumstance which remained in evidence even months after the Wall had been removed. A telephone call between West and East Berlin was more difficult to establish than one between West Berlin and, for example, Tokyo. It was also almost as expensive. A call between the western and eastern sectors was counted as a long-distance connection. For East Berliners, West Berlin remained – literally – a blank area on the map. All East German plans of the city showed the area beyond the Wall as No Man's Land; the Wall was depicted as a national border; everything beyond was a "non-socialist foreign country".

The Wall's victims: One of the more grisly sights on offer to western tourists was the array of crosses in the Bernauer Strasse.

a sheet to catch them after the secret signal had been given. Four escapers missed the sheet and died of their injuries. Later on, most of the houses were demolished or the windows and doors blocked up.

There were deaths, too, on the west side of the Wall. On a number of occasions, West Berliners tired of life drove at full tilt at the Wall – as if they wished by their suicide to register a formal protest at any restrictions of any kind.

Only on one occasion was there a protest on the East Berlin side. On 13 August 1987, on the 26th anniversary of the building of the Wall, some 300 people demonstrated against

Marked in each case with the name and date of death, they recall the people who died, drowned or were shot attempting to flee to the West. Here the houses are still in East Berlin but the pavements lie across the border. During the weeks after the Wall was constructed, the street was the scene of numerous tragic escape attempts. Many people tried to jump from a window to freedom. The West Berlin fire brigade was permanently on duty, ready to move forward and spread out

Left, at Pink Floyd's "The Wall" concert on 21 July 1990. **Above**, the Wall is besieged.

it on Unter den Linden. According to witnesses, the People's Police was remarkably restrained. It seems that no one was arrested, but the demonstration was too lacking in numbers to be effective.

Shortly after the Wall was built, there was a confrontation between Soviet and American tanks near what was then known as Checkpoint Charlie at the junction of Friedrichstrasse and Kochstrasse. The Americans rushed at full speed up to the border crossing when they saw the Soviet vehicles advancing. They stopped just in front of the white line painted on the road marking the actual frontier. Berlin held its breath, but the danger of a military confrontation passed.

The Museum of the Wall stands today by the site of the former Checkpoint Charlie. Displayed here by the "Association of August 13" are the hazardous implements with which some refugees managed to escape. These include a home-made miniature submarine and an armoured Opel P4. Then there are photographs depicting events before the Wall was built as well as its history, with film lectures and literature on the subject and an exhibition which is entitled "Artists' Interpretations of the Wall".

The flight to the East: On another occasion

during its existence, the Wall was worth a headline in the international press. An amusing event which amazed the entire world has gone down in history. On 1 July 1988 there was a mass escape over the apparently impregnable Wall – what is more, with the connivance of the East German border police. The direction of flight was eastwards, not westwards.

For weeks a group of some 200 young people had been occupying the Lenné Triangle, a small area of land directly beside the Wall. At this precise spot the Wall stood slightly back from the actual border on East

German territory, so that an area of land on the West side actually belonged to the GDR. The Lenné Triangle was to be exchanged and subsequently concreted over by the Western authorities. The squatters used the area, which fell under neither country's jurisdiction (the western authorities were not allowed to lift a finger here), not only to protect the ecotope but also to create living space for themselves. A few hours after the land had been handed over, the West Berlin Senator for Domestic Affairs had the police clear the young people away.

The squatters fled from the police over the Wall to East Berlin. The GDR border police gave them a helping hand – even their dogs and bicycles were given a friendly reception. In East Berlin they were served an opulent breakfast and permitted forthwith to return to the West by suburban train. The entire city – except for the senator in question – laughed heartily. It was the only occasion in its history that the Wall gave rise to quiet merriment.

"Thank you, Gorbachev": "Rejoice, Berlin!" exalted the Mayor of West Berlin, Walter Momper (SPD), the day after the Wall fell. And how the city rejoiced! But the opening of the Wall did not happen completely out of the blue. Near the Brandenburg Gate was written, in small black letters – long since painted over – the simple statement: "Thanks, Gorbi!" Someone had remembered who was ultimately responsible for the original initiative which had prompted the change of heart in the Warsaw Pact countries.

Mikhail Gorbachev, the powerful leader of the Soviet Union, was the man. He prescribed for the decaying system in the USSR *glasnost* and *perestroika*, "openness" and "restructuring" – a process which finally led to a reawakening of national interests in the countries of the Eastern bloc, and to a new freedom of expression.

Hungary took the first step. During the summer of 1989 it opened its border with Austria. No one guessed how significant this removal of travel restrictions would prove to be. Thousands of East German citizens spending their holiday in a country belonging to the "socialist brotherhood" took advantage of the new situation to flee via Austria to

West Germany. The West German embassies in Budapest and Prague were filled to bursting point with refugees demanding the right to leave their home country. Despite Wall and border security the flood of those voting with their feet rapidly reached unstoppable proportions.

In East Germany, work came to a halt as many holidaymakers failed to return home, fathers disappeared and parents abandoned their children. The economy was on the point of collapse. The protest of those who had stayed became louder – "We're staying!" was their watchword. But under one condition: changes must take place at the highest

inch. It later became known that Honecker even considered the "Chinese" solution – a repetition of the bloody repression of the revolt which had taken place a few months previously on Peking's Tiananmen Square. But the eclipse of the moribund regime was now only a matter of time. Hundreds of thousands of East German citizens took up the cry "We are the people!"

On 18 October the SED government made what was probably their first concession by dismissing their leader, Erich Honecker, who had held the reins of power for many years. His successor, Egon Krenz, was Honecker's protégé. But he, too, was too slow to react to

level. The leaders of the SED, however, remained impervious to such demands. In towns throughout East Germany, spontaneous demonstrations were held every Monday. At first only a few thousand citizens took part, but the numbers increased every week. In October, 70,000 people marched through Leipzig. In Berlin the first minor street skirmishes took place. The SED party leadership was unwilling to move even an

Left, a reception fit for rally drivers – cars from East Germany enter West Berlin. **Above**, the wall comes down at the end of an era.

the people's mood.

The fall of the Wall: On 4 November, a few days before the Wall finally fell, a crowd of almost one million East Germans gathered on the Alexanderplatz in East Berlin. With unprecedented directness and remarkable imagination they demanded the right to govern their own lives in freedom: "No visas for Hawaii!", "We want our daily bread, not peanuts – the moment of truth has arrived!" and "No protection orders for wrynecks". The SED government remained silent, until the evening of 9 November, when the opening of the Berlin Wall unleashed unprecedented expressions of delight all over the world.

There was now no stopping the course of events. On Christmas Day 1989 the Wall was opened at the Brandenburg Gate, traditionally the symbol of German unity. Hundreds of television cameras had been waiting for weeks for just this moment. The New Year celebrations of 1989/90 at this historic place became a party of mammoth proportions – unfortunately with tragic results. The Quadriga was destroyed, a section of scaffolding collapsed under the weight of spectators and a number of people were injured. One man was found dead on the street in

impromptu concert in the Deutschlandhalle; with tears in their eyes, the audience of thousands from East and West sang *With a Little Help from my Friends* in chorus. The West German chancellor, Helmut Kohl, was less rapturously received when, to mark the "historic hour", he cut short his visit to Poland and hurried to Berlin with Foreign Minister Hans-Dietrich Genscher and the Honorary Charirman of the SPD, Willy Brandt. Their attempt to sing the national anthem in front of the Schöneberg Town Hall unfortunately failed to strike the right note. The citizens of Berlin had no time for demonstrations of nationalist fervour.

Unter den Linden.

After their long closure the underground stations were gradually opened again. The public transport system collapsed under the strain. The city, hopelessly overcrowded, was on the verge of grinding to a complete halt as thousands of East Germans from the surrounding area converged on the metropolis. The department stores were jubilant at their unprecedented profits. Foreign heads of state and artists arrived upon the scene. Mstislav Rostropovich, the world-famous cellist, played "free and for nothing" by the Wall. The pop singer Joe Cocker gave an

In the whirl of events there were others for whom the "Golden West" had hitherto been forbidden territory, but who now found their way over the border and asked for asylum. Refugees from Vietnam and Mozambique in particular, exploited as temporary workers in East Germany, described themselves as "forced labour" and used the chaos at the crossing points as an opportunity to escape.

Wall-peckers and national profit: The "Anti-Fascist Protective Wall" finally became a victim of capitalism. The next people to enrich the language after the "wrynecks" – East German politicians who suddenly

76

claimed to have known nothing and who were always against it anyway – were the "Wall-peckers". They attacked the Wall with hammer and chisel. Some, no doubt, did so from political conviction, but most were souvenir hunters. A tiny chunk of Wall in a glass frame served as proof that one had actually been there. Quick-witted traders made earrings or brooches from tiny pieces of Wall – a procedure not without its dangers, for the fabric was contaminated with highly toxic asbestos. Larger specimens appeared in American stores with certificates of authenticity. The East German government, quick off the mark, contracted its ex-

port trade firm Limex to sell for profit segments of the Wall – it was – after all, the property of the state and the funds would improve the moribund national economy.

In the first six months of trading the company earned more than DM2 million: universities in the United States and Japanese banks purchased slabs, weighing nearly three tonnes, complete with certificate of authenticity, for DM60,000 a piece. Two sections of the Wall, one next to Potsdamer Platz and

Left, "wall-peckers" chip away souvenirs for the tourists. **Above**, checking for authenticity?

the other on Bernauer Strasse, have been declared to be protected monuments.

The first protests from those who "wanted their Wall back" began to get louder. The hothouse society of West Berlin was anxious about the loss of provincial sleepiness to which it had become accustomed. "The 'Ossis' will rob us of our jobs and housing, which are in short supply anyway", they claimed. The melting-pot culture of Kreuzberg, whose residents were "Wallflowers" in the true sense of the word, complained at the unaccustomed noise in the new through roads, which they only knew as dead-end streets. Land prices in previously neglected districts suddenly rocketed as the latter became desirable areas overnight. A former watch-tower was crowned with a blue neon three-pointed Mercedes star as a pointed commentary on the rush towards Western market capitalism.

The East Germans in their Trabants, previously greeted with enthusiasm, were suddenly cursed as disruptive, pestilential additions to the traffic chaos. And, in the shops, some items were in short supply – "The 'Ossis' are buying up all our goods." There was aggression on all sides. West Berlin's peace had been shattered – a fact which would take some getting accustomed to.

An ecological no man's land: In 1989, Erich Honecker had confidently asserted that the Wall would still be standing in 100 years. Today, there is virtually nothing left of what was for several decades the city's most notable landmark. Tourists seek in vain a brightly painted section which will serve as backdrop for their photos; at best, they may come across a crumbling, badly damaged ruin. Segments may be seen in the "Museum of German History".

East German artists had eventually been allowed to paint the Wall on the Eastern side. But even this work of art, known as the "East Side Gallery", has been reduced to rubble. The frontier complex has disappeared from the city centre. So well-camouflaged are the former crossings that visitors traversing Berlin on foot, by bicycle or by car will suddenly find themselves in the "Eastern Sector".

Checkpoint Charlie: On 22 June 1990 the most famous border crossing point, Checkpoint Charlie, was dismantled in the presence of representatives and foreign ministers of the Allied powers. It was an historic moment. The former crossing point used by diplomats and the Allies had provided the setting for countless tales of espionage. *The spy who came in from the cold* was the most famous of them. For tourists, too, it exerted a legendary attraction. Floodlit by night and guarded by motionless East German sentries, together with the punctilious military drill of the Allied forces it produced an atmosphere to arouse everyone's imagination. Might one become the witness of an attempt to escape? Would shots be fired here

that very night – only to be denied later by official sources? Nowadays, such fantasies are no longer appropriate. The traffic streams steadily through the former barriers; the famous guard's shelter now stands in a museum across the Atlantic. Today, Checkpoint Charlie is simply Friedrichstrasse again.

Apart from a few short sections, the land previously occupied by the Wall is waste ground. As you walk past you may see rabbits hopping by – an unusual sight in a city of the size of Berlin. Bicycle trips through the inner-city ecotope have become popular. The former Death Strip has become a favourite

recreational area. Children play happily on their new adventure playground. Town planners fall over each other to present their schemes for putting the land to good use. And historians are demanding that a section of the Wall should be preserved as a permanent reminder of the divided city which already seems an unreal nightmare.

The Wall in people's heads: The idyll which has replaced the Wall is deceptive. "It will take longer to demolish the Wall in people's heads than contractors will need to deal with the visible Wall in the city", wrote the author Peter Schneider in 1982 in his novel *The Wall-Jumper*. Berliners will remain Berliners, it seems. There is no doubt that they can still be divided into East Berliners and West Berliners, and that they will continue to be so for some time to come. Their customs and social habits have been too different for too long. Everyday reality has succeeded the tears of emotion and the joy. Until currency union in July 1990, West Berliners were wont to demonstrate arrogance and a know-all attitude as they explored East Berlin as if it were a newly conquered colony. They exchanged their hard-currency D-Marks for the socialist "slot machine" money at a rate of one to 10, and threw it ostentatiously around. Their behaviour was referred to as the "East Germans' Closing-Down Sale".

East Berliners descended on West Berlin shops like vultures. West Berliners mocked these "stone-washed people". East Berliners were annoyed at the West Berliners' large cars, who seemed to take it for granted that they would have right of way. Envy and a ghetto mentality were widespread. Forty years of two different social systems and different education, 28 years of almost total separation from the "other half" of Berlin became painfully obvious.

Reunited Berlin's struggle to regain its identity as a European metropolis rather than the "capital of an extended German Reich" is also the struggle of its citizens, not of governments. The acceptance of the city's new identity is developing slowly. Walls, real or imaginary, cannot be demolished in a day.

Left, watchtowers have been made redundant. **Right**, the Wall turned into museum pieces.

THE BERLINERS

Just what constitutes a true Berliner? As long ago as 1822, Heinrich Heine discovered that this was a subject worthy of endless argument, writing: "Berlin is not a city at all; it is simply a town where a lot of people, many of them of lively temperament, are gathered together. The place itself is of no significance." Another chronicler wrote in 1880: "It is very difficult to find a genuine Berliner; the town is largely full of foreigners, who make it a colourful place."

A glimpse at local statistics would appear to confirm this observation. Conservative estimates seem to indicate that barely half of West Berlin's 1.9 million inhabitants are natives of the city. For 130,000 of those who are registered as living here, the residence on the Spree is their second home; for safety's sake they still have at least a suitcase waiting for them in the Federal Republic. This means that more than half the city's population actually came from elsewhere – a characteristic which was typical of Berlin from the very beginning.

The home of the homeless: The first settlers who made their homes in the Berlin area during the 13th and 14th centuries came from the region between the Harz mountains and the Thuringian forest, from the native district of the Ascanians around Bellenstedt and Bernburg, or from the Lower Rhine or Flanders. It seems highly probable that the name of Cölln on the Spree was derived from that of Cologne – *Köln* – on the Rhine.

The seat of the electors of Brandenburg experienced a considerable influx of new residents towards the end of the 16th century, when settlers from the Netherlands under the protection of Johann Georg were encouraged to move to Berlin to improve the chronic shortage of underlings.

Then came the plague, carrying off 3,000 of the city's 12,000 inhabitants. The Thirty Years' War made further inroads. Berlin would still be just a small town in the Marches

Preceding pages: the start of the Berlin Marathon in Tiergarten. **Left**, the face of a Berliner.

today if fresh blood had not flowed in from elsewhere. During the 17th and 18th centuries the new arrivals were mostly refugees: Huguenots and Waldenses from France, Moravian Brethren from Bohemia, and 20,000 Salzburg Protestants from Austria. Swiss settlers and Jews swelled the ranks under Frederick the Great. During the Empire and thereafter, country-dwellers – Poles, Silesians, East Prussians and Pomeranians – were attracted by the city's expanding industry. After World War II the new residents were refugees from the Eastern zone, and guest workers. It is therefore impossible to generalise about origins when discussing the citizens of Berlin.

Goethe, an inveterate traveller, described Berliners as "that saucy race". Berlin was, in fact, a sort of America set in the middle of east Germany, enjoying no particular advantages of climate or topography. Newcomers had mostly endured injustice of some description and had mostly been borne or driven along by forces of one kind or another. Berlin offered them the chance of a new beginning, coupled with the attraction of the unknown, of "the chance deal; the city was a pawnbroker's shop of possibilities for making a living. Here the future was cheap for the asking; there were prospects to be enjoyed without bothering to climb a tower; there was pleasure to be had – if you knew how to take advantage of it." – thus the writer Dieter Hildebrandt described the capital's inhabitants in his work *Deutschland, deine Berliner* ("Germany, your Berliners").

In order to assert oneself in a place like Berlin, one needed to "be a tough customer, and a bit coarse with it", once more to quote Goethe, one of the city's most illustrious visitors.

Until the Wall was built, West Berlin served as reception centre for the stream of immigrants from East Germany. In addition, with the assistance of the employment exchange, it recruited 370,000 new workers from the Federal Republic, the so-called *Wessis*.

Roughly two-thirds of all *Wessis* became

permanent residents. They now consider themselves to be "true Berliners".

Since the end of the 1960s increasing numbers of Italians, Yugoslavs, Greeks and Turks have moved to the city. Today, roughly one resident in 10 is a foreigner; one quarter of all children under six have foreign parents. Workers from the surrounding German Democratic Republic and "socialist foreign countries" streamed into East Berlin. According to a local joke, the "reason they built the television tower at the Alexanderplatz so tall was so that the Saxons could see more clearly where there was an empty flat".

Tolerance and dry humour: It is virtually

his home here, and who learns to love the city, can become a Berliner.

To do so, however, he must come to terms with the local mentality. This reveals itself above all in a sharp tongue and a predilection for a typical, unmistakable brand of humour. A Berliner prefers to call a spade a spade. It disturbs him not at all whether, in doing so, he appears brash or puts his foot in it.

And then there is the Berliner's frequently quoted desire for amusement. During the last century it gave rise to the city's Ballhouse society – *Resi*, *Walterchen, der Seelentröster* and many more. On the outskirts of the city, popular pleasure *établissements* were already

impossible to produce a character portrait of the "true Berliner". And yet, there are a number of traits which have always been cultivated by those who live here.

First of all, there is the Berliner's traditional tolerance of foreigners. It does not matter where any one may have come from; half of the city's residents are elective Berliners – "trained Berliners" – anyway. And so, there are practically no pejorative nicknames for newcomers.

Virtually none of the city's mayors – at least, none of those who made their mark – was a native Berliner. Anybody who makes

flourishing: *Neue Welt* in the Hasenheide and *Krolls* in the Tiergarten. Here the local citizenry amused themselves with music, dancing, theatrical performances and artistry like *Bolle uuf'm Milchwagen* (the once-famous painter).

The call of the countryside: Also typical of the Berliner is his love of nature – all the more surprising in this city of tenement houses and back yards, where greenness is a rarity. A Berliner loves to grow flowers on his balcony, or at least a row of pot-plants on his window-sill. A popular long-standing tradition is the Sunday trip "into the country".

Picknickers by the Havel will produce from their baskets meatballs, home-made potato salad, an adequate supply of beer and maybe even their skat cards. They feel they are in seventh heaven, as if they were sitting on a palm-fringed beach instead of under a few sparse spruces and pines. On Sundays it even seems as if each family has its own particular place, as they all sit there cheek by jowl.

It may have been because so many participating fathers were suddenly overcome by thirst that these weekly trips into the country invariably ended up in the nearest pub. For this reason a ring of tourist cafés mushroomed up around the former city wall, an-

in the large numbers of dogs living in the city. Despite the overcrowding there are, comparatively speaking, more dogs here than in any other city in Germany: five for every hundred citizens. This statistic is also linked to the particular age and social structure of Berlin's inhabitants. More than one quarter of Germany's population is over 60 years old. Many of these often lonely elderly people live alone in anonymous council flats with their dog as their only companion. A study produced by the Technical University glossed over the sad reality by describing the city's numerous "consolation dogs" as "social functionaries".

nouncing "Let the family make coffee here!" One just paid for the hot water and then unpacked the home-made cake; the landlord would still make a profit, because father would be bound to treat himself to a beer; mother and children were also entitled to their *Weiße mit Schuß* – local white beer with a dash of raspberry juice.

The dogs' capital: The Berliner's love of animals is proverbial and, at times, borders on the pathological. It is particularly evident

Taking one's four-legged friend for his daily constitutional causes problems in Berlin as in other big cities. Another statistic reveals that, every year, a 16-tone mountain of dog dirt is deposited on Berlin's streets. In a well-meaning campaign, the local senator for the environment drew attention to the need for consideration with posters claiming "Goodwill can move heaps!"

Native wit: Berliners are famous – and feared – for their quick-wittedness, for they take a delight in mockery and sarcastic repartee. They enjoy complaining about everyone and everything which may come be-

Left, the new generation, young and affluent.
Above, a backyard in Wedding.

"BERLINESE" FOR VISITORS

Linguists are fond of arguing as to whether "Berlinese" is a proper dialect or merely a degenerate city patois. Whatever the truth, a Berliner's language is without doubt one of his most unmistakable characteristics. A Berliner is instantly recognisable by the twang in his voice and the brash way he has of expressing himself.

The Berlin vernacular has never been short of ribald phrases and witty expressions. A host of publishers make a living from local anecdotes and examples of the Berliner's sense of humour. To foreign ears the latter sounds more vitriolic than it actually is. People tend to forget that the Berliner's colourful irreverence is more an expression of delight in his own eloquence than a wish to hurt the feelings of another.

Rationality is one of the typical traits of the city. This is reflected in the speech of its inhabitants. "Without much ado" they come straight to the point, usually mutating the "g" of standard German into a "j" – at least at the beginning of a word. One mannerism which lends Berlinese its unique tone pattern is the habit of pronouncing consonants in a lazy way, or even swallowing them entirely – as in the case of "Wa?" instead of *Was*? ("What?").

A Berliner has problems with a short "i". He finds it easier to pronounce it as a rounded "ü". And so, on the Spree, one goes to church in the *Kürche* rather than the *Kirche*. Or, one may be warned that it is not a good idea to "get m*ü*xed up with a tw*ü*t like that". Berlinese contains no equivalent of the Standard German accusative case; Berliners always say "mir" and "dir" instead of "mich" and "dich" – "even when it's wrong".

Those who wish to learn more about the typical expressions used in Berlinese should study Walter Kiaulehn's book *Der richtige Berliner* ("The true Berliner"). Here they can study the language's earthiness and informality, its sauciness and lack of respect. One could fill a booklet with the nicknames conferred on the city's churches and official buildings; inevitably, someone actually did, calling the result *Baptized with Spree water*. The gallery owner Jule Hammer dedicated an entire dictionary to Berlin's favourite terms of mockery and abuse. One seldom encounters the poetic side of Berlinese, which is overwhelming. One of the finest examples is the lyricism of Kurt Tucholsky's *Mother's Hands*.

The origins of the Berlin dialect lie in the Low German group of languages. Settlers and merchants brought it from the region between the Harz and the Elbe. During the Middle Ages the people there spoke a pure Plattdeutsch which then took root in the district around Berlin and Cölln.

In the 16th-century Berlin experienced a linguistic transformation. The city's main trading links moved away from the Hanseatic towns towards Frankfurt an der Oder and Leipzig. The dominant dialect here was High Saxon – a Middle German vernacular resembling the written language of Martin Luther some time later. In 1504 the town clerk Johann Rether took up residence on the Spree and introduced the High Saxon dialect of Meissen as the new official language. This did not mean that Berliners were in danger of falling prey to the sing-song tones of Saxony; in time, the two languages fused with each other. And so true Berlinese developed between the extremes of Low German and the new High German of Luther.

Traces of the traditional Plattdeutsch dialect do not remain only in the classic *ick* (for *ich*), or the emphatic *icke*. If you listen carefully you will notice that Berlinese retains a large number of Low German constructions – *Appel* (*Apfel* – apple), *Männeken* (*Männchen* – manikin), *Töle* (*Köter* – cur), *schnoddrig* (cocky) and *doof* (daft).

In Berlin, the colloquial language was greatly enriched by the city's Huguenot immigrants. They added such words as *Boulette* (meat ball), *Roulade* (beef olive) and *Destille* (brandy shop). Other words have become so firmly adopted by the Berliners that their French origins are now hardly recognisable. This applies to *Botten* (from the French *bottes*) and *Kinkerlitzchen* (from *quincaillerie*). And, from the French *mocca faux* the Berliner made their own *ersatz* coffee – *Muckefuck*.

tween them and their desire for freedom – especially those in authority. The latter have always found it difficult to extract from their Berlin subjects a modicum of respect.

Frederick the Great, who wisely decided to release Berliners from military conscription, also deliberately ignored the sarcastic jokes in circulation concerning his person. "Let him get drunk himself!" he wrote in the margin on a letter in which an informer denounced the treasonable remarks of a drunken man.

Adolf Glassbrenner, the creator of *Eckensteher Nante*, a Berlin original, described 150 years ago how Berliners used to grouse in order to let off steam in the newly-established coffee houses of the post-Napoleonic era. "Only army officers eat cake for the sake of eating. All other Berliners eat cake in order to be able to read the newspaper; most of them also go to the taverns for the same reason, because there are no other public places. Wine, however, makes them reveal their true nature, and criticism and humour soon give way to a mood of enthusiasm. Before an hour has passed the newspapers have been swept from the tables and a conversation begins, becoming steadily more lively and delightful, as well as more animated, by the minute. The attraction of wit and freedom of expression know no bounds, and the champagne corks pop like the souls of Berliners who are released from convention and police repression…"

Claire Waldoff, alias *Rosine von's Projramm* in the Linden cabaret (*Who's throwing mud around here?*), ran into difficulties during the Third Reich. Berliners had no compunction about drawing parallels between *They call him Herrrmann*, one of her songs written long before the Nazis came to power, and the prime minister of Prussia, Hermann Göring, Hitler's henchman and subsequent Reichsmarschall. The latter was known throughout Berlin as "the bulging Teuton" because of his vast girth.

The Berliners had long been used to such ambiguities from their adored and fêted Claire. The chorus of one of her most popular

songs went *William, don't talk so much, I'm just sick of it.*

Hitler, whose rise to fame had taken place in the beer cellars of Bavaria, enjoyed little popularity in Berlin – largely due to his lack of humour. During the Third Reich the motto ran "I'd rather believe than feel too surprised". Later, as the bombs fell on their capital, the citizens of Berlin satirised the air raids with bitter irony: "*Be practical – give him a coffin!*" Districts which were razed to the ground acquired new nicknames: Charlottenburg became *Klamottendorf* ("Rag Village"), Lichterfelde was known as *Trichterfelde* ("Craterfield"), and Steglitz was

rechristened *Steht nichts* ("Nothing left").

Kurt Tucholsky described the Berliner's everyday routine thus: "There is much work done in this city – the people really slave away. (Even pleasure is hard work here; you roll up your sleeves before you get down to it, and you expect something in return.) The average Berliner is not industrious; he is permanently wound up. Unfortunately he seems to have forgotten the real reason for living. Even if he were in heaven – assuming he actually went to heaven in the first place – he would have an appointment at four o'clock."

THE TURKISH MINORITY

At present some 254,000 foreigners living in Berlin. Approximately 150 different nationalities are represented, from Afghans to Zaïrese. There are large contingents of Yugoslavs (12.1 percent), Poles (4.6 percent), Italians (3 percent) and Greeks (2.8 percent). With a total of 114,000, however, Turks constitute the largest minority group (almost 45 percent). Berlin is the city with the largest Turkish population outside Turkey.

The boom years of the 1960s, when the Federal Institute of Employment advertised for guest workers from the remote villages of Anatolia are past. Many of these first immigrant workers, whose time in Germany was originally intended to be of a temporary nature, have since sent for their wives and families to join them and have found cheap accommodation in the traditional working-class districts. Nowadays the Turks represent a clearly defined ethnic minority group; they have developed a strong sense of community in every way, with their own tradesmen and wholesalers, restaurants and banks, their own clubs and religious practices and even their own travel agents, who arrange regular flights to Ankara and Istanbul.

Turkish doctors treat (not only) their compatriots, Turkish secretarial agencies help them with the pitfalls of the German language, and Turkish driving schools assist with the obstacle race of the German driving test. The Turks have their own daily newspapers, radio programmes, video libraries and – the latest service – their own cable television channel.

In Moabit, Wedding, Kreuzberg and Neukölln, districts where the further influx of foreigners has been banned by the authorities, Turkish immigrants, most of whom are Muslims, dominate the everyday street scene. The women wear headscarves – some are even veiled – and the men, all with a dark moustache, wear the *takke*, the Muslim cap. The highest percentage of Turks can be found in Kreuzberg, where the district surrounding the Kottbusser Tor and Görlitz station has been transformed into a sort of Istanbul on the Spree. The underground line

No. 1 is even known as the Orient Express. Most traders on the market along the Maybachufer are Turkish and offer for sale piles of brightly coloured fruits, clothing, fabrics and household goods.

The differences of language, culture, religion and attitude to life of the Turks has caused the city headaches greeted with incomprehension on the part of many native Berliners. Their idea of Turkey as an oriental fairy-tale country with minarets, bazaars and harem beauties was very different from this daily confrontation with Turkish extended families. It is true that the numerous Doner kebab stands have been accepted as a popular

enrichment of the gastronomic scene, and native Berliners may even appreciate Turkish restaurants as a welcome change from local food. As an alternative to the anonymity of supermarkets they also like the personal service in the little corner shops – revived by the Turkish community. Nor would they want to do without the Turkish cobbler and tailor down the road.

Nonetheless, for the majority of Berliners, the "garlic eaters" remain foreigners. For the considerable number of Berliners for whom the Turks epitomise the word, prejudice has been further fuelled by the high unemployment rates of the past few years, coupled with the general shortage of available apprenticeships.

Such people see the Turks as competitors for jobs. They even turn them into whipping boys for their own financial difficulties, although they would not want the immigrant worker's poorly paid job as refuse collector or office cleaner. The Turks' relatively high birth rate aroused fears that the city would be overrun. Racialism and xenophobia were fuelled by members of the extreme right, resulting in chants of "Turks out" or even violence.

The Turks, on the other hand, who before their arrival had only a vague idea of the city which was to become their new home, feel increasingly insecure and discriminated against. The more difficult it becomes for them to establish contact with their new German neighbours, the more inclined they are to retreat into the reassuring familiarity of their traditional lifestyle, which provides them with clear guidelines for everyday life and behaviour.

Some 25 mosques have been built in Berlin over the past years: most are housed in former factory premises and are unobtrusive. Strictly segregated according to sex, children learn to recite sections of the Koran in Arabic as well as receiving from the imam value judgments which are difficult to reconcile with those they encounter in everyday life, and which largely serve to alienate them still further from their German peers.

This also causes crises and family conflicts within the Turkish community. Torn between the relative freedom they experience at school and advertisements based on materialistic consumption and the rigidly patriarchal society within their families at home, second and third-generation Turks divide their world in accordance with the principle "Germany in the morning, Turkey at night". Parents who would prefer to keep their daughters under lock and key in order to marry them off later on to an orthodox Turkish husband, show little understanding for their children's desire to dress fashionably rather than wearing the traditional headscarf or even the veil.

In recent years there have been a number of attempts to encourage understanding and interaction between the two cultures. In addition to joint Turkish-German playgroups and women's groups and the "mixed" district self-help associations, there are many common activities, particularly in the cultural sphere – German-Turkish theatre groups, rock festivals and street parties.

The *Treffpunkt Berlin* was created as a coordinating body for integrated activities of all kinds. A publicity campaign under the rubric "Living together in Berlin" was started by the Berlin senator for immigrant problems, with the aim of encouraging more tolerance. It is hoped that the readiness of young Turks of the second and third generation to orientate their lives according to their new environment will be encouraged by the gradual elimination of prejudice on both sides.

Many of the Turks living in Berlin still cling to their cultural and religious traditions in order to maintain their sense of identity. Their aim in life is to be able to return home to their native land one day with sufficient savings – and possibly with the Senate's repatriation allowance – in order to make a fresh start.

Most young Turks set their sights on assimilation and integration, yet it is frequently difficult for young Turks to participate in the more casual lifestyle enjoyed by young Germans of similar age. They are often refused entry to discothèques; obviously, such discrimination leads to further aggression and conflicts. However, many will take advantage of the possibility of acquiring German nationality: more than half the Turks living in Berlin already meet the naturalisation requirements. It seems likely that several generations, possibly even several centuries, will pass before the integration process is complete.

The conflicting feelings of expatriate Turks are summarised in a poem by Aras Ören, a Turkish writer living in Berlin:

In my case,
Whichever life they create for me,
I know it is a coat which does not fit.
But how will the next generation
Pass judgment on me?
If not on my reality,
Then on their own.

THE MUSEUMS

Like so many other things in Berlin, some museums exist in duplicate. For decades the divided city developed two parallel collections. Both halves claimed to be the rightful trustees of the Prussian heritage. East Berlin expanded the historic Museum Island, and West Berlin countered with the "Foundation for Prussian Cultural Possessions". Now former differences of opinion concerning the city's cultural legacy have become superfluous and it is planned to unite all the capital's museums under the simple title "The State Museums of Berlin".

A beginning has already been made: the famous Egyptian bust of Nefertiti, a bone of contention between East and West for many years, will be returned from the Egyptian Museum in Charlottenburg to its original place on the Museum Island as soon as restoration work is complete.

Regardless of their geographical location, all Berlin's art treasures are infinitely worth a visit.

The Museum Island: Whether you plan to explore Berlin at leisure or only have time for a short visit, an excursion to the Museum Island lying between the two arms of the Spree is a "must". Four of the five buildings within the complex have been reopened following extensive restoration work: the last was the Bode Museum with Schlüter's equestrian statue of the Great Elector dominant in the domed entrance hall. Building work is still in progress on the New Museum, one of the last ruins left after World War II.

The **Pergamon Museum** houses the most valuable art treasure in the city: the Altar of Zeus and Athene (180–160 BC) from Pergamon in west Turkey. Since 1986 the town council of Bergama has been attempting to have the altar returned. The Turkish Republic no longer recognises the export permit granted by the Ottoman Sultan Abdulhamid II. It is unlikely, however, that the monument will be returned without a murmur. Also on view in the Collection of

<u>Left</u>, Nefertiti as souvenirs.

Antiquities is the Market Gate from Miletus. Amongst the most important exhibits in the Near East section are the Ishtar Gate, the Processional Way and the facade of the Audience Room of the wealthy Babylonian King Nebuchadnezzar II.

The most valuable item in the Islamic Museum is an 8th-century desert castle. The complex also includes the East Asia Museum and the Museum of Folklore.

The **Bode Museum** contains Egyptian antiques (mummies, sarcophagi and burial gifts) from prehistoric (pharaonic) until Graeco-Roman times. The papyrus collection, which includes 25,000 papyri, parchments and wax and wooden tablets, is one of the most important in the world. The Palaeo-christian and Byzantine galleries house works of art from the 3rd–13th centuries from the Mediterranean area.

The sculpture collection is particularly rich in South German, Dutch and Italian works from the late Gothic era. The art gallery traces the development of the history of art in Germany, Italy and the Netherlands between the 15th and the 18th centuries.

The Museum of Prehistory and Early History contains some of Heinrich Schliemann's collection of Trojan antiquities as well as finds from virtually every period of prehistory and early history in Europe. The Berlin Numismatic Museum houses 500,000 exhibits, which makes it one of the largest coin collections in the world.

The **National Gallery** displays paintings and sculptures from the beginning of the 18th century until the present day. During the Nazi era more than 600 exhibits were classified as "degenerate" and were confiscated and destroyed or sold for export.

Contemporary art and a collection of etchings can be viewed in the **Old Museum** (*Altes Museum*), which is situated near the Lustgarten. (Opening times for all museums: Wed-Sun 9 a.m.–6 p.m.; Mon–Tues – only the architectural galleries of the Pergamon Museum.)

The **Museum of Natural History** (*Museum für Naturkunde*) in the Invalidenstrasse (Tues–Sun 9.30 a.m.–5 p.m.) houses the zoological, mineralogical and palaeontological collections of Humboldt University. The focal point in a 38-ft (12-metre) high skeleton of a brachiosaurus – the largest dinosaur skeleton on display in any museum in the world.

The **Arts and Crafts Museum** (*Kunstgewerbemuseum*) (Wed–Sat 9 a.m.–5 p.m.;

Sun 10 a.m.–6 p.m.) is housed in the baroque palace of Köpenick. The main emphasis of the collection lies in its antique furniture, porcelain and leather items from various periods. The Treasury contains the Gisela Jewels dating from around AD 1000.

In the eastern part of the city, art collections are not only to be found on the Museum Island. The **Museum of German History** (*Museum für Deutsche Geschichte*), including exhibits from the earliest periods of history in Eastern Germany, is housed – ironically enough – in the Arsenal on Unter den Linden. The building, an impressive example of monumental baroque, was built in

Cathedral on the Platz der Akademie documents the persecution of the Huguenots in France and their contribution to the historical, intellectual and cultural development of Berlin and the Brandenburg Marches.

The **Brandenburg Marches Museum** (*Märkisches Museum*), near the Köllnischer Park, traces the intellectual and cultural history of Berlin from earliest times until the (socialist) present – or past.

Also of interest is the **Museum of Post and Telecommunications** in the Leipziger Strasse. Reopened in 1987, it contains an exhibition describing "The Development of Post, Telephone and Radio Services" as well

1695 as a magazine for weapons and instruments of war. The inner courtyard is decorated with 22 masks of dying warriors symbolising the agonies of war. The facades, by contrast, celebrate victory. Between 1875 and 1944 the building was used exclusively as a museum of weapons and war. Its present use dates from 1969, after reconstruction was complete.

The **Huguenot Museum** in the French

Left, peering into the magic of Rembrandt's *The Man with the Golden Helmet*. **Above**, encounters with an exotic deity in the Anthropology Museum.

as a comprehensive stamp collection.

Three centres: The principal art collections in West Berlin are concentrated in three areas: in Dahlem, in the Charlottenburg and in the new Art Forum in the Tiergarten, not far from the Philharmonie.

There are also a large number of smaller museums – for visiting cards, sugar production, or in memory of individual artists such as Georg Kolbe or Käthe Kollwitz. And then there are museums with special exhibitions for environmental protection, postal history, the Berlin Wall, resistance during the Third Reich and the Anti-War Museum in the

Genter Strasse 9 in Wedding. A point to remember: all the museums listed below are closed on Mondays unless there is an indication to the contrary.

The Prussian legacy: The **Foundation for Prussian Cultural Possessions** is situated not far from the Dahlem Dorf underground station. The exhibition rooms of the Painting Gallery are filled with Old Masters. The complex also contains the Sculpture Gallery, the Museum of Indian Art, the Drawings and Prints Department, the Museum of Far Eastern Art, the Museum of Islamic Art and – not far away – the Museums of Anthropology and German Folklore.

body knows nothing definite no more", as they say in Berlinese. But the Gallery houses a further 25 works by the master; to date, the authenticity of none of the others has been questioned.

In addition to the Rembrandts, the collection contains magnificient examples of virtually every movement in Western art before 1800. From the Italian School there are works by Giotto, Mantegna, Botticelli, Raphael and Titian; the German Gothic and Renaissance is represented by Albrecht Dürer, Lukas Cranach and Hans Holbein, and the Dutch masters on display include Rogier van der Weyden, Hugo van der Goes, Brueghel,

Visitors with limited time available should at least make a point of seeing the masterpieces in the **Painting Gallery** (*Gemäldegalerie*). Those who maintain that Berlin has not a single fake Rembrandt are mistaken. It does possess one – although its status was established only recently. Following exhaustive research the Gallery in Dahlem came to the conclusion that the *Man with the Golden Helmet*, one of its most valuable paintings, was not painted by Rembrandt, but most probably by one of his pupils. The date of the painting remains unchanged; experts still believe that it originated around 1650. "No-

Vermeer, Franz Hals and Peter Paul Rubens. There are also paintings from the French rococo (Antoine Pesne) and the late Spanish Renaissance (El Greco). Sharing a room with works by two other Dutch artists is a painting by Pieter Breughel the Elder – *The Dutch Proverbs*, painted about 1650. The meaning of the various sayings is explained in German.

Adjoining the painting gallery is the **Sculpture Gallery**. The Brandenburg-Prussian art treasury, which has existed since the mid-17th century, formed the basis of the collection. The works were housed in the Old

Museum from 1830. In 1904 the sculpture section received its own rooms in what was then the Kaiser Friedrich Museum, now the Bode Museum. The masterpieces were put in storage during the war; good numbers of them then ended up in the West.

Apart from the works of the baroque, Renaissance and rococo the gallery contains a collection of Palaeochristian and Byzantine works in various media. There are also fine examples of typical medieval sacred art, including a section of the Münnerstadt Altar by Riemenschneider.

The **Prints and Drawings Department** (*Kupferstichkabinett*) houses one of the most

Islamic religion from its foundation in about AD 600 as reflected in its paintings and decorative arts. Carpets and textiles, glass, pottery, enamel, book illustration, miniatures etc. tell the story of Islam.

A journey of discovery for young and old: The largest museum in West Berlin is the **Museum of Anthropology** (*Museum für Völkerkunde*), which is subdivided into departments covering Africa, Old America, East Asia and the South Seas. Founded in 1873, the museum brings together under one roof cultural artefacts produced by exotic, sometimes extinct, peoples. The collections from four continents include paintings, sculp-

extensive collections of its kind in the world: 25,000 hand drawings by world-famous artists, 50,000 sheets of prints and 1,500 illustrated books. There are examples of work by every painter of significance, from Dürer to Brueghel and from Botticelli to Picasso. There is also an illustrated Bible. The holdings are displayed in rotating exhibitions.

The **Museum of Islamic Art** was founded in 1904. It traces the development of the

Left, the Martin Gropius Building at the Anhalter Station. **Above**, the Bode Museum is situated on the Museum Island.

ture, religious objects and utensils of every description. A complete clubhouse used by the men of the Pacific island of Palau has been reconstructed here. Children in particular are enchanted by the imaginative dolls and masks on display. The junior section offers special educational activities which are sure to arouse their interest.

The Far Eastern Section was founded in 1907. It now forms a complete museum-within-a-museum with a wealth of porcelain, pottery, bronze and lacquer work from China, Japan and Korea.

The newest of the specialist departments is

the **Museum of Indian Art** (*Museum für Indische Kunst*), opened in 1963. Its 12,000 exhibits make it the most important collection of its kind in the German-speaking world. Here the visitor will find bronzes, scroll paintings, ivory, glass, metal and wood *objets d'art*, and miniatures from India, Burma, Cambodia and East Turkestan.

In the vicinity of this major complex of musuems and galleries, in Winkel 6/8, lies the **Museum of German Folklore** (*Museum für Deutsche Volkskunde*), founded by private initiative in 1889 and since 1904 a constituent part of the national cultural heritage. Until 1935 the collection was known as the *Museum for German National Costumes and Cottage Industries*. For some years it was housed in Bellevue Palace, today the Berlin residence of the President of the Federal Republic.

A visit to ancient Egypt: Moving on to the Charlottenburg and its surroundings, the visitor will find a mixture of Prussia, Egypt, antiquity and – a recent addition – the Gallery of Romantic Art, containing the principal works of Caspar David Friedrich.

The **Egyptian Museum** (*Ägyptisches Museum*), in the Schloßstrasse 70, is housed in a barracks for officers which was designed by the master builder Friedrich August Stühler. The collection contains items covering the period from approximately 5000 BC until AD 300.

The most famous exhibit of all is the bust of Nefertiti, a limestone sculpture of the wife of Akhenaton, the Egyptian Pharaoh who reigned from 1375–58 BC. Some 18 inches (48 cm) tall, it was discovered in 1912 by the German archaeologist Ludwig Borchardt in the atelier of the master sculptor Tutmosis, as he was excavating on the banks of the Nile in the hope of finding the lost royal city of Akhetaton. There is no satisfactory explanation, merely a host of theories, as to why Tutmosis depicted his model as being blind in the left eye. The bust arrived in Berlin in the 1920s as part of an exchange.

Nefertiti is not, however, the only exhibit of note. Other celebrated exhibits include the "Green Man", a bald head in green stone from about 300 BC,, the ebony head of Queen Tiy and the remarkably well pre-

served Kalabasha Gate. Ancient papyri, the oldest bearing a text over 3,000 years old, also recall the remarkable civilisations of the land of the Nile. Utensils, pottery, and instruments for measuring time bear witness to everyday life in Pharaonic Egypt.

The building across the road, Schloßstrasse 1, which is almost the mirror image of the Egyptian Museum, has housed the **Museum of Antiquity** (*Antikenmuseum*) since 1960. The collection consists of Greek and Roman works of art, including statues, portraits and antique miniature art. Special sections cover the Etruscan, Roman and Hellenic periods.

Near here, on Sophie-Charlotte-Strasse 17/

18, are the workshops of the National Plaster Casting Company. From their stock of over 6,000 casts you can purchase a plaster copy of the Nefertiti bust or of many of the other works in the various national museums. The exhibition and sales rooms are closed at the weekend.

Early history and Early Romanticism: The Palace of Charlottenburg was built by a succession of architects of the baroque and the rococo. It was the last remaining Hohenzollern residence to be left standing in Berlin after the City Palace on the Spree and the Monbijou Palace both fell victim to the destruction of war. The Belvedere, in the palace gardens, houses a collection of Berlin porcelain; the Schinkel Pavilion, an unadorned building with a square ground plan, contains Biedermeier miniatures and vases. On the second floor of the Knobelsdorff Wing are works formerly in the possession of Frederick the Great, by court painters such as Watteau and Pesne.

The ground floor houses one of Berlin's latest museums: the **Gallery of Romanticism**: (*Galerie der Romantik*) Displayed here are the National Gallery's finest early 19th-century paintings, including some of the most famous works of Caspar David

Friedrich, Schinkel, Spitzweg etc. Architectural subjects from the Biedermeier by Gaertner, Hummel *et al*, are also represented.

The Langhans building houses the fourth of the Charlottenburg museums comprising the Foundation for Prussian Cultural Possessions: the **Museum of Prehistory and Early History** (*Museum für Vor- und Frühgeschichte*). The collection was located in the Palace of Monbijou and formerly included the legendary *Priam Treasure*, dis-

covered by Heinrich Schliemann in 1873 on the site of Troy and eventually transported to Berlin after the circumvention of various official channels. Unfortunately the treasure disappeared without trace during the course of World War II.

Finally, there is the **Bröhan Collection** (*Sammlung Bröhan*) at Schloßstrasse 1a in Charlottenburg. It was founded some 15 years ago on the initiative of a local storekeeper who is now the museum's director although the entire collection has since been taken over by the municipality. The museum consists of a series of mock drawing rooms displaying splendid examples of art nouveau and art deco works by Berlin artists and hung with outstanding contemporary paintings. Each room is named after a leading designer or furniture manufacturer from the first 30 years of the present century, including Hector Guimard, Louis Majorelle and Edgar Brandt.

Near the radio tower is the Radio museum, with exhibits ranging from granny's steam radio to the first colour television camera. The museum offers a complete summary of the history of German radio from the first wireless exhibition to the début of colour television in Berlin in 1967 (Closed on Tuesdays).

From Menzel to Beuys: The next museum complex lies on the south side of the Tiergarten. Bordering the Landwehrkanal, on the corner of Potsdamer Strasse 50, is the **New National Gallery**, containing late 19th-century and 20th-century paintings up to the present day. The basis of the collection was a legacy of 262 contemporary works of art which the Swedish consul and banker Joachim Friedrich Wagener bequeathed to King Wilhelm I of Prussia.

The original home of the collection lay on the Museum Island (Museumsinsel), but after being put into storage during the war a number of the paintings ended up in West Berlin. They were exhibited at various locations throughout the city until the present gallery was completed in 1968 in accordance with a design by the Bauhaus architect Ludwig Mies van der Rohe.

World-famous contemporary artists are represented in the collection – Kandinsky,

Klee, Malevich, Grosz, Dix, Beuys, Newman and Rothko – as are 19th-century Realists and Impressionists including Menzel, Liebermann, Böcklin and Monet.

A short walk away lies the **Arts and Crafts Museum** (*Museum für Kunstgewerbe*). Originally housed in the so-called *Gropius Building* near the Anhalter Bahnhof, after World War II it was transferred to its home at the Charlottenburg. The collection, which is extensive, is distributed throughout 10 rooms, each dedicated to a specific period from the Middle Ages to the present day. Here there are Brussels tapestries, period furnishings, chinoiseries and a variety of

other items – Bugatti chairs and art-deco furniture designed by Muthesius for an Indian maharajah.

From the cembalo to the Wurlitzer: A modern building on the opposite side of the road houses the **Musical Instruments Museum**. The collection, which includes a valuable assortment of old instruments including a Wurlitzer organ (with regular demonstrations), was housed at a variety of locations after World War II before being moved to its permanent location by the Tiergarten.

The **Bauhaus Museum** occupies premises by the Landwehr Canal, at Klingelhöfer-

strasse 14. During the 1920s the world-famous school of architecture, crafts and fine arts provided a forum for a number of progressive teachers and students who attempted to achieve a unity of art, technology and science. The museum exhibits teaching material and works by artists who graduated from the Bauhaus or taught there: Gropius, Mies van der Rohe, Kandinsky, Klee, Breuer and Itten (Closed on Tuesdays).

Across the city: The **Brücke Museum** lies on the Bussardsteig in Zehlendorf, not far from the Clayallee. It contains a collection of paintings by great German Expressionists of the "Bridge" – Karl Schmidt-Rottluff, Ernst-Ludwig Kirchner etc. The gallery was partly financed by Schmidt-Rottluff (Closed on Tuesdays).

At the other end of the city, in Kreuzberg, a former cold store near the Gleisdreieck underground station houses the **Transport and Technical Museum** (*Museum für Verkehr und Technik*). Opened in 1983, it continues a 400-year-old tradition, for the capital city of Berlin once boasted a large number of important technical and scientific collections. Historic exhibits and contemporary models provide an insight into the development of various branches of technology, including road and rail transport, shipping, aircraft, hydraulics, data processing and printing.

Every city needs to document its own history. The **Berlin Museum**, in Lindenstrasse 14 in Kreuzberg, is housed in a baroque building dating from 1735, which was formerly the Prussian Supreme Court. With its models and maps, furniture and fashions, signs, prints, pictures, portraits, busts, china and household utensils, the collection provides a cross-section of the cultural history of the city.

The **Berlin Gallery**, in the Gropius Building near the Anhalter Bahnhof, displays a collection of pictures and historic photographs originating in Berlin or associated with the city.

Left, the man who gave Berlin its neoclassical countenance: Karl-Friedrich Schinkel stands before his Alte Museum. **Right**, the Porcelain Collection in Charlottenburg Palace.

Berlin assumed its role as a national centre of music and drama somewhat later than, for example, Paris or Vienna. Such a position was unobtainable as long as the town was nothing more than the residence of a provincial potentate in the backwoods of the Holy Roman Empire. In order to act as a magnet for artists and the arts, Berlin first had to become the capital of a state of international significance. During the age of absolutism, this in turn was dependent on the personality of the ruling prince. Here, too, there was room for improvement.

In 1740 the throne of Prussia was ascended by a new king who realised that the identity of state and subjects would be more worthily and permanently enhanced by cultural achievement than by rigid discipline and the militarisation of every aspect of life, as the miserly "King-Sergeant" Friedrich Wilhelm I had prescribed. The monarch in question was his artistically talented son Friedrich II – Frederick the Great, who lost no time in putting theory into practice.

A mecca for musical drama: Under the patronage of Frederick the Great (1740–86), himself a philosopher and musician, Berlin blossomed into cultural vitality. Opera lovers of today still benefit from the legacy of the enlightened Hohenzollern despot. During the First Silesian War he had the Royal Opera House built on Unter den Linden. It was formally opened in 1742 with a performance of Graun's *Cesare e Cleopatra*.

During the next two centuries Berlin gained a reputation as a glittering metropolis through the presence of Spontini, Meyerbeer, Richard Strauß, Erich Kleiber and Wilhelm Furtwängler. After World War II, the Opera House was one of the first cultural buildings in the Eastern half of the city to be rebuilt. Rechristened the German State Opera, since 1955 it has established its reputation as one of the leading German opera companies.

Left, "Ruski go home" was realised quicker than the "Theatre of the West" could ever have imagined.

Its natural rival is the Berlin German Opera Company. This West Berlin counterpart was built in accordance with Fritz Bornemann's design on the ruins of the old Charlottenburg opera house. It opened in 1961 with Ferenc Fricsay as musical director of Carl Ebert's production of *Don Giovanni*. Under the direction of Gustav Rudolf Sellner and Götz Friedrich the new company soon rose to international fame. Audiences who have experienced a *Tosca* fit for the recording studio under Lorin Maazel, a brilliantly cast *Cosi fan tutte* under Karl Böhm, a sparklingly witty *Figaro* or a daringly psychological *Ring* will have felt as thrilled in the functional building on Bismarckstrasse as in Covent Garden or the "Met".

The Theater des Westens: During the mid-1980s Götz Friedrich took over the directorship of the Theater des Westens. Occupying the building near the Bahnhof Zoo, where the City Opera Company had occupied temporary quarters, the "Theatre of the West's" production of *My Fair Lady* in 1961 marked a runaway victory for the American musical on the German stage. In recent years the producer and choreographer Helmut Baumann has been the theatre's artistic director; his intelligently designed Kurt Weill revue and cosmopolitan production of *A Cageful of Idiots* were rapturously received far beyond the city boundaries. Since then, the Theater des Westens has established a leading reputation for its musical and operetta productions.

At the Comic Opera House, Walter Felsenstein began in 1947 his much-admired campaign for the revival of realistic musical drama. His attention was devoted primarily to the *Opéra comique*, and to a lesser extent to classical operetta and the musical. His productions of Janáček's *The Cunning Little Vixen* and Verdi's *Othello* were hailed as the work of a genius. Nowadays, innovative producers of great fantasy, such as Harry Kupfer, ensure that the theatre in the Behrensstrasse remains true to the reputation it acquired in the Felsenstein era, when it was a world centre for modern musical theatre in the best sense of the word.

World-ranking orchestras: For the citizens of Berlin, music and singing are a fundamental form of expression in spheres beyond that of opera. Numerous amateur choirs with fine reputations will sing you not only a litany, but also songs, cantatas and oratorios on the subject. These nightingales include the Philharmonic Chorus, the Choir of St Hedwige's Cathedral and the Berlin Oratorio Choir, not to mention the RIAS chamber chorus and a long list of small vocal groups and church choirs.

All of them are following in the footsteps of the Academy of Singing, which first raised its melodic voice in 1791 and which, with its 1829 performance of the long-forgotten *St. Matthew Passion* under the direction of the young Felix Mendelssohn-Bartholdy, inaugurated a revival of interest in the music of J.S. Bach which has lasted to this day.

Berlin's musical potential was not always used to the full, because it took some time for the city to mature into its new role as capital. Its governors were sometimes more well-meaning than competent. And so the triumphant première of *Der Freischütz* at the Royal Theatre in 1821 was an important step in the development of Romantic opera, but had little lasting effect on the career of its composer, Carl Maria von Weber.

The King, blind to the talents of everyone except the Italian composer Spontini, failed to persuade Weber to remain in Berlin. When Mendelssohn applied for the position of director of the Academy of Singing as successor to the illustrious Carl Friedrich Zelter, he was passed over in favour of a worthy but insignificant fellow-applicant. "Berlin", he remarked – not without bitterness – "is the sourest apple into which anyone can bite."

The Berlin Philharmonic Orchestra, founded in 1882, played its way to international fame under Hans von Bülow, Arthur Nikisch and Wilhelm Furtwängler. By the end of the Karajan era it could claim a reputation, not only amongst local patriots, as one of the best orchestras in the world.

Serious competition is present in the form of the Radio Symphony Orchestra, which has reached a first-class standing under Fricsay, Maazel and Riccardo Chailly. In contrast to the relative conservatism of its more venerable rival, the RSO is well-known for its open-minded approach even to music of the avant-garde. That same critical interest in innovation which made the Berlin of the legendary "Golden Twenties" the most exciting cultural centre in the world ensures that attitudes today still remain open to experiment.

Progressive unrest: If a hidden message can be heard, or at least sensed, in the unfamiliar, revolutionary tones, a Berlin audience will be the most rewarding one imaginable. In 1974 the 30 informative concerts of the first

– but by no means the last – Meta Music Festival provided a summary of new and previously ignored developments between Tibet and San Francisco. To the surprise of the organisers it was welcomed with enthusiasm by the city's youth. As far as music lovers of Berlin are concerned, half the fun is simply having been present and being able to express an opinion. A festival première of a new work by Mauricio Kagel will receive the same attention as a fringe performance in the Academy of Fine Arts or the Bethanien Artists' Centre.

Both these places have developed into

settings where innovators can experiment with the frontiers of the arts, thus preventing any risk of stagnation. This is a characteristic of contemporary musical life in Berlin: as soon as an institution starts to sit back comfortably on its laurels, someone else appears on the scene to challenge its reputation with something better, or at least more interesting. Often enough, they succeed.

The Jazz Days, for example, had hardly established themselves in the Philharmonie as the most important festival on the jazz scene after America's Newport, when the Free Music Workshop was formed in the Quartier Latin, taking up the theme more or less where the Jazz Days stopped. And the modern series by the Philharmonic and Radio Symphony Orchestras had just found favour with their audiences when the New Music Group piped up to show that you can tackle matters quite differently with a smaller group.

Theatrical rivals in East and West: The drama scene in Berlin is just as varied. The decades during which the city was divided led to a parallel dual development which has in some respects enriched the result. During the post-war years each sector of the city strove to demonstrate its cultural independence or even superiority as part of the general rivalry between the two systems.

One example is the Volksbühne, the People's Theatre Organisation which made theatrical history during the Wilhelminian Era with its performances of censored plays by Gerhard Hauptmann, Strindberg and Ibsen, which lay in the Eastern sector. Because the corresponding organisation in West Berlin also needed a stage for its performances, it built its own Theater der Freien Volksbühne in the Schaperstrasse. The Free People's Theatre opened in 1963. The first director was Erwin Piscator, famous as the creator of the "proletarian theatre" during the 1920s. He had recently celebrated his comeback as a committed man of the theatre with the première of Rolf Hochhuth's *The Deputy* in the Theater am Kurfürstendamm.

Berlin's principal theatres were mostly located in the old city centre. They were the scene of many a triumph for the most famous producers of their times – Werner Krauss, Gustav Gründgens, Paul Wegener, Elisabeth Bergner, Käthe Dorsch and Käthe Gold.

Left, *Der Hauptmann von Köpenick* prformed in the Schiller Theatre. Above, "One, two, three" in the Theatre of the West.

The première of Brecht and Weill's *Three-penny Opera* in the **Theater am Schiff-bauerdamm** in 1928 achieved world fame. After the war, Brecht returned from exile in the United States to East Berlin. Largely as a result of his inspiration and authority, coupled with generous state subsidies, the Berliner Ensemble established a world-wide reputation for the East German stage.

The **Grips-Theater** at the Hansaplatz has also achieved international fame. Youth drama performed here in exemplary productions is imitated in many countries and languages. One musical, *Line 1*, can even claim to have become a hit. At its première in 1986,

amazed critics and audience witnessed a performance which could be considered to represent the birth of the Berlin – or even the German – musical. With Line 1 (which refers to the underground railway line between Bahnhof Zoo and the Schlesisches Tor), the German musical emancipated itself from its American forerunners. With typical Berlin wit it has come of age, thereby becoming both cosmopolitan and exportable.

A pilgrimage to the show stage: In 1970, when it suddenly hit the headlines, the Schaubühne was on Hallesches Ufer in Kreuzberg – a location which, in those days,

was far from the city's official temples of culture. When it opened with Brecht/Gorki's *The Mother* with Therese Giehse in the main role, it set a standard that was surpassed only by its own performances. It achieved the impossible with Ibsen's *Peer Gynt* and Gorki's *Summer Visitors* in a production by Peter Stein, and with its trend-setting Shakespeare cycles and classical plays. In 1981 the "Show Stage" acquired a theatre with the latest technology in its new home near the Lehniner Platz.

The Schaubühne was in many respects a belated West-Berlin answer to the Berliner Ensemble and Brecht's epic theatre in the Eastern zone. The latter still produces outstanding performances, based as before, on specific stage directions of the master dramatist. East Berlin was also the home of the city's only world-standard revue: in the Friedrichstadtpalast in Friedrichstrasse, artistes, ice dancers and jugglers present classical variety theatre in a form most people would think is long since dead.

Regaining former glory: Thanks to its countless stages, many of which must be counted amongst the most celebrated in the German-speaking world and which can stand comparison with the best anywhere, since reunification Berlin has the opportunity to regain its former position as one of the most important cities on the European cultural scene. A varied programme is available virtually all the year round.

"Official" and "alternative" culture alternates in Berlin. The 200 or so unofficial groups make it impossible to keep track of the fringe scene; this very unpredictability introduces a welcome element of surprise, contributing a lively eccentricity as well as innovation. The work – indeed, the very existence of all these alternative stages and theatre groups, which in the past gave birth to the celebrated Schaubühne – can be relied upon to ensure that in future the "official" music and drama will not be permitted to fossilise in subsidised complacency and repetitive routine.

Left, a revealing performance on Breitscheid-platz. **Right**, a performance of *Hamlet Machine* in the Deutsche Theater.

It is not easy to establish when night begins in Berlin – and even more difficult to decide when it ends. Night-time here is not just a cocktail at sunset on the rooftop terrace of the Intercontinental, or a steamer trip under the reunited German stars on the Wannsee – or even an expense-account cowboy's surreptitious taxi ride to the Madame Club in Grunewald after the evening's television programmes have given way to the test card. Even when the yawning barmaid counts the takings and the waitress calls "No more oxtail soup!" through the swing doors, the night is still not over for many a reveller propping up the long, empty bar.

For Uschi, the municipal bus driver, the night begins when she steers her big yellow vehicle into the omnibus station in the Helmholtzstrasse. Before she goes out she will just have time to dash round the supermarket, casting a quick glimpse into her letter box and exchanging a few words with her daughter, who is glued to the video being played on television. This evening her mother is going dancing in the Café Keese in the Bismarckstrasse. Here the ladies rule the roost, and the men follow them hesitantly, but ready for anything, onto the dance floor.

The Big Eden on the corner of the "Ku'-damm" and Knesebeckstrasse has already opened its doors. But who would want to rave it up in the old-fashioned disco cavern whilst the temperature outside is still 26 degrees and a sweet-toothed queue is waiting impatiently in front of the Old San Francisco Ice Salon? Yet, for some it's never too early. In front of the disco entrance they have already surveyed the ancient publicity photos in the showcases – the nominal owner, aging playboy Rolf Eden, with Elke Sommer, Telly Savalas and other celebrities whose images are as faded as their old-fashioned photos. They have said to themselves: "Per-

haps it'll click with a hot number straightaway, and then we'll have the entire evening ahead of us."

Susi switches the video recorder to "The Denver Clan" and rolls over again. For her, the day has not even started yet: it is 6 p.m. Susi's night begins when, for most other people, it is almost dawn. Susi is a practitioner of the world's oldest profession, and knows that the night will be half over before a client dares to approach her.

Between the stage and the buffet: In boozers, bars, pubs and saloons the Happy Hour is just beginning at the buffet. Everything is half price until half past seven, and then, when you've got into practice, you can keep going until 5 a.m. Not that the 5,000 beer taverns and schnapps bars ever close. As everybody knows, Berlin is open right round the clock. The door will be locked when the landlord has had enough. But in any case, everybody has to go home sometime – to get changed for the office. The cat will want its supper at some stage, and from time to time even the flowers on the balcony need a drink. Then

<u>Left</u>, a send-up of Marilyn Monroe in the transvestite theatre "Dream Boy's Lachbühne". <u>Above</u>, German rock-star Nina Hagen on stage before the Reichstag.

the taxi drivers from the night shift come in for "lunch". Otto, the baker's boy puts down his empty basket after his round of the local bars and orders. Somebody buys all the shy Tamil youth's flowers "So that he can buy himself a square meal for once", whilst in the Kleine Philharmonie on Schaperstrasse (at the Bundesallee junction), Wanja and his aging friends recall how splendid the coy gay Tefi Balls once were, whilst nowadays Andreas's gaudy "Queens' Ball" in late autumn merely attracts showy butchers' wives and upstart building pimps to a pseudo-carnival of commercially calculated despicableness.

Andreas is the king of parties for men who get on well with other men. Andreas' Kneipe on the Wittenbergplatz, diagonally opposite the KaDeWe department store, encourages pensioners to come for coffee and cake during the afternoon. Any man caught making a pass at a man at that time of day will be evicted. The old girl with the floral hat and the strangely rapt smile is still sitting in front of her schnapps at her favourite table in front of the toilet door when, later on, the decorators and buffet servers from the delicatessen section at KaDeWe appear. One of them, who once served the vegetables at Bolle, now stands behind the counter as "Romanova". Careers in Berlin are often like that.

The transvestites, who every evening invite the guests in Chez Nous in the Marburger Strasse to join them in the can-can, have aged gracefully between their tulle, sequins and ostrich feathers. Lunchtime customers at Kaiser's complaining that the bacon wasn't sufficiently smoked last time have no idea that, a few hours later, they can see the short-tempered elderly gentleman with a paunch and a bald patch swinging his hips like Mae West in Chez Nous.

Mascha leans over the crystal ball. The black student from Upper Volta wants to know what the future has in store for him. Mascha has already given a number of prominent friends useful tips. "It runs in the family. We have the power", he explains curtly. All Berliners must be superstitious – otherwise the city would not be so full of soothsayers, card-readers, pendulum-swingers and star-gazers.

Marion believes in the future too. She hopes to make it to the top. At half-past nine in the evening she is sitting in the Hansa Studio in the Tiergarten, crooning a hackneyed pop song into the microphone for the umpteenth time. The sound engineer yawns; the technician grins and thinks of the Rolling Stones. Marion does her best. The song is stupid, but her agent has managed to arrange an appearance for her in a television show and another at the Solicitors' Ball. It's a start, anyway: what else will come will come. Also waiting in the wings for the big break are some 2,000 rock bands, pop combos, singers, folk groups and jazz trios.

The local rock tearaways are sitting on the lakeshore in Grunewald. They have parked their powerful motorbikes (BMWs, Harley Davidsons and souped-up Moto-Guzzis) on the sandy footpath and have lit a bonfire. Don Gibson, Buddy Holly, Elvis and Carl Perkins croon away at full volume from the huge portable radio. A crate of beer stands on one side; one of the girls plans to grill curry-flavoured sausages; the gang leader's "Missis" has brought some macaroni salad.

There will be plenty of drinking, singing and laughing before the night is over. One of the boys is bound to fall in the lake and almost drown. Some of the others will suggest that they all go "Turk-bashing", but another will point out – with the insight of one who has drunk more than he should – that it would be better to "leave the poor bastards in peace".

Carpe diem: Heike Ruschmeyer is sitting in her studio in the Kulmer Strasse and thinking. It is half past one and she has just completed another picture. She doesn't really want to look at it: at first glance, she may not like some aspect of her work. She needs to sleep on it first. Maybe she should go to the Dschungel in the Nürnberger Strasse. They usually don't just let anyone in, but if you do

make it you can feel honoured. It doesn't matter whether you are unemployed or in the throes of cold turkey. As you sail majestically down the magnificent 1950s staircase you will feel as if you are taking part in one of the spectacular films of the olden days. The "olden days" are in at the moment. Looking the way your parents once did is the very latest trend. In the Dschungel nobody looks at what you are wearing, but they still notice it all the same. The mail-order catalogue look is the hottest thing of all – crêpe shoes, nylon shirts and a carefully Brylcreemed short-back-and-sides. And, in the background, cool jazz imported from the West Indian district of London.

The streetlamps are still burning although day is beginning to dawn over the Tiergarten. Susi is fed up. She has been prowling back and forth between Kurfürstenstrasse and Genthiner Strasse but there was hardly a prospective client in sight. So she wanders into Tom's (on the junction of Eisenacher Strasse and Motzstrasse), knocks back a few sherries and tells her gay friends in building labourers' gear about her previous life as Hans-Bernd, the photographer's assistant in Cottbus. Her parents accept their son's leanings even though her father is a member of the Party.

The conspirators of the night: The snack bar at the corner of Trautenaustrasse and the Bundesallee is open until 5 a.m. That is a record in this city which although it never sleeps, has few nocturnal rendezvous for empty stomachs. Taxi drivers swear by the fiery shashlik, but decide to do without the beer when they see the occupants of the police patrol car approaching to treat themselves to a plateful of Thuringian sausages ("with chips, but hold the salt"). How many times has the man in the white overall already dipped his strainer into the hot fat, and how many times has he chopped up burst sausages before smothering them in watery ketchup? The light music programme RIAS 2 tootles away from the small transistor radio next to the coffee machine.

These are the conspirators of the night, the allies between midnight and dawn. The children of Bahnhof Zoo: the aging transvestite in Hollywood glitter, the rock gang by the camp fire, the wistful girl by the tape recorder. There is no night, and the morning will never come. When the early risers stagger out of bed, the others are not yet ready to sleep; when one group says goodbye, the others have not yet greeted each other. The 24-hour city: there are 3.2 million souls in this impossible metropolis. And between them they have 3.2 million stories to tell. Who can judge when one of them should stop talking?

Above, cabaret girls let it all hang out in the Friedrichstadtpalast.

There are supposedly visitors who come to Berlin not to see the Kurfürstendamm or the Alexanderplatz, nor even the consumer's paradise *Kaufhaus des Westens* or the monumental avenue Unter den Linden. They come because "things happen here", because "the whole place has a different feeling about it"; it is irrelevant whether they themselves are from the old Federal Republic, from the former GDR, or from abroad.

The attraction of which they speak is neither a specific establishment nor the pestilential Berlin air. The Berlin scene has no official opening times, like a museum or is it a clearly defined area like the zoo within a sea of normality. The scene is everywhere where people set store by shaking a bit of life into the sleepy provincial atmosphere. The scene is made up of people who have new ideas, who are seeking new experiences and a new brand of creativity.

During the era of the Wall, West Berlin became a mecca for restless souls who found the prospect of a carefully planned existence in some Federal provincial town too restrictive. "Normal" people found little attraction in the idea of scaling the ladder of professional success in the permanently threatened island-city. Correspondingly, individualists, survival experts and opponents of the system found opportunities within the hothouse atmosphere of the western half of Berlin even more enticing.

During the complacent, ignorant time of the Economic Miracle such "deviants" had few chances of being accepted in the "frontier town" of the Western world. But during the 1960s a new generation accustomed to an affluent lifestyle had grown up in both the Federal Republic and West Berlin – a generation which longed for fresh ideals and which revolted against the black-and-white clichéd images of the Cold War. They dismissed as irrelevant the slogan formulated by Konrad Adenauer, the first Chancellor of the Federal Republic of Germany: "No experimenting!"

Protest and alternative lifestyles: As the horrors of the US involvement in the war in the Vietnam jungle became known, America's credibility as a "guardian of the peace" was also destroyed. The student movement shook up not only the way the universities saw themselves politically; but it also blew away the fustiness hidden under academic gowns and with it the structure of private life as a whole, which was now seen to be repressive. The first communes and flat-sharing groups were formed. People became accustomed, slowly at first, to the existence of alternative lifestyles and to the unorthodox appearance of angry young people.

Skeletons were soon discovered not only in the cupboard of world politics, but on the domestic front as well. Some protesters went underground and used violence in the fight against the capitalist system. Others became involved in citizens' initiatives in an attempt to put an end to the destruction being wreaked on the environment and to the quality of life in the name of social progress. Today, there is scarcely a sphere of life where private initiative does not exist independently of state control.

Playgroups and women's refuges, gay meeting places and women's centres are all part of the daily scene. Bar-keepers' and taxi-drivers' collectives, bicycle shops and craftsmen's associations are all part of the left-of-centre city infrastructure. There are local magazines like *Zitty* published for the entire metropolitan area, and smaller periodicals for the individual districts. And the biggest alternative publishing project of all, originally serving only the Federal Republic and since reunification covering the entire country is the leftist daily newspaper *taz*, founded in 1979 in protest against the conservative press monopoly within the city.

Finally, at the end of the 1970s, a new political force of the Alternative List (AL) – was born, a "Green" party which in 1989 stood for the Berlin Senate in alliance with

Left, Left-wing "68" student leader Rudi Dutschke speaks to fellow activists.

the SPD. In 1990 it became the Association of Greens.

The desperate housing shortage: The alternative lifestyle has not yet brought peace to the social system and there was a fresh storm of protest in the autumn of 1980. In spite of a serious shortage of housing, unscrupulous landlords, including non-profit-making associations, continued to permit some 20,000 cheap flats to remain empty. Entire blocks were like ghost towns. Once they were dilapidated it was easy to obtain a demolition order and to make an exorbitant profit from the new building, especially with the assistance of public subsidies. By adopting this tional and occasionally violent manner in which they defended the houses against the authorities, the local citizenry was aware of the social problems to which they were drawing attention.

The popular newspapers published by the House of Springer and the senator for domestic affairs, Heinrich Lummer – notorious at the time as an agitator – roused public opinion against the "anarchists", who were disturbing the peace of their smug fellow-citizens. With a large contingent of police, Lummer arrogantly had some of the houses cleared. On 22 September 1981 there was a bloody street battle, during the course of

approach, many speculators destroyed and subsequently "restored" entire blocks.

To fight against machinations of this kind, a front was formed by people who over the course of two years occupied and renovated, with skill and imagination, some 170 old buildings which were standing empty. Most of them, unemployed young people, were not interested in spectacular protest: their concern was to create for themselves enough space to be able to determine their own lives. Most Berliners adopted an understanding attitude towards the squatters. Although they were sometimes shocked at the unconven- which an 18-year-old youth, Klaus-Jürgen Rattay, was knocked down and killed by a bus in the Potsdamer Strasse as he attempted to flee the police baton charge. The powerless rage of many of the demonstrators was unleashed in the shattering of shop windows in several streets. After the Conservative CDU-ruled senate under the mayor of the time, Richard von Weizsäcker, had maintained a hard-line approach, the increased pressure of numerous supporters led to a change of heart. One-third of the occupations was legalised and the squatters were given right of tenure. What was more, the

CDU senator for social matters, Ulf Fink, released over the next years a total of DM10 million from the senate's budget for self-help groups and self-administered businesses.

The subsidy, which came to be known as the "Fink Bank", was not merely the result of sympathy for alternative lifestyles. Conservative politicians had long since recognised that these alternatives also served to correct the tense situation within the labour market. When the state itself was not able to offer more job vacancies, such measures at least provided support in the alternative sphere. Furthermore, environmental protection, the use of natural resources rather than a slavish

makers like Lothar Lambert or Rosa von Praunheim has become too loud for that.

For some time now, Berlin has been a centre for alternative large-scale industry. One example is the Mehringhof, a former factory which contains almost 30 businesses and institutions ranging from *Alternative Energy* to the *Network*, the financing body for self-administered projects, and *Ecotopia* – not forgetting *Ex*, the pub and meeting place which always seems to be packed.

Another popular gathering place is the UFA factory for culture, sport and handicrafts in the Victoriastrasse in Tempelhof. The varied activities range from ecological

adherence to technological progress, and a rejection of the throwaway society, can be regarded as conservative, rather than capitalist, objectives.

The development of a subculture: The cultural and social criticism stemming from this subculture can no longer be ignored by the Establishment. The alternative voice in the shape of the *Grips* children's and youth theatre, young writers and painters, musicians from punk to jazz, and subculture film

Left, contrasting uniforms. **Above**, baking wholemeal bread in the UFA Factory.

projects – for example the planting of trees and shrubs on roofs, a café and a cinema – via dozens of courses and workshops to the active organisation of leisure time or self-fulfilment, or to a wholemeal bakery which produces 2,500 loaves of bread per week. "No chiefs, one kitchen, one kitty and lots of beds" is the philosophy of some 70 alternative-minded Berliners, who live and work together in an extended family. Popular throughout the city and beyond is the UFA circus, in which 35 members of the commune perform as jugglers, animal tamers, clowns, artists and magicians.

Already something of an institution, at least during the summer months, is the Tempodrom, a permanent circus tent in which alternative entertainment of every kind is offered. The Tempodrom stands on the historic site of *In den Zelten* (by the tents) which is the name of the square in the Tiergarten, opposite the Reichstag. Tents stood here 150 years ago, when the local citizens congregated at weekends to enjoy beer and dancing.

The Eastern scene: Those who believe that there was no opportunity for the development of a subculture in East Berlin similar to that in the West are quite mistaken. For the youth of the German Democratic Republic,

ited adventurous undertakings, not to mention official recognition such as the "Fink Bank". Resistance was expressed most usually in refusal or in the risky exposure of social and political misdeeds – a sort of alternative *glasnost*. This was an approach which required considerable courage and imagination in the former GDR.

Nonetheless, the young people of East Berlin made for themselves their own "alternative" niches, such as on the Prenzlauer Berg, a district which is often compared with Kreuzberg in the West. As long ago as the 1980s there were alternative bars there – albeit not so loud as those in the West – and

East Berlin always represented a glittering, cosmopolitan ideal – even if the latter was relatively seldom visible under the stranglehold of the SED. The proximity of the "Showcase of the Western World", combined with the traditional tolerance of a metropolis, permitted the creation of an alternative scene which stands comparison with the liveliness, if not the violence, of its counterpart across the Wall.

It is clear that life on the Eastern side of the Wall was less spectacular than in the West, and that the censorship imposed by the omnipresent SED agents of repression prohib-

gay meeting places and flat-sharing schemes in occupied flats and houses. Apart from the official cultural scene, independent groups were formed; their performances were watched with enthusiasm by visitors from West Berlin. Eccentric fashions were created and shown in private. Artists created galleries in back yards and garages; fringe theatre provided countless opportunities to publicise matters usually veiled in silence.

Only since the removal of the Wall has it been clear just how extensive the alternative scene of East Berlin was. Freed of the restrictions of life in a socialist society, within a few months a considerable number of projects took off. Entire housing complexes, hitherto abandoned to decay, were occupied and renovated in an improvised manner in order to experiment – as in West Berlin – with new lifestyles. One example is the Oranienburger Strasse in the Central District. Here the remains of the Friedrichspassagen were earmarked for demolition, because a street was to be built there. Yet, today some 30 people live and work in the "Tacheles multi-cultural artists' centre and meeting place". Original works of art can be viewed, and there are numerous musical and theatrical performances. Many have a good chance of being

ment of a political attitude different to that in the West. Before the 1989 "October Revolution" the struggle against the potentates of the SED and their destructive approach to environmental and social questions was fought with great determination and personal energy. Now the scene must defend its beliefs against the bourgeois man-in-the-street as he chases his personal longed-for Economic Miracle and against the radical right-wing youth who see a peaceful alternative lifestyle as pure provocation.

The members of East Berlin's alternative scene are determined to pursue their aims in a peaceful manner. Their lack of experience

allowed to establish themselves as permanent fixtures.

However, the alternative scene in the East has other problems to solve. Here, it is not just a matter of the realisation of chosen lifestyles, but a question of basic survival. The years of resistance to a system intolerant of non-conformists has led to the develop-

in hard street fighting, and the years of repression – experienced every day and usually directed towards the individual – have given them a different resistance potential from their counterparts in the West. The involvement of church-like institutions has played a role. Solidarity and a feeling of community lend the alternative scene of East Berlin a touch of Woodstock.

Left and **above**, on St Christopher's day gays and lesbians throng the streets – just like in the USA. **Following pages**: it was Berlin's women who cleared away all the rubble; squatters in residence.

Both scenes, however, have quite a lot in common. Their aims are basically the same – an environment in which life is worth living, a lovable city and the creation of a framework for peaceful co-existence.

WOMEN'S LIB

Berlin is a feminine city. "Berlin", enthuses Johanna passionately, "Berlin is like a love affair. First comes the tingling sensation of attraction, then the confrontation with the unexpected harshness of reality, and finally the realisation that you must be prepared to take your life into your own hands, and that then everything is possible." Her eyes sparkling, this young woman from Swabian Stuttgart laughs as only true Berliners can, even if they were born in Munich, Dresden or Istanbul. It is a full-throated laugh with the charm of those who do not take themselves unduly seriously.

A women's city. No other metropolis has been so indelibly imprinted by the character of its women. The famous 19th-century salons of Rahel Varnhagen, Henriette Hertz and Bettina von Arnim are just a handful of obvious examples. Everybody who could lay claim to be somebody gathered here, provided they were also quick-witted. Those who wished to match up to these well-educated women needed to be in possession of more than an academic title and a literary reputation. And it was Queen Sophie-Charlotte who during the 18th century supervised the founding of the Academy of Science and summoned scientists like Leibniz to Berlin.

Over the years, the women of Berlin have added a fighting spirit and social commitment to this propensity for wit. The artist Käthe Kollwitz took up the cause of the poorest of the poor, the children who lived in abject poverty. At the end of the last century Lina Morgenstern founded the first educational association for women factory workers, and Else Lasker-Schüler chose Berlin as the city in which to find inspiration for her literary works.

But the women of Berlin have sometimes won back their city in a highly subversive, even a radical, way. The first women's centre in Germany was opened in the Stresemannstrasse; during the student revolts the "Women's Council" threw tomatoes at the SDS, the male-dominated socialist student union. Playgroups were formed as a way of escaping domestic isolation; refuges were set up for maltreated women and girls; prostitutes joined together to form the association known as *Hydra*, which fought for their rights and recognition. In 1990 the first old people's home run exclusively by women was established.

Women have also achieved a great deal in less spectacular ways. Their early efforts were often greeted with derision, which rapidly changed to admiration in the light of their successes. The first house to be occupied exclusively by women, a former sweet factory, is now a feminist centre for the entire district. Today there are galleries, cafés, bars, information offices, health centres, even a hotel for women (*Artemisia*, tel: 878905). The list is endless. It sometimes seems as if masculine establishments have become totally superfluous.

Even the Senate of West Berlin was dominated by women from 1989. There were, admittedly, reasons for this: it was a clever move to gain popularity by the newly elected Socialist mayor, Walter Momper. He chose five women to fill senatorial posts, and a further three were proposed by the Alternative List, the SPD's smaller coalition partner. Eight women against five men - a situation greeted with scepticism and celebrated with euphoria. In any case they were observed far more critically than their masculine colleagues.

One of these woman senators instilled fear which spread far beyond her opponents in Berlin: she pitted herself against the entire atomic power industry of the land. Michaela Schreyer, the Senator for Development and Environmental Protection, was an independent appointed by the Alternative List. Despite opposition from the highest quarters she refused to license the controversial atomic research reactor of the Hahn-Meitner Institute because of insufficient provision for waste disposal. During her period in office she asserted herself in an expert manner which won her lasting respect.

The women of Berlin are simply tougher when it is a question of claiming their rights. They are also fairer when it comes to sharing – a fact documented by past history as well as the present. Come what may, Berlin's future is bound to be feminine or nothing.

Change, probably the most constant factor about Berlin, leads Berliners ironically to say: "As long as the Spree is still flowing through Berlin...". There's scarcely a place in the city but there's some elderly Berliner who can tell you how it used to look once upon a time. There's scarcely a street that hasn't altered, if not its outward appearance, at least its general air. And so many squares have changed both in look and in name.

One of the main reasons for the city's strange new profile is without doubt the devastation left behind after World War II. Reconstruction was not always along historical lines. And there was the Wall, which necessitated two separate city plans. Once central and bustling places like Potsdamer Platz and Friedrichstrasse became wasteland. Finding your way around this vast city, which is large enough in area to take almost the entire Ruhr, can seem an almost impossible task. Even 150 years ago Adolf Glassbrenner asked: "Where is Berlin in Berlin? Just because you had a glass of the popular *Weißbier* doesn't mean you know anything about Berlin".

Berlin has no city centre in the sense that Paris or London has, although there's the historic centre, known as Berlin Mitte. And there's a kind of City, the "Neuer Westen" or New West along Kurfürstendamm, which is no longer quite the cultural boom area it was in the 1920s but which now enjoys a commercial boom. But essentially Berlin is made up of lots of little towns, and in part even village communities.

Altogether, Berlin is divided into 23 districts, each with its own distinctive features and each with its own infrastructure. Twelve of these districts are in western Berlin and 11 in eastern Berlin. To give an idea of the diverse faces of the city, these districts are described one by one in the following chapters. In addition, a separate chapter is devoted to the Kurfürstendamm, which isn't really a district, but which is one of the main attractions for visitors to the city. For that reason, it is placed at the very beginning of this section.

The individual districts are not divided into east and west but presented from the centre of the city outwards. After Kurfürstendamm the logical next chapter is Berlin Mitte, with its historic centre, Alexanderplatz, and of course that ancient boulevard Unter den Linden, once glorious and maybe glorious again. Then, as now, the two territories of Berlin Mitte and Charlottenburg, the centre and the New West, were separated by Tiergarten. Schöneberg, Kreuzberg, Friedrichshahn and Prenzlauer Berg follow. These, with their old tenement blocks and back courtyards and above all their animated atmosphere are the most "urban" areas of Berlin. Not for nothing is Prenzlauer Berg often called the Kreuzberg of East Berlin. As far as liveliness is concerned, it looks like it will soon be the other way round.

Pankow and Wedding are Prenzlauer Berg's immediate neighbours and are typical traditional working-class districts. Weißensee, Lichtenberg, Treptow, Neukölln and Tempelhof were originally planned as suburbs and have developed their own individual identity.

Steglitz, Zehlendorf and Wilmersdorf are traditional middle-class districts, with lots of open spaces and elegant houses. Zehlendorf is the most sought-after of all the districts. And Reinickendorf is the "green north", a district of contrasts. Agricultural Lübars is as much a part of it as the dormitory town of Märkisches Viertel.

Spandau and Köpenick are places in their own right, not only in this book. Both are older than Berlin, which was founded over 750 years ago as a small trading post. Finally, the three districts of Hohenschönhausen, Marzahn and Hellersdorf are treated together. They did not emerge as independent districts until later, in the 1970s and 1980s.

Welcome to Berlin!

Preceding pages: sledging on the Teufelsberg; the Memorial Church and the Kurfürstendamm; slow dancing. Left, topless in an oasis of green.

Berlin and Environs

4 km/ 2,5 miles

Hohen - Neuendorf

Mühlenbeck

Mathiasberg
▲ 56

Bötzow

Henningsdorf

E46

Sc

Glienicke / Nordb.

Schönwalde

FROHNAU

BERLINER
FORST
TEGEL

HERMSDF.

LÜBAR

HEILIGENSEE

WAIDMANNS-
LUST

Humboldt Palace

NC

KONRADS-
HÖHE

BORSIG-
WALDE

WITTENAU

WILH
R

BERLINER FORST
SPANDAU

Falkensee

TEGEL

TEGELORT

REINICKENDORF

HAKENFELDE

F.-FALKENHÖH

SPANDAU-
NEUSTADT

Airport

K.-Schumacher-
Damm

WEDDING

SPANDAU

Citadel

HASELHORST

SIEMENS-
STADT

KLOSTER-
FELDE

STRESOW

Charlottenburg
Palace

TIERGARTE

STAAKEN

WILHELM-
STADT

WESTEND

Bellevue Palace

Brande
Ga

Seeburg

PICHELSDORF

CHARLOTTENBG

Victory Column

Radio Tower

WILMERS-
DF.

SCHÖN

Finkenberg
▲ 75

GATOW

Karlsbg.
▲ 78

BERLINER

GRUNEWALD

Fahrland

Groß-
Glienicke

Gatow Airfield

FORST

Grunewald
Hunting Lodge

SCHMARGEN-
DF.

FRIEDENAU

2

KLADOW

GRUNEWALD

DAHLEM

STEGLITZ

Havel

ZEHLENDF.

P.-NEDLITZ

NIKOLASSEE

LICHTER-
FELDE

LANKWITZ

P.-BORNIM

P.-SACROW

WANNSEE

Berlin-
Zehlendorf

273

Cecilienhof
Palace

Kl. Glienicke
Palace

SCHÖNOW

MARIEN

Sans Souci
Palace

Babelsberg
Palace

P.-KLEIN-
GLIENICKE

Kleinmachnow

Potsdam

STEIN-
STÜCKEN

Teltow

P.-
BABELSBERG

Stahnsdorf

1

101

2

Kl.
Ravensberg
▲ 114

P.-DREWITZ

Güterfelde

Großbeeren

Bergholz

Rehbrücke

126

BE.-NIBELUNGEN

Zepernick

Börnicke

BE.-EICHWERDER

BE.-BIRKENHÖHE

Weesow

Abzweig.
Berlin - Pankow

BUCH

109

Birkholz

Löhme

Werneuchen

E 74

158

Lindenberg

KAROW

Blumberg

DER-
ÖNHSN.

BLANKENBG.

Krummensee

MALCHOW

WARTENBG.

Ahrensfelde

NKOW

Mehrow

Altlandsberg

HEINERSDORF

FALKENBG.

Eiche

WEISSENSEE

HOHEN-
SCHÖNHSN.

Bruchmühle

ENZLAUER
BERG

BERLIN

Neuenhagen

Tower

LICHTENBG.

Fredersdorf

FRIEDRICHS-
HAIN

Socialist Memorial

TE

FRIEDRICHS-
FELDE

BIESDF.

KAULS-
DORF

MAHLS-
DORF

1/5

UZBG.

STRALAU

Münchehofe

Vogelsdorf

TREPTOW

Spree

Soviet
Memorial

KARLSHORST

MAHLSDF.-
SÜD

Schöneiche

E 74

NEU-
KÖLLN

OBER-
SCHÖNEWEIDE

UHLEN-
HORST

PEL-
F

NIEDER-
SCHÖNEWEIDE

Spree

FRIEDRICH-
HAGEN

WILHELMS-
HAGEN

Wolters-
dorf

EN-

BRITZ

JOHANNISTHAL

ADLERSHOF

Gr. Müggelsee

OW I

BUCKOW II

KÖPENICK

RAHNSDORF

Erkner

BUCKOW

ALT-
GLIENICKE

GRÜNAU

Müggelberge
▲
115

HESSEN-
WINKEL

MÜGGELHEIM

RUDOW

Abzweig.
Berlin - Zentrum

BOHNSDORF

Langer
See

Große
Krampe

TEN-
DE

KAROLINEN-
HOF

Seddinsee

Schönefeld Airport

Eichwalde

Neu - Zittau

96

E 15

179

SCHMÖCK-
WITZ

Wernsdorf

Zeuthener
See

Schulzendorf

Zeuthen

127

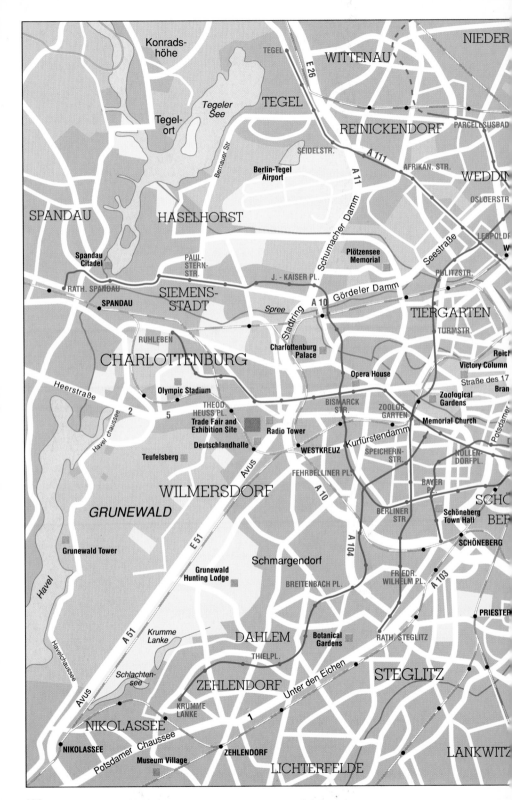

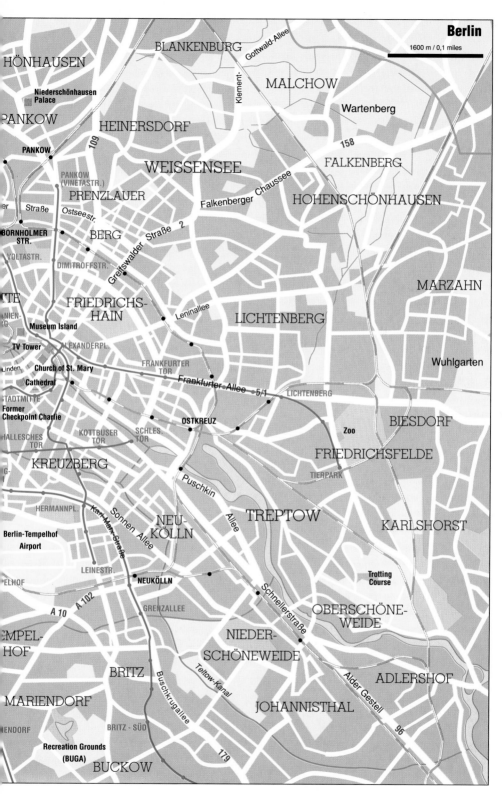

Berlin

1600 m / 0,1 miles

HÖNHAUSEN

BLANKENBURG

Gottwald-Allee

MALCHOW

Klement-

Niederschönhausen
Palace

PANKOW

HEINERSDORF

Wartenberg

109

PANKOW

158

WEISSENSEE

FALKENBERG

PANKOW
(VINETASTR.)

PRENZLAUER

Falkenberger Chaussee

HOHENSCHÖNHAUSEN

er   Straße

Ostseestr.

BORNHOLMER
STR.

BERG

Greifswalder Straße 2

VOLTASTR.

DIMITROFFSTR.

MARZAHN

TE

FRIEDRICHS-
HAIN

Leninallee

LICHTENBERG

NIEN-
G

Museum Island

Wuhlgarten

TV Tower

ALEXANDERPL.

FRANKFURTER
TOR

Linden

Church of St. Mary

Frankfurter Allee   5/1

LICHTENBERG

Cathedral

STADTMITTE

BIESDORF

Former
Checkpoint Charlie

OSTKREUZ

Zoo

HALLESCHES
TOR

KOTTBUSER
TOR

SCHLES.
TOR

FRIEDRICHSFELDE

KREUZBERG

TIERPARK

G-

Puschkin

HERMANNPL.

Sonnen-Allee

NEU-
KÖLLN

Allee

TREPTOW

KARLSHORST

Berlin-Tempelhof
Airport

Karl-Marx-Straße

LEINESTR.

Trotting
Course

ELHOF

NEUKÖLLN

A 10   A 102

GRENZALLEE

OBERSCHÖNE-
WEIDE

EMPEL-
HOF

NIEDER-
SCHÖNEWEIDE

Schnellerstraße

BRITZ

Buschkrugallee

Teltow-Kanal

ADLERSHOF

MARIENDORF

Alder Gestell

JOHANNISTHAL

96

ENDORF

BRITZ - SÜD

Recreation Grounds
(BUGA)

179

BUCKOW

Berliner Nahverkehrsnetz
Schnellbahnnetz

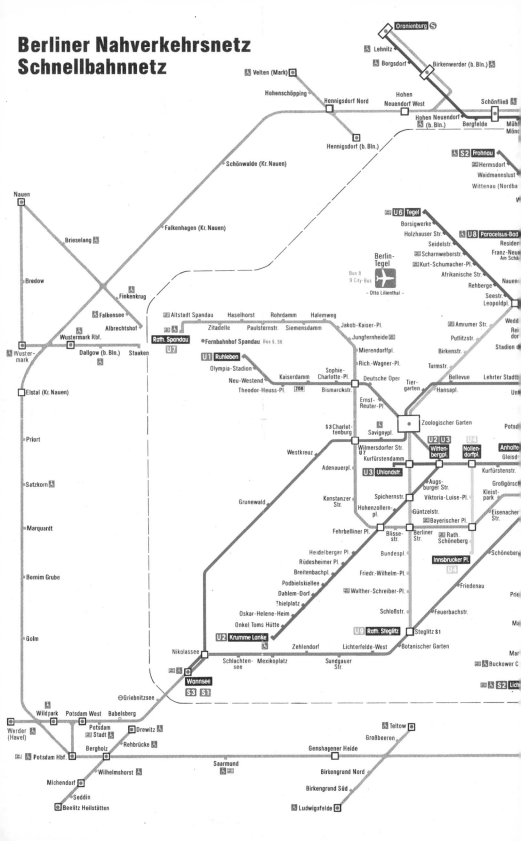

Oranienburg **S**

Lehnitz

Borgsdorf   Birkenwerder (b. Bln.)

Velten (Mark)

Hohenschöpping   Hohen
                        Neuendorf West   Schönfließ

Hennigsdorf Nord   Hohen Neuendorf   Bergfelde   Müh
                                    (b. Bln.)   Mönc

Schönwalde (Kr. Nauen)   Hennigsdorf (b. Bln.)

                                                            S2 Frohnau
                                                            Hermsdorf
                                                            Waidmannslust
Nauen   Wittenau (Nordba

Brieselang   **U6** Tegel
                                    Borsigwerke
Falkenhagen (Kr. Nauen)   Holzhauser Str.   **U8** Paracelsus-Bad
                                    Seidelstr.   Resider
Bredow   Scharnweberstr.   Franz-Neu
                                    Kurt-Schumacher-Pl.   Am Schä
Finkenkrug   Berlin-
                    Tegel   Afrikanische Str.
Falkensee   Bus 8   Rehberge   Nauen
Albrechtshof   9 City-Bus   Seestr.
Wustermark Rbf.   - Otto Lilienthal - Leopoldpl.
Dallgow (b. Bln.)   Staaken   Altstadt Spandau Haselhorst Rohrdamm Halemweg   Amrumer Str.   Wedd
Wuster-   Zitadelle   Paulsternstr. Siemensdamm   Jakob-Kaiser-Pl. Putlitzstr. Rei
mark   Rath. Spandau   Jungfernheide   dor
                    U7   Fernbahnhof Spandau Bus 5, 56   Mierendorffpl. Birkenstr. Stadion d
Elstal (Kr. Nauen) **U1** Ruhleben   Rich.-Wagner-Pl. Turmstr.
                    Olympia-Stadion   Deutsche Oper   Bellevue Lehrter Stadt
Priort   Neu-Westend   Kaiserdamm   Sophie-   Tier-   Hansapl.
                    Theodor-Heuss-Pl. ZOB   Charlotte-Pl. Bismarckstr.   garten   Un
                                                            Deutsche Oper
Satzkorn   S3 Charlot-   Zoologischer Garten
                                    tenburg   Savignypl.   Potsd
Marquardt   Westkreuz   Wilmersdorfer Str.   **U2 U3**
                                    U7   Witten-   Nollen- **U4** Anhalte
                    Adenauerpl.   Kurfürstendamm   bergpl.   dorfpl.   Gleisd
Bornim Grube   **U3** Uhlandstr.   Kurfürstenstr.
                                    Augs-   Großgörsc
                    Grunewald   Konstanzer burger Str. Spichernstr. Viktoria-Luise-Pl. Kleist-
                                    Str.   park
Golm   Hohenzollern- Güntzelstr.   Eisenacher
                                    pl.   Bayerischer Pl.   Str.
                    Fehrbelliner Pl. Blisse-   Berliner Rath.
                                    str.   Str.   Schöneberg
                    Heidelberger Pl. Bundespl.   Schöneber
                    Rüdesheimer Pl.   **U4**
                    Breitenbachpl. Friedr.-Wilhelm-Pl.   Innsbrucker Pl.
                    Podbielskiallee   Friedenau
                    Dahlem-Dorf   Walther-Schreiber-Pl.   Prie
                    Thielplatz   Feuerbachstr.
                    Oskar-Helene-Heim Schloßstr.
                    Onkel Toms Hütte   **U9** Rath. Steglitz Ma
Wildpark   **U2** Krumme Lanke   Steglitz S1
Potsdam West Babelsberg Nikolassee Zehlendorf Lichterfelde-West Botanischer Garten
                    Schlachten- Mexikoplatz Sundgauer   Buckower C
Werder   see   Str.
(Havel) Griebnitzsee
         Potsdam   Wannsee   **S2** Lich
         Stadt Drewitz **S3 S1**
Bergholz Rehbrücke
Potsdam Hbf.   Teltow
         Wilhelmshorst Großbeeren
Michendorf   Genshagener Heide
Seddin   Saarmund   Birkengrund Nord
Beelitz Heilstätten   Birkengrund Süd
                    Ludwigsfelde

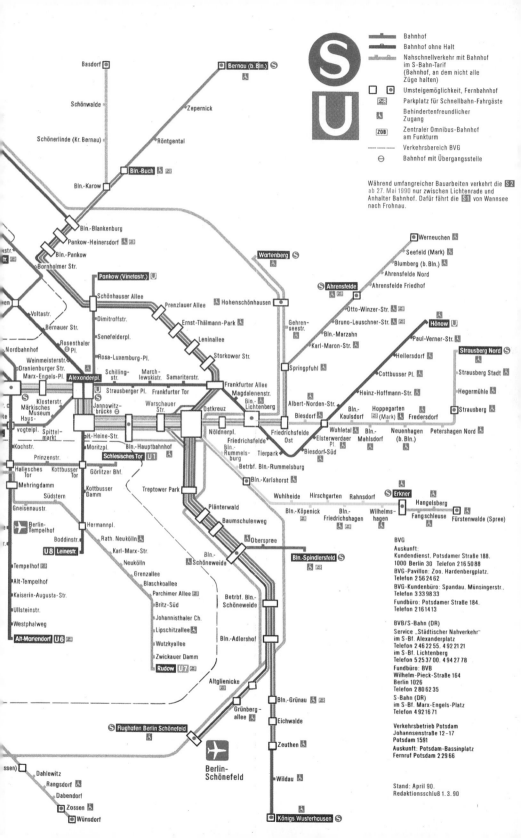

KURFÜRSTENDAMM

"Without the Ku'damm, no Berlin," runs the birthday chorus sung by the Schöneberg Boys' Choir to mark the centenary of their "glorious boulevard" in 1986. They were right, the little choristers. The Kurfürstendamm was, is and will remain the focal point of the western part of Berlin. It's difficult to imagine the present city without it.

Opinion is divided on the question of the exact birthday of the Ku'damm. The street existed as "Knüppeldamm" as far back as 1542. In the beginning it was a rough bridleway for Joachim II to his Grunewald hunting lodge. For centuries, the renowned boulevard was a track across the fields, through sand and marsh, until in 1871 Chancellor Bismarck set his eyes upon the Champs-Elysées in Paris, a thoroughfare through the Bois de Boulogne which had been drawn up by the ingenious master builder Le Nôtre "with a single chalk line through a wasteland".

The Iron Chancellor became obsessed with plans for a similar mighty avenue for the capital of the newly formed German Empire. In 1875 his cabinet issued the following order: length 3.8 km from the zoo to Grunewald, total width 53 metres, space for 7.5-metre gardens on either side, 4-metre pavement and 10-metre carriageway, 5-metre bridleway in the middle and 5-metre promenade, all to enable "the Berlin population to circulate with ease in the open air" and to facilitate "the equestrian training of the upper classes".

Construction on the country road proceeded slowly but by May 1886 steam-driven street cars began running between Grunewald and the zoo. This event marked the real beginning of the Kurfürstendamm. But, as with many things on the Ku'damm, the street cars did not last long. What, however, has lasted since the 1930s, is the Ku'damm myth, which expresses itself in an unde-fined longing called "homesickness for the Kurfürstendamm".

Full speed ahead: Those who wander among the hundred years of history on the Ku'damm today have to look very closely to detect traces of its brilliant past: little remain. But you shouldn't approach the boulevard with the reverential fervour of a pilgrim, or expect to find the golden good old days – the bad times are far too evident. One thing's for sure: a brisk wind blows in this part of Berlin. This is no place to gather dust or dawdle in the slow lane. The Kurfürstendamm is as lively as ever, fun-loving, fast-living, as full of contradictions as it was at the beginning of the century.

The "hollow tooth": With the exception of the protests against the threatened demolition of the ruins of the Gedächtniskirche Kurfürstendamm escaped political demonstrations until the mid-1960s. After the war the ruins were left standing where the church had always stood: in the thick of the traffic surging around **Breitscheidplatz** (named after the Social Democrat politician Rudolf Breitscheid, who was murdered in 1944 in Buchenwald concentration camp). The bare skeleton of the church was a thorn in the sides of the Senate's architectural bureaucrats. It didn't fit in with their concept of an "auto-friendly city".

The *Tagesspiegel* newspaper carried out a survey in 1957, in which 90 per cent of the city's population voted to keep the "hollow tooth". Eventually in 1961 the ruins were integrated into a new **Gedächtniskirche** (Memorial Church), designed by Professor Egon Eiermann. A plaque was erected in the ruined tower, outlining its significance as a memorial: "The tower of the old church serves as a reminder of the judgement that God passed upon our people during the years of the war."

Thanks to its location in the heart of the city, the Gedächtniskirche has also been drawn into the political headlines. In the 1960s and 1970s services were repeatedly interrupted because student leader Rudi Dutschke of the SDS (Association of Socialist German Students) wanted to discuss the Vietnam war with the church-going Christians. Many of the clergy and congregation supported the students' protests; other parishioners resorted to violence.

Excellent gold-inlaid mosaics on the ceiling of the nave celebrating military campaigns from the Crusades on give a good idea of the original church.

Once a year Breitscheidplatz is inundated with hundreds of Hondas and BMWs, when Berlin's bikers gather in their leathers for a memorial service to their friends killed in accidents.

The "Water Meatball": The rest of this area is usually taken over by kids doing flips and wheelies on their skateboards, roller skates and bikes. The square is alive until late at night. People sit on benches, steps and the granite seats around the **Weltkugelbrunnen** (Fountain of the Globe). The "Wasserklops" or "Water Meatball" as it is popularly known, is a massive angular sphere of rust-coloured granite, which was built in 1983. Here they listen to the buskers or have their portraits drawn by one of the street artists. Or they read the fliers distributed by political groups and cults of every imaginable persuasion. Others linger over the market stalls – leather belts always seem cheaper here than in the shops, jewellery brighter, silk scarves more exotic.

The Europa Centre: A wrestling tent and a few wooden snack stands were all that stood on the present site of the **Europa Center** in the 1950s. It sprang up from the ground in 1965, prompting unprecedented debate and no shortage of deprecatory remarks. Strolling, shopping, recreation – these three little words sum up the Europa Center. There are some 100 shops, restaurants, bars and cafés here, as well as a five-screen cinema, a 40-minute "multivisual show" providing a crash course in Berlin history, the VIP-Club disco, the Berlin Casino (entrance on Budapester Strasse), the cabaret "Die Stachelschweine", a revue bar and Berlin's biggest sauna,

The showcase of the Western world in the 1950s.

not forgetting the observation platform 353-ft (106-metres) up, where there's a row of telescopes and a panoramic view. It's easy to spend a whole day and not get bored exploring inside this externally rather ugly construction.

The "Romanisches Café": This was also the site of the neo-romantic apartment house, home of the legendary "Romanisches Café", until it was destroyed in 1943. Just as bohemian Berlin congregated at the "Café des Westens", nicknamed "Café Größenwahn" (Megalomania) in the years before World War II, so the "Romantic" flourished during the Weimar period, to become the centre of the literary expressionist movement, a place to exchange opinions, a meeting-place for the avant-garde and their outrageously dressed followers. Inside, the smoke-filled coffee house wasn't particularly interesting. Diagonally opposite the revolving door was a buffet offering the same unappetising fare you might find in any railway station. The regulars used to sit, split into different cliques, in the rectangular "non-swimmers' pool" or the square "swimmers' pool". The mezzanine was the haunt of the chess players.

Today, the legendary coffee house is synonymous with cosmopolitan Berlin and the hedonism of the "Roaring '20s". The names of all the clientele who passed through the Romanischen in its heyday, and the other artists' haunts around Kurfürstendamm, reads like a *Who's Who* of modern literature, stage and screen: Else Lasker-Schüler, Kurt Tucholsky, Alfred Kerr, Robert Musil, Joseph Roth, Egon Erwin Kisch, Gottfried Benn, Carl Zuckmayer, the Manns, Klabund and many others. Billy Wilder, another regular, made his reputation as a journalist with his report on life as "A Gigolo at the Hotel Eden". Film directors Robert Siodmak and Ernst Lubitsch were already on the road to fame – then along came Hitler.

When the Nazis expelled the Jewish intelligentsia from Kurfürstendamm, they also destroyed its spirit of liberal-

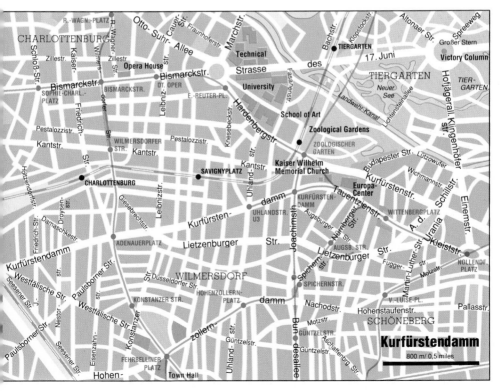

ism "We watched the café and its terrace blow away, disappear with its spirit cargo, dissolve into nothing, as though it had never existed…" wrote the poet Wolfgang Koeppen, describing the end of the Romanisches Café. "The clientele… scattered throughout the world or were imprisoned or were killed or killed themselves or they sat on in the café, cowering over their books, ashamed of the meekness of the press and their great treachery…"

Ten years later British bombers reduced the zoo district to rubble and ashes in a single November night. The remainder was accomplished in the mania for demolition and modernisation in the 1950s and 1960s, which was on a scale barely imaginable even today. Thus the boulevard that exists today is a hotch-potch of modern glass architecture and historical stucco, lacking any coherent line.

Fluid boundaries: So exactly where does the Kurfürstendamm begin? The answer is at No. 11 on the north side of the avenue directly behind Breitscheidplatz… There's no point looking for the first 10 houses. In 1925 the first part of Kurfürstendamm, where the Hotel Intercontinental stands now, was renamed Budapester Strasse. Very few people are aware that the Damm once began on the outskirts of Tiergarten, on the Corneliusbrücke (bridge) over the Landwehr canal.

Others maintain that the street starts at Wittenbergplatz, where it goes under the guise of **Tauentzienstrasse**, but this isn't true. The boundary may be unclear, but there is a difference: on "Tauentzien", an out and out commercial street, there are no street cafés. In their place, on the corner of Wittenbergplatz, stands the **Kaufhaus des Westens** or KaDeWe (pronounced kar-day-vay). The famous cathedral to consumerism is Europe's largest department store, with 51,400 sq. yards (43,000 sq. metres) of sales floor. About 3,000 employees are on hand to serve you with the 250,000 items on sale, from pins to

Ku'damm – hectic city high life…

computers. Here you'll find any and everything under the sun. In particular, the **delicatessen floor** (Feinschmecker-Etage) on the sixth floor is worth a visit, and not only on Saturdays, when the jet set come in from Grunewald to throng around the champagne counter and oyster bar. Gourmets claim that there is nothing that's edible that can't be found in the KaDeWe food department.

"Burger boulevard": The Ku'damm no longer shares the elegance of the KaDeWe. It's a sorry shame, claim those who have watched more and more stylish small businesses being driven out by escalating rents. No independent retailer can afford commercial rents in excess of DM200 per sq. yard. Who cares, say others, who see Kurfürstendamm as a commercial centre where only the financially fit survive.

In the 1970s the Kurfürstendamm came under increasing fire from its critics. People talked of a "pizza, pop and porno promenade", of the "kebab mentality" and "meatball palaces". Kur-

fürstendamm had become the "nation's rubbish tip", complained others, while carefully overlooking the fact that tourists in trainers and American fast-food chains had also invaded the Champs-Elysées. Nevertheless, responsible local politicians realised that the acclaimed "showcase of the Western world" was losing élan through ill-conceived urban development. This was especially evident in the "the depressing, neon-lit strongholds of consumerism", as the new shopping centres were described. Others warned of a "St Paulisation", as porn cinemas and peep-shows began to multiply in various corners.

New facades: There was no doubt about it, the Ku'damm was fast degenerating into just another street, losing its unique character. To halt the decline, a City Commission was set up by the City Business Association, a group of concerned business people, with representatives from the three relevant administrative bodies of Charlottenburg, Wilmersdorf and Schöneberg. Since it was

...and thoughtful portrait-painting, an investment for your loved one or your descendants.

ANIMAL OASES

Many a visitor will scarcely believe his ears when, emerging from Bahnhof Zoo, he is greeted by the sound of squawking parrots and trumpeting elephants. Berlin's rapid development resulted in the fact that today its Zoological Garden lies in the heart of the city. At the suggestion of naturalist Alexander von Humboldt, zoologist Martin Lichtenstein and landscape gardener Peter Lenné, construction of a menagerie began in the grounds of the Royal Pheasant Houses in 1844. In those days the zoo, situated within the Tiergarten park, lay outside the city limits. It began in quite a modest way; later, however, during the feverish expansion of the *Grün-derzeit*, the entire city was caught up in a fever of speculation. The zoo administration offered shares for sale, and the money began to flow in.

It was at this time that Germany began to show increased interest in its colonies. The officers of the Imperial Colonial Army had their headquarters not far from the zoo. They enriched the menagerie with animals which no other collection in Europe possessed. The first "colonial elephant" from Cameroon, with its downward-pointing tusks, caused a scientific sensation.

The animal houses in the growing zoo were disguised as pagodas, temples and mosques. Completed in 1891, the Elephant Gate on the Budapester Strasse provided a magnificent entrance to the exotic animal world. Destroyed during the war, it was reconstructed in 1984. An aquarium was added in 1913 under the aegis of the zoo's "father", Alfred Brehm. Today, housing some 4,000 species, it is one of the largest in the world.

With the addition of the baboon rock and the open-air seal pond during the 1930s the zoo curator of the time, Lutz Heck, began the replacement of the barred cages which had been standard until then with modern enclosures and safety ditches.

In November 1943 the work of an entire century was almost completely destroyed by a 15-minute air raid. During the final stages of the Battle of Berlin in April 1945 the "Eastern Front" ran right

through the middle of the zoo; one of the last defences also stood there, a huge air raid shelter. When the smoke had cleared only 91 animals were still alive.

The hippopotamus "Knautschke" – since deceased – became the hero and the symbol of the Berliners' will to survive. The creature, which weighed several tons, survived the last few days of the war under water. When reconstruction started it lay quietly in its muddy pond and allowed rescuers to feed it up again. All Berlin rejoiced when, in 1986, Knautschke became a grandfather. In 1981 it was joined by two pandas, a present from the People's Republic of China. A magnificent bungalow was even built for the zoo's most illustrious residents.

Today the zoo (opening hours: 9 a.m. until dusk) can claim to have the largest number of species of any zoo in the world – 11,758. As soon as he walks through the entrance on Hardenbergplatz, the visitor is transported from the big-city bustle into an animal paradise. He will be greeted by the elephants on the right, whilst opposite lie the large birds' aviary and the monkeyhouse, followed by the lions' enclosure, the baboons' rock and the polar bears' pool. And then there is the enchanted world of the nocturnal animals and the aquarium. A children's zoo delights young visitors.

The eastern half of the city also has an animal sanctuary. In order to provide a menagerie for the residents of the capital of the GDR, the Friedrichsfelde Zoo was opened in July 1955 in the grounds of Friedrichsfelde Castle. The landscaping was carried out according to the plans of Peter Josef Lenné.

It then boasted 400 animals and 120 species. Today, it has more than 5,000 creatures and 890 species, distributed over 160 hectares (400 acres). Friedrichsfelde Zoo was the first to sucessfully breed musk oxen in captivity. The zoo's layout compares well with its West-Berlin counterpart. Its pools and ditches, glass aviary with tropical vegetation and glass enclosures for exotic birds and giant snakes in the Alfred Brem House, and its cafés and children's playground make it an oasis for city-dwellers. It is open in summer from 7 a.m. and in winter from 8 a.m. until dusk.

founded in 1981, the commission has been responsible for ensuring that development on Kurfürstendamm is in accordance with "the interests of the boulevard". The intention is to discourage amusement arcades, peepshows and snack bars in the "heart of the city". But the official line is that the clean-up will be carried out in a spirit of "liberalism, pluralism and multi-functionalism".

Stroll along Ku'damm and the commission's efforts are evident all around you. Between Breitscheidplatz and Joachimstrasse, Berlin's most expensive building land at between DM3,000 and DM5,000 per sq. yard, the last gap has been filled between Marmorhaus and Café Wien. The Wertheim department store has replaced its horrible concrete facade with a decorative glass frontage. Kiosks and advertising columns have been given an old-fashioned look, and stucco facades restored to brighten up the rather tired-looking face of the Ku'damm.

The thin line between elitism and modern mass tourism appears to have been reasonably well negotiated. The critics are steadily being silenced, Kurfürstendamm is once more "in".

Cultural choice: There's certainly no shortage of cultural activities on offer, beginning with the old-established première cinemas, mostly concentrated between the Gedächtniskirche and Uhlandstrasse, and stretching as far as the **Schaubühne am Lehniner Platz**, the holy of holies of modern German theatre. The **Staatliche Kunsthalle** (State Gallery) at Budapester Strasse 46, with its two airy exhibition floors and caféteria, could be described as its counterpart in the realm of fine art. It is chiefly devoted to contemporary artists, but now and then it does run notable retrospectives, such as those not so long ago on Otto Dix and George Grosz.

Next door at No. 48 is the information bureau of the **Berliner Festspiele** and its gallery. For those who want to stroll around the Ku'damm galleries, the Naive Art at Wölffer's (No. 206) is recom-

mended, or the modern masters at Brusberg's (No. 213) or the Majakowski Gallery further along, which features work by contemporary East European artists.

The **Maison de France** on the junction with Uhlandstrasse runs lectures, films and language courses promoting the culture of Germany's western neighbour. If you want to know the time from the **Mengenlehre-Uhr** on the central reservation, you'll have to solve a conundrum first, as the clock is based on mathematical set theory. You simply add up the numbers from top to bottom. The flashing light denotes the seconds, then you calculate the remainder with the following formula: in the first row, one box equals five hours; in the second, one hour; in the third, five minutes and in the fourth row, one minute.

Kurfürstendamm 218 was the former residence of the Chinese ambassador and is now the house of the Ho Lin Wah restaurant. Next door, in the **King's Teagarden**, there's a choice of 170 sorts of tea – you can even partake of a cup to the civilised accompaniment of classical music.

The American poet Thomas Wolfe described the Kurfürstendamm as "Europe's biggest coffee house". Everywhere you turn, there's another ambient corner. Café Kranzler (Nos. 18–19) and Café Möhring (No. 213) carefully preserve the feel of the good old days, while the Kaffeehaus Edinger (No. 194) is the haunt of the young trendies or "Schickimickis".

Even the dreaded tourist traps are good for a few surprises. "Over 40 of the most interesting people in Europe" (according to the signs) await you in the Berlin waxworks at Ku'damm Corner, where the Ku'damm meets Joachimstaler Strasse. In Ku'damm-Karree there's a flea market and a **Teddy-bear Museum** to entice you. Because the closing times of the shops in the city are fairly liberal, the café terraces and pavements are crowded until late on warm summer nights.

Off-Ku'damm: Whoever has been along Ku'damm may be familiar with Berlin's cosmopolitan face, but not the city itself, not by a long way. A detour into the side streets "off-Ku'damm" gives a wider picture. In Fasanenstrasse, which in recent years has become the art and gallery mile, you can catch a glimpse of life on the other side of the tracks. The street's crowning glory was the opening in 1986 of **Villa Grieseback** (No. 25). This city villa dating from the years of rapid industrial expansion in the latter half of the 19th century, together with the adjoining winter garden, had stood derelict for years and they were to be knocked down to make way for a multi-storey car park. Local people launched a campaign and successfully defended the building from demolition. Today, the house is used by the Gallery Pels-Leusden for exhibitions and auctions.

The **Käthe-Kollwitz Museum** moved in immediately next door. In the **Wintergarten** (No. 25), Berlin's literary scene has once again found a focal point,

Off-Ku'damm – a flea market on Fasanenstrasse.

while the **Literaturhaus Berlin** (No. 23) has a basement bookshop and a beautifully restored café-restaurant with a garden.

Along to Kantstrasse: On the northern side of Fasanenstrasse, diagonally opposite Hotel Bristol-Kempinski, is the **Jewish Community Centre**. There was once a synagogue on this street, but it was burnt down by the SA gangs on 9 November 1938 – "Kristallnacht". Only a portal remains, but it sits very comfortably with the simple new building, dating from 1959. The large hall on the top floor is used as a prayer room on Jewish holidays. The building also houses the Jewish College, where courses are conducted in Hebrew, a library and a kosher restaurant.

The theatre on the corner of Kantstrasse, with Latin inscriptions along the gables, has had a chequered past. As a private venue for comedy and operetta, it went bankrupt several times. From 1950 to 1961, as the **Theater des Westens**, it was the home of the Berlin City Opera, under Michael Bohnen, Heinz Tietjen and Carl Ebert. In 1987 the première of *Cabaret* starring Horst Buchholz Ende heralded a new era for the theatre staging musicals. Box office hits like *Peter Pan* and *La Cage aux Folles* have secured the theatre's artistic reputation, while visiting companies from New York bring a real Broadway atmosphere to the lavishly renovated building which dates from the Kaiser's time (1896).

Among the city's landmarks are the old-fashioned clock and the glass concourse of **Bahnhof Zoo** (Zoo station), for decades a blot on the whole district. In conjunction with the East German State Railways, the station underwent a 40-million mark overhaul for the jubilee celebrations in 1987. Before that, many a traveller arriving in West Berlin's only major rail terminal has been tempted to turn around and go straight home.

Rather St Germain: To the west, Kantstrasse opens out into Savignyplatz. The numerous booksellers and trendy bars are reminiscent of St Germain. And, like its Parisian counterpart, apartments in this corner of the city are much sought after. In contrast to Kurfürstendamm, the side streets here are fairly quiet. But a stroll through Bleibtreu, Knesebeck, Mommsen and Giesebrecht streets reveals plenty that's lacking in the main boulevard: delightful little boutiques, side by side with junk and secondhand shops.

The neighbourhood makes a pleasant contrast to the honky-tonk atmosphere around **Lietzenburger Strasse**. Here in **Sperlingsgasse** you'll find an assortment of watering holes which claim to be "olde Berlin", but Berliners are rarely found here. On "Lietze", between Uhlandstrasse and Knesebeckstrasse, clip joints, strip shows and brothels abound. One popular exception is the **Loretta im Garten**, a charmingly lit beer garden with several pavilions, where in the evenings you can enjoy a sociable drink under the trees.

Life in the international metropolis.

BERLIN CENTRAL

Historically speaking, Berlin Central is the true heart of the city. Here, on the island in the Spree, the twin village trading settlements of Berlin and Cölln first grew up some 800 years ago. Here, too, was the centre of the residential cities of ruling electors, kings and emperors. Berlin Central was the power hub of the Nazi regime, and the seat of government of the German Democratic Republic. Here, the visitor comes face to face with Berlin's long history.

Berlin Central begins where East Germany once ended: at the **Brandenburg Gate**. This symbol of Prussian glory and inter-German destiny must be the most-painted, most-photographed monument in the city. Built in 1788–91 as a triumphal focal point for the capital's magnificent boulevard **Unter den Linden**, its history has often been a turbulent one.

The Gate's famous **Quadriga**, the goddess of victory driving her four-horse chariot, has experienced a difficult fate as the representative of the "Triumph of Peace" – as the Gate's architect, Langhans, described her symbolic importance. Captured by Napoleon in 1800 and returned to her original site eight years later, badly damaged in crossfire in 1945 and replaced in replica in 1958, the statue was destroyed once more by over-enthusiastic revellers in 1989–90, during the first New Year celebrations following the opening of the Wall, but since has been restored.

Walking from the Brandenburg Gate along the avenue Unter den Linden, the visitor will gain an impression of the magnificence and splendour created by Frederick the Great when he had this symbol of Prussian supremacy constructed. Every stone bears witness to historical events, whether hidden behind a modern facade or carefully restored. The first section, starting at the **Pariser Platz**, is dominated by contemporary buildings in which Britain, France and Italy have set up their embassies. Here, too, once stood the Adlon, the most famous hotel in Berlin.

Further evidence of a less glorious past can be found in the former "political corner" of Berlin, surrounding the Pariser Platz. Hitler's architect, Albert Speer, was responsible for the construction in 1939 of the vast New Imperial Chancellery at the junction of what was then the Wilhelmstrasse (now Otto-Grotewohl-Strasse) and Vossstrasse. Beneath it lay the bunker which was to be the Führer's last refuge. Today, nothing can be seen of all this; the site is occupied by apartment blocks and a park. Continuing towards the city, the visitor passes the monumental building of the **Soviet Embassy**, constructed in the style of the Stalinist Era. Completed in 1953, it was the first building along this section of the avenue.

The pulsating heart of the city once lay at the junction of Unter den Linden and Friedrichstrasse. However, the drabness characteristic of social realism lent the scene an air of desolation rather liveliness. Since the Wall was removed the boulevard is gradually becoming a promenade once more, an avenue where the masses throng and push – more, at present, out of historical interest than in pursuit of pleasure. Gone are many of the shops and cafés such as the original Café Kranzler.

Turning right into Friedrichstrasse, one soon arrives at the **Platz der Akademie**. On the corner of Friedrichstrasse and Behrensstrasse stands the Grand Hotel, the most prestigious hotel in East Berlin, opened in time for the city's 750-year celebrations in 1987. Its nostalgic décor and Old-Berlin pomp evoke memories of the luxurious lives of the haute bourgeoisie.

The Platz der Akademie is dominated by the **Evangelical Lutheran Church** (1708) and the **French Reformed Church** (1705), the latter built by the Huguenots. Their towers dominate the entire district. Today the dome of the French Church houses a wine bar, whilst the meeting room is the setting for the **Huguenot Museum**.

The **Schauspielhaus** (1871), flanked by the two churches, is one of the finest buildings designed by that most Prussian of all architects, Karl Friedrich Schinkel. In his time the neo-classical masterpiece was described as "tangible music". Since its re-opening as a concert hall in 1984, it has remained true to the challenge contained in that description. The marble pedestrian statue of Friedrich Schiller was returned to its original site here in 1986 as part of an exchange of cultural assets. The Nazis had banished the statue during the 1930s.

Continuing along the Französische Strasse towards the Spree, the visitor next comes to the Werderscher Markt. The building on the right was once occupied by the **Central Committee of the SED**.

If you take the Oberwallstrasse you will soon find yourself back on Unter den Linden, at the **Lindenforum**. "Here

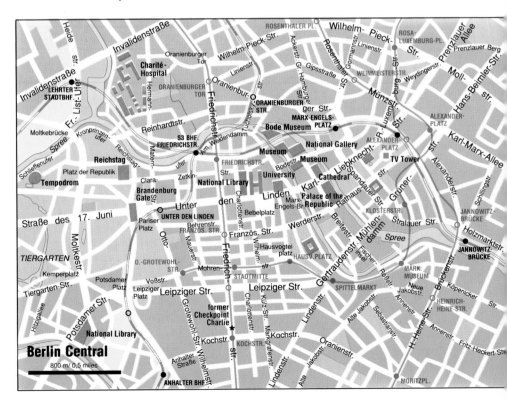

Berlin Central

800 m/ 0.5 miles

one magnificent building rubs shoulders with the next", enthused the poet Heinrich Heine. The baroque splendour of the old Arsenal, constructed in 1695, marked the first stage in the development of what was to become Berlin's show avenue. Today the Zeughaus houses the **Museum of German History**. The four allegorical female figures by the entrance represent pyrotechnics, arithmetic, geometry and mechanics. Particularly moving are the 22 masks of dying warriors in the inner courtyard.

A few steps further on is the **Memorial to the Victims of Fascism and Militarism**, housed in Schinkel's first neo-classical style building, the former **Neue Wache** (1818). Eternal flames burn above the graves of the Unknown Soldier and the Unknown Resistance Fighter, recalling the 50 million deaths caused by National Socialism and World War II.

The students of the **Humboldt University**, next to the memorial, tread in the footsteps of many famous men. Their spiritual rector is Wilhelm von Humboldt, at whose suggestion the institute of learning was founded in 1809. The East and West wings encircling the courtyard of honour are extensions dating from the early years of this century. The **National Library** next door contains a collection of more than seven million books.

Also part of the university buildings are the former **Governor's House** (Unter den Linden 11) and the **Altes Palais** (Unter den Linden 9). The Governor's House originally stood in the Rathausstrasse, but had to make way for new buildings during the reconstruction of the city centre. In order to preserve the baroque facade it was transported and used to fill a gap left by a war ruin.

The **Opernplatz** opposite the University acquired a certain tragic notoriety at the beginning of the 1930s. On 10 May 1933, at the height of Nazi propaganda minister Joseph Goebbels' "Campaign against the Un-German Spirit", it was the scene of the burning of over 20,000 books by those authors whose works were abhorred by the National Socialists. Today the square has been rechristened in memory of the workers' leader August Bebel. The building on the west side exists in duplicate; as part of the Hofburg in Vienna, and here. The **Old Library** is affectionately known by Berlin residents as the "Dressing Table" because of its arched facade. Since its restoration in 1969 it has been used as a reading room.

The neo-classical jewel on the other side of the Bebelplatz is the **German State Opera House**. During the course of its history it was completely redesigned and rebuilt on two occasions, and was also destroyed twice – in 1941 and 1945 – during World War II. The reconstruction at the beginning of the 1950s followed as precisely as possible the plans of the rococo architect Georg von Knobelsdorff.

Friedrich II had the domed **St Hedwige's Cathedral**, on the edge of the Bebelplatz, built for the 10,000 Catho-

A view of the cathedral.

lics resident in Berlin during his reign. The former **Crown Prince's Palais** closes the square off from Unter den Linden.

Schinkel was responsible for the design of the former Castle Bridge, now rechristened the **Marx-Engels Bridge**, which crosses the Kupfergraben – one of the arms of the Spree – to the island. The "Gallery of Goddesses", depicting Nike and Pallas Athene, formed a cycle inspired by the anti-Napoleonic wars of independence.

To the left, a footpath leads through the Lustgarten, the former pleasure gardens, towards the oldest museum in Germany other than the Glyptothek in Munich. Also designed by Schinkel, the **Old Museum** boasts an Ionic colonnade which encloses the park to the north. The enormous bowl in front of the entrance – an Ice-Age granite erratic weighing 80 tonnes and with a diameter of 7 metres (23 ft) – was greeted with rapture as a Biedermeier-style wonder of the world in 1834.

The Old Museum forms part of the **Museum Island**, a series of five buildings in which are housed countless priceless treasures from every period of world history. The complete rebuilding of the complex, approved in 1976, is still under way. The **National Gallery**, in the form of a Corinthian temple, the **Pergamon Museum**, the first museum of architecture in the world, and the **Bode Museum**, contain the finest collections under the curatorship of the Berlin State Museums.

The **Berlin Cathedral** is a typical example of Wilhelminian historicism; it stands on the eastern periphery of the park. Since 1980 the church, a favourite for baptisms and weddings, has once again been in use by the Lutheran community. The crypt, containing the tombs of the Hohenzollern emperors, has been transformed into a museum.

The cathedral is reflected in the vast 180-metre (600-ft) long bronze-coloured glass facade of the monumental **Palace of the Republic**. Locals refer to it as the Palazzo Prozzo, the "Show-offs Palace". It was dedicated in April 1976, having taken barely 1,000 days to build. The wing on the Lustgarten side contained the East German People's Chamber; the assembly hall on the mews side boasted a wooden floor which could be raised or lowered at will, providing space for congresses and cultural functions for between 500 and 5,000 people.

On the eastern bank of the Spree, the Marx-Engels forum situated on the Karl-Liebknecht-Strasse is adorned with statues by East German sculptors. Rising up in the middle of the star-shaped square, dwarfing all the other exhibits, are twin bronze figures of the forerunners of Socialism, Karl Marx and Friedrich Engels. With their fondness for nicknames, local Berliners were not slow to christen them 'Vest and Jacket'.

The Gothic **Church of St Mary** is dwarfed by its modern surroundings in the shadow of the Television Tower. Visitors seeking refuge here from the roaring traffic of the Karl-Liebknecht-

The Neue Wache on Unter den Linden.

146

Strasse will find amongst the treasures in this 13th-century place of worship a 22-metre (70-ft) long late-Gothic fresco, *The Dance of Death* (1485), and a marble pulpit by Andreas Schlüter.

The **Fountain of Neptune** between St Mary's and the Red Town Hall demonstrates the Berliners' predilection for Wilhelminian opulence. The bronze statue was completed by Reinhold Begas in 1891 as a gift from the citizens of Berlin to their emperor. The four beauties splashing around the basin represent four rivers: the Rhine, the Elbe, the Oder and the Vistula.

Alexanderplatz: Visitors and locals can be seen rushing or strolling between the 39-storey hotel Stadt Berlin, the department store Centrum and the Teacher's House with its mural painting by Walter Womacka (also known as "Cummerbund"). They pass the World Time Clock and the Fountain of International Friendship, all seeming somewhat lost in the shadow of the overpowering architecture.

Two of the pre-war buildings alongside the suburban train overpass, the Berolina-Haus and the Alexanderhaus, are both representative of the New Functionalism at the end of the 1920s. They blend unobtrusively with the characteristic Socialist architectural style. The 365-metres (1,168-ft) high Television Tower with its unusual futuristic, triangular form at the base has become East Berlin's most familiar landmark. Despite its weight of some 26,000 tonnes it is affectionately known as the "Tele-Beanpole".

The **Red Town Hall** owes its name less to its political inclinations than to the red bricks from the Brandenburg Marches of which it was built. The fifth town hall in the history of Berlin, it was completed in 1869.

The East Berlin authorities were particularly painstaking in their restoration of the **Nikolai District**. With meticulous attention to detail they reconstructed many buildings which originally stood somewhere else. The result was an island of history in the centre of East Berlin, a collage of antiquity which fulfils admirably the desire for a "showcase of the past". The houses clustered around the Church of St Nicholas were all restored, at least externally, with great attention to historical accuracy and loving insistence on period detail. One of the most important structures is the arcade in front of the Courts, dating from the year 1270. Today few court orders are passed here; instead, orders for drinks can be heard by day and night. The historical inn Zum Nussbaum, on permanent loan from the Fischerinsel, is a familiar sight to those who know the drawings by Heinrich Zille and Otto Nagel.

The **Church of St Nicholas**, the oldest building in Berlin, is mentioned in records for the first time in 1264. In the surrounding district the nooks and crannies of the cobbled streets invite the visitor to take a leisurely stroll past little shops, craftsmen's workshops, bars and restaurants.

Meeting place of couples and families: the world clock on Alexanderplatz.

The **Ephraim Palais** by the Mühlendamm Bridge is one of 20 historic houses grouped around St Nicholas's. It was formerly considered to be the finest residence in the city and when completed in 1764 its magnificent rococo facade aroused considerable attention. Nowadays it houses changing exhibitions from the Marches Museum. Diagonally opposite, from the Molkenmarkt, the oldest market square in the city, the round domed tower of the former Town Hall can be glimpsed.

Having crossed the Mühlendamm Bridge, remember to glance down the Breite Strasse. It was formerly one of the most exclusive addresses in the city, with the 17th-century **Ribbeckhaus**, built in the Renaissance style, and the **Old Royal Mews**. To the left lies the **Fischerinsel**: nothing indicates that the island was once the cradle of the twin founding settlements of Berlin and Cölln. After the war, plans for the reconstruction of the district, although technically feasible, were rejected in favour of total demolition and a policy of radical "rebuilding without nostalgia". In concrete terms, this meant that between 1967 and 1971 the entire area was razed to the ground before the construction of six 21-storey buildings. The traditional charm of the saucer-shaped Ahornblatt inn adds little to the attractions of the area, despite its historic associations.

You will feel more at home in the **Köllnischer Park**. Focal point is the Wusterhauser Bär, a tower which was once part of the 17th-century fortifications. The city's furry mascots romp and play in the nearby bear pits. Passing the Zille monument, you will arrive at the **Marches Museum** (Märkisches Museum), which houses the most extensive local history collection in the former GDR. Returning to the Fischerinsel, the visitor may be tempted to stop at the restaurant in the **Ermelerhaus** on the Märkisches Ufer – a rococo palais – or at the **Otto-Nagel-Haus**, whose permanent exhibitions display

Smothered in ivy: the exterior of the National Library.

paintings, drawings and pastels by the Berlin proletarian artists. From the Gertrauden Bridge there is a fine view of the oldest railway bridge in the city, the Jungfernbrücke (1798).

There is still a faint air of disreputableness hanging over the **Friedrichstrasse**, for over 300 years a boundary as well as the city's north-south axis. During the long, hot nights of the "GoldenTwenties" the street vibrated with wild vitality. Here the pulse of the metropolis beat more quickly than elsewhere; here its citizens revelled in the High Life in the velvet-and-kitsch atmosphere of the cafés, hotels and variety theatres. The citizens of East Berlin were consequently amazed when, in 1985, it was announced that along its entire 3-km (4-mile) length, the Friedrichstrasse was to be reconstructed in an attempt to recreate the "Berlin milieu of past decades".

Today, the Friedrichstrasse is the setting for a number of outstanding buildings: the Hotel Metropol (on the junc-tion of Unter den Linden); the International Trade Centre (on the junction of Clara-Zetkin-Strasse) – built according to Japanese design, and unfortunately too high, too box-like and too close to the suburban railway lines; the Metropol Theatre in the Admiral's Palais, offering highlights of light comedy as well as providing a permanent home for the East Berlin cabaret Die Distel; the Weidendamm Bridge, with an 1890s balustrade adorned once more by wrought-iron light fittings; the Berliner Ensemble on the Schiffbauerdamm – Brecht's home theatre, with a reputation extending far beyond the boundaries of East Germany; and – last but not least – the Friedrichstadt Palais, mockingly known as the "Stalactite Cave".

What is served up behind the stained glass of the facade is described as "Metropolitan variety theatre". International singers and artistes, a famous ballet and perfect production techniques are supported by a movable stage with every refinement from an artificial ice rink to

Neptune could not bear to be alone.

a retractable swimming pool for underwater shows – Las Vegas in miniature, made in East Germany.

Famous names: For more than 40 years the producer Max Reinhardt was the dominant influence at the Deutsches Theater and the nearby Studio Theatre in the Schumannstrasse, where he was director between 1905 and 1933. Both establishments continue to support the tradition of critical drama as a mirror of contemporary issues.

Not far away stands the **Charité**, the archetypal Berlin hospital. In 1710 Friedrich I had constructed on this site – purely as a precautionary measure – the "Plague Hospital", since he feared that the plague, which at the time was already devastating nearby Prenzlau, might also spread to Berlin itself. Once the danger of epidemic was over, the "Great Royal Hospital" was given over for the care of the indigent sick and rechristened the Charité ("Mercy"). The ivy-clad brick building was the penultimate extension (1917); since 1982 the hospital has boasted a 15-storey tower and has beds for 7,000 patients. Testifying to the fame of the establishment are the names of distinguished medical men such as Ferdinand Sauerbruch, Rudolf Virchow and Robert Koch.

Berthold Brecht and his wife Helene Weigel are both buried in the **Dorotheenstadt Cemetery** on the Chausseestrasse, near the town flat where they once lived and which has become their memorial museum. If you study the inscriptions on the graves as you pass you will notice a number of famous names. The philosophers Johann Gottlieb Fichte and Georg Wilhelm Friedrich Hegel lie here, as do the writers Arnold Zweig, Heinrich Mann and Johannes R. Becher and the artists Daniel Chodowiecki and John Heartfield, as well as many other famous personalities from German history and the recent East German past.

Another chapter of Germany's history can be studied in the occasional faded inscriptions, memorial plaques and buildings scattered across the city: the paltry remains of the world created by 160,000 Jewish citizens and wiped out by the events of history. The Scheunen District, behind the **Oranienburg Gate**, was the centre of their quarter. This disreputable, impoverished region, inhabited primarily by the Jewish proletariat, provided the scenario for numerous novels and stories.

Nowadays the Jewish community totals not more than a few hundred souls; their former synagogue in the Oranienburger Strasse, burnt down during the Crystal Night and bombed during the war, still stands in ruins as a "place of warning and remembrance for all time".

The passage of the years wrought havoc on the rest of the imposing building until, in 1985, as a result of pressure from the Jewish community, it was decided to renovate the complex. On the 50th anniversary of the Crystal Night a museum was opened here to preserve the memories of Jewish culture and traditions.

Below, Berthold Brecht occupies a pedestal in front of his theatre. Right, a girl braves the monument to Karl Marx and Friedrich Engels.

150

TIERGARTEN

As long ago as 1764, the English travel writer James Boswell enthused about the "magnificent park on the edge of the town, with carriageways and bridle-paths". And, he noted, there was also provision for those "desiring to exercise themselves". Even today, the mention of Tiergarten immediately conjures up images of sauntering through Berlin's "green lung". Großer Tiergarten, 3 km (2 miles) long and 2 km wide, stretches on both sides of the Strasse des 17. Juni, between Tiergarten S-Bahn station and the Brandenburg Gate. On sunny weekends, the playgrounds and lawns teem with umpteen thousand holidaymakers, and Turkish families at home with their barbecues – much to the dismay of the city gardeners.

The 212 hectares (525 acres) of the park are the heart of the administrative district of the same name. Within its cramped 13 sq. km (5 sq. miles) the glory and decline of the former imperial capital are reflected in starkly contrasting scenes. The Großer Tiergarten is a quiet haven in the centre of the district, with its mute stone witnesses of the nation's former greatness – the Reichstag, the Brandenburg Gate and the Siegessäule. To the south lies the once gentrifed Tiergartenviertel, to the north the industrial, working-class neighbourhood of Moabit, an island surrounded by canals, where the majority of the 93,000 inhabitants live in tenements which date back to the late 19th century. Most of the district was incorporated into Berlin in 1861.

In the years before and after World War I, representatives of numerous foreign countries settled in Tiergartenviertel, with the result that the area north of the Landwehr canal became known as the Diplomatenviertel (Diplomatic Quarter). In recognition of the Axis federation with Hitler's Germany, Japan and Italy built prestigious mansions on **Tiergartenstrasse**. Left as wasteground for a long time, the area is slowly coming to life again. The Japanese embassy, destroyed in the bombing, has been faithfully restored and how houses the **Japanese-German Centre**. The ruins of the former Italian embassy are still in the process of being restored, and will house the future **Akademie der Wissenschaften** (Academy of Sciences).

At Stauffenbergstrasse 14, immediately south of the embassies, is the **Gedenkstätte Deutscher Widerstand** (Memorial to German Resistance), a permanent exhibition in the former Wehrmacht headquarters. It was here in the courtyard of the former Bendler block that Colonel von Stauffenberg and four of his co-conspirators were executed by firing squad on 20 July 1944 for the abortive attempt on Hitler's life. They are commemorated in a sculpture by Richard Scheibe, *Der gefesselte Jüngling* (*Youth in Chains*). From here, your attention will be auto-

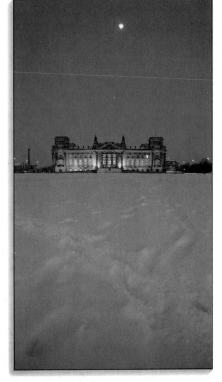

matically drawn to the **Kulturforum**, a seemingly permanent building site and location for a third museum district to complement the traditional centres of Dahlem and Charlottenburg. Originally conceived by Hans Scharoun, it is still undecided precisely what form the completed Kulturforum will take.

The **Nationalgalerie** (National Gallery) on Potsdamer Brücke, designed by Mies van der Rohr, provides the southern focus of the Kulturforum. The simple symmetry and colossal expanse of glass are a lively contrast to the **Philharmonie** (Philharmonic Hall) on the northern edge of the campus. The neighbouring concert hall for chamber music is also by Scharoun, as is the **Staatsbibliothek** (State Library).

The **Musical Instrument Museum** adjoining the Philharmonie, and the comparatively simple red tiled building housing the **Kunstgewerbemuseum** (Crafts Museum) complete the complex. Development has begun on new buildings to house a museum of copper-plate engravings and an arts library.

Continue past the Staatsbibliothek and under the monorail and arrive in Potsdamer Platz (Potsdam Square). The Nazi People's Court used to sit in the buildings of an old school alongside the ruined Grand Hotel Esplanade on Bellevue-Strasse. This was the scene of the notorious terror trials under "Bloody" Judge Roland Freisler. Opposite, you can still see a section of the "old" Potsdamer Strasse, which in pre-war times led to what was one of Europe's busiest squares. The Staatsbibliothek was built on the axis of this street. In the face of considerable public opposition, an office block is to be built on this historic square for the Daimler-Benz company.

All routes to Großer Tiergarten, including the **Liechtensteinbrücke** (bridge) in the extension of the Zoological Gardens, cross the Landwehr canal. After protracted political wrangling, two monuments now commemorate the murders of Rosa Luxemburg and Karl

An open-air concert in Tiergarten.

Liebknecht by members of the Reichswehr in 1919. The **Berlin Pavilion** at Tiergarten S-Bahn station is only a short walk away and features exhibitions on architectural history. En route you pass the **Lantern Museum**, a collection of antique gas lamps from around the world.

Monuments to victory: At the centre of Großer Tiergarten stands the 67-metre (223-ft) **Siegessäule** (Victory Column). Friedrich Drake's golden "Viktoria" – also known as "Gold Elsie" – was erected in 1873 to commemorate Prussia's victory in the wars against Denmark (1864), Austria (1866) and France (1870–71). The last of the four patriotic bronze reliefs around the base that were removed by the occupation forces in 1945 was brought back to Berlin from Paris by French President Mitterand as a gift on the occasion of the city's 750th jubilee. The reliefs show events from the successful campaigns.

The Siegessäule originally stood in Königsplatz (now Platz der Republik)

but was moved to Großer Stern in 1938 as part of the development of the east-west axis into a parade ground and boulevard for Hitler's new "Germania". The bronze **Bismarck memorial** by court sculptor R Begas (1901) and the monuments to Generals Roon and Moltke (1904) were moved at the same time to the northern side of the square.

A footpath leads past statues of Lessing, Goethe, Wagner, Lortzing, Fontane and many others who were honoured during a veritable mania for monuments at the turn of the century. Finally, you arrive at the **Brandenburger Tor** (Brandenburg Gate). The once proud symbol of the imperial capital Berlin was completed by C.G. Langhans in 1791 and is 20 metres (67 ft) high and 65 metres (213 ft) wide. It heralded the classical era in Prussia.

Modelled on the entrance to the Acropolis in Athens, the middle of the five arches was reserved exclusively for the members of the imperial court until the November Revolution of 1918. The customs houses in the wings were converted into hallways for pedestrians after the toll wall was pulled down in 1868.

The Siegeswagen (Victory Chariot) on top of the Gate is the work of sculptor Gottfried Schadow (1794) and was created from moulds which managed to survive the war.

The Reichstag: The Reichstag and the Swiss consulate buildings are all that remain of the grand buildings from the former Alsenviertel on the bend of the Spree. The Kroll Opera House and the General Staff Headquarters, not to mention the buildings around Königsplatz which were designed as the centrepiece of the Empire and which lined the vast area of what is now **Platz der Republik**, were casualties of the fighting in 1945. The **Reichstag precinct** was built between 1884 and 1894 by Paul Wallot and cost more than 26 million gold marks. Based on the style of the Italian high renaissance, the over-ornate facades and grandiose interiors exempli-

MAN, MUSIC AND SPACE

The honey-coloured facade shimmers in the sun as the tent-shaped gable curves boldly skywards above the auditorium. The most striking silhouettes amongst the new buildings in the Culture Forum in the Tiergarten are those of the Philharmonia and its smaller sister, the Chamber Music Concert Hall.

At the opening ceremony on 15 October 1963, the former was praised as one of the great concert halls of the world, an architectural wonder with remarkably excellent acoustics. Echoing the avant-garde lines of the exterior is the unconventional interior, designed by Hans Scharoun. He created a new relationship among the trio of man, music and space by moving the orchestra and its conductor to the centre of the auditorium. The audience is distributed on nine levels around the pentagonal podium. Rising up like vineyard terraces, they enclose the platform on all sides so that the sound soars unhindered to the furthest of the 2,200 places.

In the evening, the staircases and foyers become the festive focus of West Berlin's musical life. The symphonic repertoire dominates most evenings, but the Philharmonia also provides the scenario for the Berlin Jazz days, the Festival of World Cultures and the

occasional hot rock performance. The building is first and foremost the home of a much-celebrated, world-famous orchestra which exists in two different, but very similar, forms. Firstly, there is the Berlin Philharmonic Orchestra, which is in some respects the official orchestra of the entire nation and which travels the globe as a musical ambassador for the city of Berlin. When the same 120 musicians gather together to make a recording they become the Berlin Philharmonic.

The Philharmonia's tent-shaped silhouette has given it the popular nickname "Karajan's Circus" after Herbert von Karajan. Born on 5 April 1908 in Salzburg, he came to Berlin to the State Opera and the State Chorus in 1938. From 1947, von Karajan conducted the Vienna Philharmonic Orchestra and from 1956 until 1964 directed the Vienna State Opera. His artistic reputation, however, achieved global fame after 1964, when he was appointed musical director of the Berlin Philharmonic. The Herbert von Karajan Foundation, which he founded in 1969, aims to further the career of young conductors with its biennial competition. Conflict between the maestro and the equally self-confident orchestra was exacerbated by von Karajan's frequent absences and autocratic behaviour, leading eventually to their final split a few months before the maestro's death on 16 July 1989 at the age of 82.

Herbert von Karajan had previously been elected the orchestra's musical director for life, thereby inheriting the legacy of three former conductors from the days when the orchestra's headquarters were in the Bernburger Strasse 22a–23 near the Anhalter Bahnhof. Here Hans von Bülow, Arthur Nikisch and Wilhelm Furtwängler wielded the baton until the concert hall was destroyed during an air raid on 30 January 1944. The Berlin Philharmonic had made its début in the former roller-skating rink on 17 October 1882. One week later the first series of subscription concerts had begun, an innovation at the time.

The formation of an independent symphony orchestra by 54 rebellious musicians during the authoritarian Wilhelminian era must have seemed quite revolutionary. On 1 May 1882 they had parted company to a man from their employer and conductor, Benjamin Bilse. The 66-year-old "musical sergeant-major" directed one of the three private orchestras which, overshadowed by the Royal Court Opera, served the city with popular concerts. Now the musicians decided to form their own orchestra along democratic principles. The statutes provided amongst other things for the election of the group's artistic director and board of directors as well as that of new members.

Enhanced by a modern payment structure, this democratic constitution continues to underline the esprit de corps of what *Le Figaro* called "the most famous orchestra in the world". In 1982 the **Centenary of the Berlin Philharmonic** was celebrated as the "anniversary of a musical republic". The current conductor, Claudio Abbado, is the first non-German in the job.

fied the Wilhelminian taste for pomp and prestige.

The glass dome and the plenary session hall were destroyed in the famous fire of 1933, and after 1945 only a bombed out shell remained with black holes for the windows. Rebuilding was completed in 1970.

The Tempodrom has struck camp to the west of the Moltke bridge. There's no question that this is its historical home. It was on this exact spot that the famous "tents" were erected in the mid-18th century, huge arenas for entertainment and recreation, originally in canvas marquees, later in stone buildings with several halls.

The **Kongreßhalle** (Congress Hall), which dates from 1957, draws on these ancient traditions from the square's past. Its concrete cantilever roof was donated by the United States. After an accident in 1980 when the roof fell in, the buildings officially opened for the second time in 1987 with an exhibition entitled "The Sciences in Berlin". Directly be-

side it stands a 42-metres (140-ft) bell tower. The carillon of 68 bells which rings out over the district was a birthday present from Daimler-Benz. Tiergarten has always been a great place for distinctive buildings.

To Moabit: Across Moltke Bridge lies Moabit. Although there is much of significance here, including the market halls on Beusselstrasse, the Westhafen (West Harbour) and the Kriminalgericht Moabit (criminal courts), this part of town was rather pushed into the shadows when the Wall went up.

Many Berliners associate the name Moabit with "the clink". They are referring to the criminal courts and detention centre on Turmstrasse, which are notorious in certain circles. Among those to have appeared in the dock of this dismal palace of justice, built in 1903 in ornate Wilhelminian style, are the captain of Köpenick and the safe-blowing Sass brothers, not to mention several of the main protagonists in the Antes & Co corruption scandal.

CHARLOTTENBURG

Those who have explored Kurfürstendamm and the surrounding area will already be familiar with a part of Charlottenburg, but only a part. The entire district covers 30 sq. km (12 sq. miles) and occupies the whole northwest of the inner city. With 190,000 inhabitants, it is as big as the towns of Kassel or Mainz, and has many sights of interest, including the radio tower and, further out, the Olympic park. Above all, though, the former royal seat represents a little piece of old Prussia in western Berlin.

The student quarter: At Zoo station cross the railway bridge and follow Hardenbergstrasse to **Steinplatz**, the heart of Charlottenburg's student quarter. En route you pass the Bundesverwaltungsgericht (Supreme Administration Court) on the corner of Jebenstrasse and the buildings of the **Industrie- und Handelskammer** (Chamber of Trade and Industry), including Berlin's hexagonal **Stock Exchange** (Börse).

The area became the student quarter in the early part of the 20th century, when an increasing number of professors, artists and wealthy citizens began to move into Uhlandstrasse, Fasanenstrasse, Carmerstrasse and Knesebeckstrasse as part of the "move West". Today the area buzzes with bars, galleries and cafés, as well as a first-class selection of bookshops.

Three of Charlottenburg's main thoroughfares: Bismarckstrasse, Otto-Suhr-Allee and Strasse des 17. Juni meet at **Ernst-Reuter-Platz** which is among the city's busiest squares for traffic. The eastern boundary of the Technische Universität campus which abuts on the square is marked by the Charlottenburg Brücke (bridge) over the Landwehr canal and the Charlottenburger Tor (gate), featuring the bronze statues of King Friedrich I and his wife Sophie-Charlotte, who gave her name to the district.

At that time the wealthiest town in Prussia, Charlottenburg erected the gateway on the border with Berlin in 1905 to mark its 200th anniversary, as an expression of civic pride. It was intended as a counterpart of the Brandenburg Gate, which stands out at the eastern end of Strasse des 17. Juni, but the imposing effect was lost when the structure had to be split into two parts to make way for the widening of the Charlottenburger Chaussee.

At the weekends a **Trödelmarkt** (flea market) is held in front of Ernst-Reuter House, the home of the German Institute of Urban Studies and the Berlin branch of the German Association of Municipal Authorities. Like the Kreuzberg Market on Reichpietschufer, this is worth a visit for its local colour. Connoisseurs of antique rococo porcelain from the time of Frederick the Great shouldn't miss the opportunity of a visit to what used to be the Royal Prussian and is now the State Porcelain Factory (Staatliche Porzellanmanufaktur, KPM)

eft, the oveliest xample of russian aroque: harlottenurg Palace. ight, ewish ervice in estalozzitrasse.

at Wegelstrasse 1 in front of Tiergarten S-Bahn station.

Bismarckstrasse – or, if you are coming from Sophie-Charlotte-Platz, the Kaiserdamm – leads to the western focus of Charlottenburg, Theodor-Heuss-Platz. On **Bismarckstrasse**, there are two prestigious buildings worth noting. Both the **Schiller-Theater** (1951) and the **Deutsche Oper** (German Opera House, 1961), next to the U-Bahn station of the same name, are on their original sites.

To the Rathaus: "The wide Berlin street which slices through Charlottenburg… runs past countless coffee houses and beer halls, all growing rich at the expense of the convivial folk of Berlin, while in between can be glimpsed the summer villas of Berlin's retired gentlefolk and bankers…" So runs a description of what is now **Otto-Suhr-Allee** around 1850. (The street was later named after West Berlin's mayor from 1955–57.) There is nothing pleasant here now. Blocks of flats provide a chilling backdrop for the traveller en route to Siemensstadt, Spandau or the airport at Tegel.

Charlottenburg's **Rathaus** (Town Hall) near Richard-Wagner-Platz underground station is unmistakable, thanks to its 88-metre (293-ft) clock tower. The rather subdued art nouveau construction was inaugurated on 20 May 1905 for the city's 200th jubilee. The townspeople are still able to appreciate its breathtaking dimensions when they lose their way in its vast corridors while on some official errand. **Alt-Lickow** street behind the Town Hall serves as a reminder of the district's origins as the village of Lützow or Lietzow. Here the former Villa Kogge from 1864 (No. 28) is worth a visit. Today it is used as a registry office. Many of Charlottenburg's famous families are buried in the **Luisenfriedhof** (cemetery) on Guerickestrasse, which dates from 1815.

In Charlottenburg's traditional petty-bourgeois district or "Kiez" around **Gierkeplatz**, one of the last smallhold-

The futuristic ICC and radio tower.

ers' home is to be found at Schuhstehrusstrasse 13. The house provides an insight into how Charlottenburg looked when it received the status of city from King Frederick 1 in 1705.

Prussian baroque: After the palace was built, Charlottenburg was planned and constructed to a strict plan as a royal seat. The palace is considered to be the most important historic building in western Berlin. Opposite the palace, at the northern end of **Schloßstrasse**, lived court officials and the militia. The two officers' barracks of the **Gardes du Corps** (1859), designed by August Stüler, a pupil of Schinkel, now house the **Ägyptisches Museum** (Egyptian Museum) and the **Stiftung Preußischer Kulturbesitz** (Foundation of Prussian Cultural Heritage).

The last Hohenzollern palace on the Spree suffered considerable fire and bomb damage in World War II. With careful restoration, it has again become one of the most lovely examples of Prussian baroque. Its magnificent 550-metre (1,830-ft) frontage is the result of almost a century of building and rebuilding. In 1695 Sophie-Charlotte, countess and later Queen of Prussia (1658–1705), had a summer residence built for her 8 km (5 miles) outside the gates of Berlin to plans by the masterbuilder Arnold Nering. During the 18th century this was extended into a royal residence, with an Ehrenhof (Memorial Courtyard) and French-style gardens. The court architect Eosander von Göthe added the 143 metres (470 ft) **Orangerie** on the west side, and erected the distinctive dome on the central section, where the temperamental goddess Fortuna spins in the wind, 48 metres (160 ft) up. Under Friedrich II, court architect von Knobelsdorff added the **Neuer Flügel** (New Wing) to the east. The **Theatre**, designed by C.G. Langhans in 1790, now the **Museum für Vor- und Frühgeschichte** (Museum of Pre- and Early History), together with the Small Orangery, completes the palace precinct.

The **Reiterdenkmal des Großen Kurfürsten** (Equestrian Monument to the Great Elector, 1698) in the Ehrenhof occupies its current location because of a wartime blunder. The bronze statue, modelled by Andreas Schlüter, originally graced the Lange Brücke (bridge) in front of the city castle on the Spree. During the war it was moved to Potsdam for safekeeping. As the baroque statue was being shipped back to Borsighafen on Tegel lake en route to Berlin, the overloaded barge sank under the weight. Several years later the statue was raised and restored and finally erected outside Charlottenburg Palace in 1965.

Restoring the historical rooms to their original state took decades of painstaking artistic work. They are now open to the public as a museum. The **Goldene Galerie** from the Frederican rococo period is particularly worth seeing. It is on the upper storey of the Knobelsdorff wing, where the collection of paintings and the library of Frederick the Great are displayed in his private rooms. The

Galerie der Romantik moved into the ground floor in late 1986.

The palace park, planned and laid out by Simon Godeau in 1697, was the first garden in Germany in the style of the French under Louis XIV. At the start of the 19th century Lenné gave the purely baroque park a face-lift along English lines.

The radio tower and the ICC: The western part of Charlottenburg is dominated by the **Funkturm** (radio tower). Including the antenna, this stands 150 metres (500 ft) high, and like a kind of little brother of the Eiffel Tower is a landmark of Berlin. The steel girder construction dates from the pioneering years of wireless. Germany's first radio broadcast was made from the Voxhaus at Potsdamer Strasse 14 on 23 October 1923. In 1926, on the occasion of the Third German Wireless Exhibition, the radio tower was officially opened. Six years later it beamed out the world's first public television broadcast. Today the aerial is only used by the police and fire brigade. There's a lift to the observation platform 125 metres (416 ft) up. Below stretch the 90,000 sq. metres (108,000 sq. yards) of the **Messegelände** (Exhibition Centre) with over 24 exhibition halls in all. Some 25 major exhibitions and trade fairs are held here every year. The **Broadcasting House** on Masurenallee opposite is one of Europe's most modern broadcasting centres and has been planned so that all its studios face onto a central courtyard. Hans Poelzig designed the blue-black clinker building, which dates from 1931. The 14-storey block next door houses the **SFB television studios**.

A covered bridge leads from the exhibition centre on Hammarskjöldplatz over the motorway to the **International Congress Centre** (ICC), which, with its silvery grey aluminium panels, resembles a terrifying futuristic spaceship. Built between 1973 and 1979 for the final sum of just under a million marks, the construction is 320 metres (1,050 ft) long and 80 metres (260 ft) wide and

Triumphal march into the Olympic Stadium in August 1936.

164

provides an area of 800,000 sq. metres (960,000 sq. yards) – more than the Kurfürstendamm if it was laid end to end. An equally outsized iron sculpture stands on the square outside – "Alexander the Great of Ectabene" by the Romanian sculptor Jean Ipousteguy. Popularly known as the "Klettermaxe", this surreal figure provides a balance to what goes on inside the ICC.

Olympic and other memories: Heerstrasse and Reichsstrasse lead to the Olympic Stadium. On the way you can make a detour to the Georg-Kolbe Museum at Sensburger Allee 25, off Heerstrasse, once the home of the famous sculptor and illustrator (1877–1947). The house and the sculpture grove in the garden feature a substantial part of his work (daily except Monday, 10 a.m.–5 p.m.).

From Olympischer Platz, you get your first view of the former Reichs sports grounds of the Third Reich. Commissioned by Hitler from Werner March for the Summer Olympics in 1936, this is still one of the largest sports complexes in Europe. It centres around the Olympic Stadium, an oval construction of whitewashed concrete, which holds about 90,000 spectators.

The neighbouring **Waldbühne** has become a Mecca for rock fans for its open-air concerts, but the Berlin Philharmonic also plays occasionally in the atmospheric arena. At the Rolling Stones' legendary appearance before 21,000 fans on 15 September 1965, the theatre was totally wrecked and for years it wasn't rented out again.

At the northeastern tip of Charlottenburg, where it borders on Wedding and where it no longer feels like you're in Charlottenburg, there is a memorial on Hüttingpfad to victims of the Third Reich. Here in what was then Plötzensee prison, 1,574 resistance fighters were executed. Berlin's Catholics dedicated the **Maria-Regina-Martyrium** church on nearby Heckerdamm to the memory of the "Martyrs for freedom of belief and conscience in 1933–45."

Well balanced: the Berlin Police's motorcycle stunt team.

SCHÖNEBERG

One image of Schöneberg is familiar to almost everyone from the television news: the city hall with its square clocktower and the flag with a bear on it. Here prominent guests from around the world enter their names in the city's golden book. On 26 June 1963, 400,000 Berliners gathered on the square outside to cheer US President Kennedy, when he bellowed those unforgettable words from the balcony: *"Ich bin ein Berliner!"* In honour of the murdered president, the place is now known as John-F.-Kennedy-Platz. At midday every day the Freedom Bell rings from the tower of the town hall, which you can climb as far as the observation platform. A copy of the Liberty Bell in Philadelphia, this was a gift from the USA.

When the mayor of the then independent district laid the foundation stone of Rathaus Schöneberg, nobody could have guessed that a bare four decades later the imposing municipal building would become the political centre of the western half of the city, the official seat of the local mayor and the mayor of West Berlin. Having been thoroughly cleaned for the 750th anniversary celebrations, the Schleswig sandstone facades are once more gleaming white.

Not much greenery: The population and architecture of the district is marked by a strong social distinction between west and east. You only need to cast a glance at Friedenau and the "Red Island", the Bavarian quarter and Potsdamer Strasse, to recognise the differences. Berlin's third smallest district in terms of area – 12 sq. km (5 sq. miles) – Schöneberg has proportionately few open spaces. To the aggravation of its 135,000 inhabitants, it also has the greatest area of roads.

Schöneberg's prettiest park, Rudolph-Wilde-Park begins immediately behind the Rathaus. On a bronze plinthe stands the Goldener Hirsch "Golden Stag", Schöneberg's heraldic mascot and a re-

minder of the original inhabitants of this once thickly forested area. At Kufsteiner Strasse, the park merges with the Wilmersdorfer Volkspark. The RIAS building has been since 1946 the home of the "Radio in the American Sector", which is Berlin's second national radio station after the SFB (Station of Free Berlin).

Village past: Dominicusstrasse leads from the town hall to the old centre of Schöneberg. The oldest building, the Frederican Dorfkirche dating from 1766, stands on a rise besides the main street, Hauptstrasse. The main section of Hauptstrasse between Kaiser-Wilhelm-Platz and Dominicusstrasse still has a grassy promenade, a throwback to its village past. The first official mention of Schöneberg in writing appeared as long ago as 1264, when the Askanian Prince Otto III of Brandenburg donated to the Benedictine nuns of Spandau "five hides of land in 'Villa sconenberch'." After the village was acquired by Elector Joachim I in 1506 and became a sovereign domain, it gradually increased in stature. It was strategically placed on the Berlin-Potsdam road, but this proved its undoing in the Seven Years' War: in 1760 Russian troops burnt the entire village to the ground.

One of the most important things to come out of the rebuilding was the surfacing of the carriageway to Potsdam. Standing on Prussia's first high road, Schöneberg was now brought even closer to Berlin. Many travellers stopped off here, and inns, craftsmen and market gardens moved in to the area. In spite of the expansion, Schöneberg retained its rural identity, and became a favourite place for day trips from Berlin – a tradition that survived into the 20th century.

Place of peace: Between 1875 and 1898, the district's population grew from 7,500 to 75,000 people. Schöneberg was given a town charter and more and more new housing was erected to accommodate the expanding population. The area of **Friedenau** in the southwest corner was a typical example. Development began there in 1871 as a genteel country estate for wealthy government officials and retired gentlefolk. The war with France had just come to its conclusion with the signing of the Treaty of Frankfurt, hence the name "Friedenau" ("peaceful meadow").

With its tree-lined streets, front gardens, leafy squares and stuccoed town houses, Friedenau retains a definite peaceful quality to this day. Its inhabitants weren't exactly delighted when Schöneberg was integrated into Greater Berlin in 1920. They felt that Steglitz would have better befitted their rank. Writers such as Max Frisch, Uwe Johnson and Günter Grass came to Friedenau in search of peace and quiet to work, and they found it here. Federal Germany's first president Theodor Heuss, lived here in Fregestrasse during the Weimar period.

Around **Friedrich-Wilhelm-Platz**, where Friedenau and Wilmersdorf merge, the geometry of the original street plan is still discernible in the curved streets. On the corner of Schmargendorfer Strasse you can marvel at the "Burg" or castle – a particularly stunning example of Friedenau villa architecture dating from around 1885. On Perelsplatz in the north of the district, there is a notable art nouveau fountain, the "Sintflut-Brunnen" (Fountain of the Flood). Like Schöneberg, Friedenau was keen to demonstrate its independence by building a prestigious town hall. The Rathaus dominates **Breslauer Platz**, on the Hauptstrasse which runs south to become Rheinstrasse.

Rusting rails: On Torgauser Strasse by Schöneberg S-Bahn station, an enormous gasometer serves as a symbol of Schöneberg's proletarian past. Railway bridges and sections of track criss-cross the area west of the Schöneberg motorway intersection. On **Priesterweg**, out towards Tempelhof, Berliners tend small garden plots in allotment colonies with romantic names such as "Spot of Happiness". The colonies are an ecological oasis, a miniature waist-high jungle,

The flags of the victorious powers on the Allied Control Council buildings signal the return of justice.

which has grown up between the rusted railway lines.

The man-made hills on Musterdamm were created after the war from the ruins of the Bavarian Quarter. Some 30 metres (100 ft) high, they have been developed as a park by the city's gardeners. On the summit of the **Insulaner**, 75 metres (250 ft) up, glistens the dome of the **Wilhelm-Foerster-Sternwarte**, the largest public observatory in the old Federal Republic and a regular meeting place for amateur astronomers. At the foot of the hill, the **Zeiss Planetarium** simulates the course of the stars under its 20-metres (67-ft) aluminium dome.

Red Island: The Insulaner hill, with its parks, swimming pool and toboggan run, provides an important recreational space for the **Schöneberger Insel**, a densely populated tenement estate between Schöneberg rail-freight station and Yorkstrasse S-Bahn station. It's known as the Insel or island because it can only be reached over various railway bridges. In the early part of this century, this working-class district developed into a stronghold of the labour movement. To this day, the "rote Insel" ("red island") is not a pleasant place. The tenements, workshops and corner bars together typify petty-bourgeois Berlin. Incidentally, two Berliners from these parts later found fame in America. Marlene Dietrich and Hildegard Knef both started life in what is now Leberstrasse, then Sedanstrasse.

The Kleist Park: From the "island" it's only a few minutes' walk to Kleist Park on Potsdamer Strasse, a neighbourhood brimming with history. From 1679 this area was used as a royal kitchen garden and courtyard. Later, Berlin's first botanical garden was founded here. The much-travelled poet and naturalist Adalbert von Chamisso, author of *Peter Schlemihl*, was custodian here from 1819 to 1839. In 1897 the botanical garden moved to Dahlem and the site was turned into a public park, named after the poet Heinrich von Kleist.

The **Königskolonnaden** (King's Col-

onnades) at the main entrance were originally designed in 1870 by Carl von Gontard for the Königsbrücke at Alexanderplatz. The baroque columns have stood here only since 1910.

The **Kammergericht** (Supreme Court) to the rear of the park dates from 1913. The *Rossebändiger* ("*Horse-Breakers*"), two bronze groups which stand in front of it, are particularly fine examples of 19th-century Russian sculptural art. The sight of this north-German baroque building provokes an involuntary shudder. During the Nazi regime this was the seat of the infamous Volksgerichtshof (People's Court) for a time, where the officers of the 20 July conspiracy and other victims were sentenced to death. From 1945 until 1948, occupied Germany was governed from here by the Allied Control Council, composed of representatives from the US, UK, France and the Soviet Union.

The **Bayrisches Viertel** (Bavarian Quarter) begins to the west of Martin-Luther-Strasse, a genteel residential district which before 1933 was known as "Jewish Switzerland". At that time many Jewish academics lived in the spacious apartments, the most famous being Professor Albert Einstein, whose home was at No. 5 Haberlandstrasse (now No. 8 Nördlinger Strasse) when he received the news that he had been awarded the Nobel Prize.

Around Nollendorfplatz: Schöneberg meets the city at Wittenbergplatz, where there is a lavishly restored U-Bahn station. North Schöneberg has a wealth of attractions to offer. On **Kleiststrasse** are the administrative offices of the cultural association "Urania".

At the rear is Berlin's **Post- und Fernmeldemuseum** (Post and Telecommunications Museum), with some interesting historical displays, while the **Landesarchiv Berlin** (Regional Museum) diagonally opposite, on the corner of Kalckreuthstrasse, occasionally holds exhibitions on the history and architecture of the city.

Treasures of another kind are waiting

A Friedenau stallholder.

to be unearthed in Schöneberg's **antique district**. The "big names" with prices to match are on Keithstrasse. Eisenacherstrasse and Motzstrasse are also treasure houses for collectors on the look-out for Meissen porcelain, Russian ikons, old militaria and other rare items. Up on the iron stilts of the disused monorail, the **Flohmarkt** (Flea Market) lords it over Nollendorfplatz, where you'll also find the tiny **Zille Museum**, full of original sketches from the Berlin "Milljöh".

The ambience of **Nollendorfplatz** is dominated by neon-lit cafés, bars, gay bars and the Metropol, Berlin's biggest disco, all of which make up Berlin's "scene". Heading towards **Winterfeldplatz** and **Goltzstrasse** you come across junk shops, antique shops and boutiques with all sorts of crazy clothing, new and second-hand.

On "Potse": In between runs **Potsdamer Strasse**, a section of the former Reichsstrasse 1 from Königsberg to Aachen. At the corner of **Pallasstrasse** is the Sportpalast (Sports Palace) where Berlin held its legendary Six Day Races. From here Goebbels proclaimed "total war" after the fiasco at Stalingrad. The Sportpalast was pulled down in 1973 and the unprepossessing "Social Palace" was built in its place, a dreary prefabricated concrete slum.

After the Wall went up, the "Potse" – as the Berliners affectionately refer to their Potsdamer Strasse – became a cul-de-sac and a problem area. Prostitution and drug-trafficking have since been forced into the side streets, and brothel owners turned their cheap hotels into more lucrative hostels for political refugees. Thus Berlin's immigrant community grew up in a district where banks alternate with amusement arcades, and supermarkets with sex shops, pawnbrokers and Turkish traders. The oldest profession, which had contributed for so many years to the ambience of the **Bülowbogen**, fell victim to the redevelopment schemes of goverment and local business.

A Schöneberg original.

BERLIN'S MAYORS

In Berlin, a man who cuts a good figure as a politician during his period in office can count on the continued affection of the citizens after his retirement – even after his death. To this very day, elderly Berliners speak with affection of "their" Ernst Reuter, and there are tears of nostalgia in their eyes when they hear his voice on the radio once more addressing the assembled crowds in front of the Reichstag on 9 September 1948 during the Blockade: "People of the world, look at this city…" Reuter, a Social Democrat, was elected mayor of the whole of Berlin in 1947, but his nomination was not accepted by the Russian forces of occupation. He became the personification of the Western Sector's resistance to the Soviet attempts at seizure, and after partition was the first incumbent of the newly created office of Mayor of West Berlin (1950–53).

The names of his successors, Walther Schreiber (CDU, 1953–55) and Otto Suhr (SPD, 1954–57), would have passed into oblivion if the authorities had not seen fit to name an important street and a square after them. A Berliner has a mercifully short memory when it comes to political mediocrity; the same also applies to the scandal-ridden terms of office of Klaus Schütz (SPD, 1967–77) and Dietrich Stobbe (SPD, 1977–81), as well as to Eberhard Diepgen (CDU, 1984-89). Five names remain as being of importance: Willy Brandt (SPD, 1957–66), Heinrich Albertz (SPD, 1966–67), Hans Jochen Vogel (SPD, 1981), Richard von Weizsäcker (CDU, 1981–84) and Walter Momper (SPD, 1989–90).

Willy Brandt remains the role model of many younger Berliners, as Ernst Reuter served as one for their older counterparts. On the day after the Berlin Wall was opened they prepared a celebratory reception for the former Federal Chancellor. The present chancellor, Helmut Kohl, hoping to receive the crowd's congratulations in front of the Schöneberg Town Hall, was booed from the platform. A chorus of "Willy! Willy!" drowned the Conservative leader of opinion's first attempts to transform the spontaneous delight into hyper-German platitudes.

When, in the autumn of 1989, the politicians' clichés were made redundant by events, Brandt was the only one to find words to express the feelings of the agitated populace. Brandt had been Mayor of West Berlin at the time the Wall was built. He subsequently made it his life's work to overcome the East-West conflict by a policy of gradual change. The goal had been achieved at last and this was perhaps why Brandt was best able to describe credibly the vision of a united Germany as an ingredient for world peace.

Brandt's successor as mayor of West Berlin, the priest Heinrich Albertz, is a well known spiritual authority. After the shooting of Benno Ohnsorg during a student riot he retired from active politics and became a leading figure of the extra-parliamentary movements of the 1970s and 1980s.

Richard von Weizsäcker, since 1984 the President of the Federal Republic of Germany, has succeeded in representing the widely ranging extremes within German society in such a manner that virtually every German feels he speaks for him personally. During his period as mayor of West Berlin he was able to ease the tensions within the city. His reputation was not damaged by the fact that whilst he was in office the fiercest street battles with squatters took place.

Nobody had really reckoned with the possibility that bald-headed Walter Momper, a virtually unknown character from Kreuzberg, would win the 1989 elections in West Berlin and form a red-green coalition government which would shortly afterwards be swept away by the process of German reunification.

The results of the first elections in the newly reunited city on 2 December 1990 were a clear rejection of Momper and his coalition, which had collapsed a few days previously. He was succeeded by his predecessor; Eberhard Diepgen (CDU), who during the election campaign had promised the Berliners order, security and peace.

Left, Willy Brandt (top right) and Richard von Weizacker (bottom left) were once mayors of Berlin, as were the less well-known Ernst Reuter and Walter Momper.

FRIEDRICHSHAIN

"In these parts, the cravat has no place in a man's basic wardrobe. More the scarf." John Stave, writing his Berlin tales in the 1920s, summed up the district of Friedrichshain perfectly and his description is as valid today as it was then. With a population of 112,000 and covering just 10 sq. km (4 sq. miles), this is Berlin's smallest district. Then as now, white-collar workers could be seen only on the outskirts.

Workers in the East: Anyone taking a walk in Friedrichshain in the first half of the 18th century would have looked out over wavering cornfields and fertile meadows. Here beyond the city gates was a rural haven. At the beginning of the 18th century, when Prussia's first king Friedrich I decided to build up Berlin as his royal seat, the city boundaries were extended to the east. A new suburb was formed which stretched to the Frankfurter Tor (gate), along Palisadenstrasse, over Leninplatz and up to the Königstor, although at that time the district did not yet have a name.

Craftsmen and workers began to settle here. But the industrial boom was just getting under way, and with it the rush to build tenements. Friedrichshain soon developed its own brand of poverty. It became a town of tenement blocks, narrow, dark apartment houses without proper sanitation, full of cramped apartments. The small workshops became manufacturing companies and later large industrial concerns.

The new factories required a lot of labour, "human resources" for badly-paid 16-hour shifts on dingy factory floors. The Berlin-Frankfurt/Oder steam railway was built specifically to guarantee supplies of manpower and raw materials, with an extra station near today's Ostbahnhof. The population expanded rapidly. By the beginning of the war Friedrichshain had the largest population in Berlin.

Friedrichshain Volkspark: The suburban population was already plagued by poverty and disease even before industrialisation brought misery on a grand scale. In 1840, during the period before the March revolution, when wealthy citizens were beginning to doubt the legitimacy of absolute rule, Berlin's city fathers decided to create a recreational park in the east of the city. In the west there was already the spacious, feudal Tiergarten, mainly frequented by the elite of the royal city, but this was far away from the poor inhabitants in eastern Berlin. Gustav Meyer, who later became the court gardener at Sanssouci Palace, laid out the Volkspark to plans by the landscape designer Lenné.

The "Poor People's Park" was called Friedrichshain to commemorate the centenary of Frederick the Great's succession to the throne. In 1868 it was reduced in size to permit the building of the city's first hospital, initiated by Rudolph Virchow because of the high incidence of sickness among the poor.

But what is most unusual about the park is the proliferation of memorials. The **Märchenbrunnen** (Fairytale Fountain) in the western corner dates from 1913 and is a token to the children of east Berlin under threat from typhoid and rickets. The neo-baroque fountain, decorated with characters from Grimm Brothers tales, was built to a design by city architect Ludwig Hoffman.

A few hundred yards to the southeast is the **Gedenkstätte für den Deutschen Interbrigadisten**, a monument to those German members of the International Brigades who fought against the fascists in the Spanish Civil War.

At the southeast corner of the park is the **Friedhof der Märzgefallenen** where many of the Berliners killed by the soldiers of King Friedrich Wilhelm IV in the unsuccessful March revolution of 1848 were buried, their internment attended by 80,000 of their fellow citizens. Until World War I many people would make the pilgrimage here to honour the dead. Wreaths with mes-

sages were banned by the Emperor while he remained in power. Here too is the **Rote Matrose** (Red Sailor) statue which recalls the Red Sailors of Kiel, who sparked off the Revolution in 1918. Engraved on the plaque is a line from the memorial address given here by Lenin in 1919: "Lay firm the foundations of working-class rule, unite against the opposition."

Dominating these monuments are two artificial hills – Großer Bunkerberg and Kleiner Bunkerberg – which were created when well over one million cubic yards of rubble from bombed-out Berlin were dumped over a couple of war-time bunkers. Between them is a small shaded lake alongside which are giant outdoor chess boards.

Vines were cultivated here, as they were on the Kreuzberg, until the middle of the last century. But the quality of this northern wine was more cause for jest than praise. The 19th-century satirist Adolf Glaßbrenner described the drink as "Three Men Wine". "If a man wants

State redevelopmen or private ownership – which will las longer?

to enjoy this grape juice, he needs two others to hold him."

Stalinist boulevard: The city's great east-west axis, Karl-Marx-Allee (Stalin-Allee) is not only astonishing for its colossal proportions but also as a monument to the Socialists' early programme of reconstruction. When the war ended, what was then Frankfurter Allee was a great expanse of ruins. In the early 1950s the SED (German Unity Party) leadership decided to build here Berlin's "first socialist street", which would not only offer comfortable living conditions for the working population but would also "take into account today's traffic conditions". The boulevard is 80 metres (260 ft) wide, a whole 20 metres (65 ft) wider than the mighty Prussian Unter den Linden. The young state pointed proudly to the fact that the first phase of building was completed in record time.

No mention was made of the fact that the construction workers had protested against the raising of construction targets, a protest which culminated in the

Writing on the wall.

storming of the Brandenburg Gate on 17 June 1953. Everything appears over-proportioned here: the shopping arcades, the gateways, the wide pavements and above all the boulevard itself, where the traffic thunders along its marked lanes and the air is thick with fumes.

Death or freedom: Cars also roar along **Leninallee**, past the ugly new buildings on the southern edge of the Volkspark. Here, on what was Landsberger Allee, the **Freie Volksbühne** was founded in the front room of the Böhmisches Brauhaus (Bohemian Brewery). The aim of the "People's Theatre" was to educate the masses, since Berlin's cultural life was mainly concentrated in the smart city centre and way beyond the means of the people of Friedrichshain. When Berlin's most famous actor at the turn of the century, Joseph Kainz, appeared as Karl Moor in Schiller's *Die Räuber*, his speech: "Now we are free comrades. I sense an army within my grasp. Death or freedom!" was greeted with thunderous applause from the audience. Berlin's "red east" was easily stirred by such talk.

On **Leninplatz** the 19-metres (62-ft) high statue of the Russian revolutionary still stands as a symbol – and not only of the SED years. However, whether it will remain in the square is questionable. The statue was hewn from red Ukrainian granite by the President of the Soviet Academy of Arts, Nikolai Tomski. Stark tower blocks ring the stone Russian master. The foundation stone for these was laid by the then head of state Walter Ulbricht on 7 November 1968, the 51st anniversary of the October Revolution.

Stralau: In the middle of the modern prefabs lies the old town of Stralau which is famous to this day for the annual Stralauer Fischzug (Fish Procession), a tradition that dates back to the Middle Ages. Then, as now, the festival was chiefly an occasion for consuming vast quantities of alcohol and recounting unsavoury jokes – two human pleasures that are absolutely timeless.

KREUZBERG

Kreuzberg may be the second smallest district in Berlin, covering just 11 sq. km (4 sq. miles), but it is the best known. The Kreuzberg legend has spread far beyond the city's boundaries, and young people especially are magically drawn here. The reason is the "Kreuzberg mix" – a certain atmosphere that comes from the combination of Turkish immigrants, students, workers, artists and the elderly all living together.

Something of the district's mobile nature can be sampled on the way there. Travel from the Zoo station on the subway (Line 1) towards Schlesisches Tor and observe that the passengers entering the car are typical of the "Kreuzberg mixture". Looking out of the car – the train travels above the ground after the Gleisdreieck station – it is clear why the district has become home to punks, social rebels, Turks and long-term welfare cases. Dilapidated houses where rents are cheap line the route and there is room for an individual existence free from the usual social structures.

Kreuzberg and its innumerable bars harbour an infinite number of eccentrics. Faraway revolutionaries dreaming of an autonomous Kreuzberg, of separating their "Kiez" from the rest of Berlin; singular artists dreaming of their big break; zealous ecologists growing their grain and herbs on balconies and outhouse roofs; old people rhapsodising over the good old days; immigrants from Anatolia (the nickname "Kruzburg" comes from their pronounciation) propagating a breath of Arabian Nights. Here life pulsates as nowhere else in Berlin.

Three parts of town: Unofficially, Kreuzberg is divided into two separate districts which co-exist in a kind of love-hate relationship. The first is known by its postcode, "61", the other by its prewar code "SO 36" or southeast 36. Anyone who lives in 61, possibly in one of the renovated town houses on Mehringdamm, Yorkstrasse or even in Riehmers Hofgarten, is automatically regarded as a "yuppie" by those from SO 36. The 61ers are not particularly popular in the area, as is apparent from the graffiti sprayed on so many of the painstakingly restored stucco facades.

By contrast, someone from "Kotti", the working-class area around Kottbusser Tor, is immediately suspected of being an anarchist. An alternative cabaret artiste in Kreuzberg once summed up this underlying rivalry rather neatly: "The guy from 61 drives a Mercedes; the guy from 36 breaks off the star emblem."

This unusual blend of people, like so much dry tinder just waiting to be sparked off, has a tradition in Kreuzberg, which isn't so very old as an independent district. It was only in 1920, with the great administrative reforms, that the newly created District IV on the southern edge of the city centre was given a name. At that time the historic districts

called "Southern Friedrichstadt", "Luisenstadt" and "Tempelhof Vorstadt" were amalgamated to form one single administrative district.

Initially some officials wanted to call the new locality "Hallesches Tor", since the gateway on the Landwehr canal was a familiar landmark to the entire population. But the name prompted all sorts of arguments, so in the end they finally settled on the district's foremost area, Kreuzberg.

In the 1920s Kreuzberg was largely a residential district, but since the turn of the century the area around Friedrichstrasse and Kochstrasse had been undergoing a fundamental change. More and more apartment blocks were being turned into commercial properties. The population fell, but its structure remained for the most part intact, unaffected by the change.

Further east in 'Luisenstadt', present-day SO 36, the vast majority of the population were workers' families, living in dingy one- or two-roomed flats without bathrooms and with a shared toilet in the corridor.

"Tempelhof Vorstadt" in the southwest was its upmarket counterpart, an elite neighbourhood of villas on the Kreuzberg, housing white-collar workers and government employees. "Southern Friedrichstadt", the lively quarter of inner-city Berlin, was very different in character to its suburban neighbour to the south. Here was newspaper land, Friedrichstrasse with its entertainment spots and elegant Wilhelmstrasse, the upper echelons of which were once the centre of government and included the presidential palace, the chancellery and the Foreign Office.

In addition, there were the two main railway terminals. Outside the city gates, Prussia's first private railway company built a station for trains to Potsdam on what is now Askanischer Platz, and there on 29 October 1838 Berlin's railway age began. Around the turn of the century millions of people streamed through the vast halls of Potsdam and

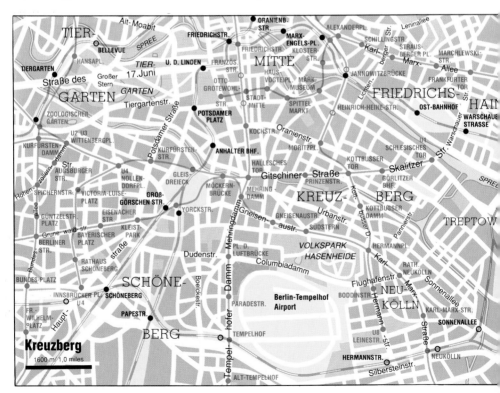

Anhalt stations every day. An old water tower in the grounds of the Museum für Verkehr und Technik (Transport and Technology) at Gleisdreieck U-Bahn dates from this period.

Around Anhalter station: Where once was city bustle, today there stretches a desolate wasteland on the edge of the city. Here film and insurance companies had their offices, here you'd find hotels like the Excelsior and the Stuttgarter Hof, and cafés, restaurants and clubs were busy late into the night. Only a single towering entrance still survives at Anhalter station which, until the end of World War II, was Berlin's main railway terminus.

The "Konzerthaus" Concert Hall once stood on **Bernburger Strasse**, where the Berlin Philharmonic celebrated their first triumphs. Among the gutted and half-gutted buildings, cleared away and levelled out after 1945, was Germany's most evil address during the Nazi period, the former Prinz Albrecht Palais at Wilhelmstrasse 102. Here and in the neighbouring buildings on Prinz-Albrecht-Strasse was the powerhouse of the Third Reich's persecution and extermination policies. This was the seat of the SS security force, and the dreaded State Secret Police (Gestapo). Here, Himmler, Heydrich, Eichmann and their henchmen had their desks.

New Kreuzberg: The architectural transgressions of the past are impossible to ignore. In the 1960s unimaginative concrete blocks were erected in east and west alike, although **Mehringplatz** is a pleasant exception, a modern complex at **Hallesches Tor** U-Bahn station which is worth seeing for its unusual structure. Admittedly, from a distance the buildings look like one massive group of uninspiring tower blocks, but when you enter the estate, laid out in the round, you find yourself in a pedestrian zone dotted with open spaces and shopping arcades. The pedestrian zone is surrounded by rings of houses of various heights, beginning with three-storey buildings in the inner circle and leading

All that remains of Anhalter station.

out to 17-storey blocks on the outside. In the middle of the ring towers a peace monument.

To one side of Mehringplatz (formerly Belle-Alliance-Platz) runs **Lindenstrasse**. Here you'll find the Berlin Museum, the former Kammergericht (Supreme Court), where the writer ETA Hoffmann once sat on the jury. Nowadays the building not only offers informative exhibitions on Berlin history but also culinary delights. The **Alt-Berliner Weißbierstube** is famous for its substantial buffet.

However, Kreuzberg's real claim to fame lies in being Berlin's number one source of talent. The artists and intellectuals who founded the reputation of the quarter in the 1920s have remained true to "their" district to this day. But before we explore the myths and special atmosphere of Kreuzberg, here's some practical advice on the best way to get to grips with the district.

A climb: Take the 19 bus or the U-Bahn (Mehringdamm station) to **Viktoria Park** and climb the 66 metres (219 ft) to the top of the **Kreuzberg**. Incidentally, this used to be called the "Round Vineyard". Vines are still grown here today, although they're not much rated. The hill owes its new name to a monument built by the architect and sculptor Schinkel to commemorate the 1813–15 war of liberation. The 20-metres (66-ft) Gothic column topped with a massive iron cross was erected in 1878 on a stone base 8 metres (27 ft) high. Iron sculptures are set into the niches around the monument, depicting successful battles and generals who fought in the campaign against Napoleon.

The visitor unfamiliar with the area will be amazed at the sight of the waterfall, which roars down towards Großbeerenstrasse. It is an imitation of the Zackelfall in the Sudeten mountains, and in summer a favourite place where dogs and small children splash around. The higher one goes up the hill, the better the view over the sea of houses. The concrete desert to the northwest, with the old-fashioned trams and solid blocks of new housing, is Kreuzberg. There's scarcely a patch of green to be seen, except maybe a few swathes which a closer glance reveals to be cemeteries. People live very close together in Kreuzberg: in 1910, more than 420,000 people were crammed together in the tiniest imaginable space. Today, Kreuzberg is still the most densely populated district in western Berlin, with about 150,000 inhabitants.

But there are perfectly pleasant places to live in Kreuzberg. **Riehmers Hofgarten** is proof of that – a historic estate within a stone's throw of the waterfall, which is protected by a preservation order. There are entrances to the estate on Yorkstrasse, Großbeerenstrasse and Hagelberger Strasse.

The complex, named after its founder Wilhelm Riehmer, a builder who made it rich in Germany's industrial boom, is built around a central courtyard and demonstrates that even in the middle of the city it is possible to find a peaceful

The immigrant minorities created their own markets: the Turkish market...

airy place to live. Entering through the imposing gateway on Yorkstrasse, you find yourself in a precinct of 24 buildings. There is plenty of evidence of the care taken by architects in planning inner-city developments before the turn of the century. The apartments are large and equipped with the necessary sanitation. The spacious grassy courtyard is so built that the various nooks and crannies effectively mask the noise of the traffic that roars along Yorkstrasse at all hours of day and night.

Riehmers Hofgarten is worth a visit, if only for the painstakingly restored stucco facades modelled on the style of the Renaissance architect Palladio. Little wonder that upmarket cafés, cinemas and a disco have moved into the neighbourhood. The **Berliner Kinomuseum** (Cinema Museum) at Großbeerenstrasse 57, an old fleapit which shows old black-and-white films from the early days of Granny's picture house, blends in very well here.

Subtle charm: Nearby is **Chamisso-Platz**, the second of Berlin's five "restricted development zones". The square is situated in an area which was largely spared in the war and during the demolition mania of the reconstruction period which followed. The attraction of the former "Tempelhofer Vorort" lies in the fact that this typical working-class, petty-bourgeois area has barely altered since it was built in the second half of the 19th century.

Today, after years of renovation work, Chamisso-Platz sparkles with a new charm. In the middle, a typical Old Berlin pissoir (men only!) has been preserved. The rectangular square is surrounded by four- and five-storey buildings distinguished by their facades, with their simple stucco ornamentation and harmoniously balanced windows. Restaurants, flea-markets and antique shops add colour to the place.

From Südstern to SO 36: Opposite the entrances to the cemetery is the Südstern (South Star) and the U-Bahn station of the same name. Seven main roads meet

.and the rempelmarkt.

here to form a star. In the middle of the traffic intersection stands the former Garnisonskirch (Garrison Church), which has not been used as a church for many years.

Further to the northeast, heading towards Kottbusser Tor, it is clear where bourgeois Berlin 61 changes into proletarian SO 36. Renovated old houses, new houses and completely derelict houses stand side by side. In this neighbourhood the "Kreuzberg mix" is also reflected externally: a trendy café stands directly next to a rough bar, which nevertheless retain the charm of the old days when Kreuzberg was still the stronghold of the bric-à-brac shop and the Naïve painters.

There is little left of the typical working-class milieu. The district has changed amazingly quickly, since the "Strategy for Kreuzberg" was unveiled in the 1970s to save it from deteriorating into a slum. The IBA international building exhibition played a major part in this, introducing the concept of "informed development", a mixture of the reconstruction of old buildings and new projects designed to blend in harmoniously with their older surroundings.

Deepest Kreuzberg: Mariannenplatz demonstrates how successful such an approach can be. Around the semi-circular square restored stucco facades alternate with angular new bays and modern glass fronts, without the old clashing with the new. The centrepiece is Kurt Mühlenhaupt's Feuerwehrbrunnen ("Fire Brigade Fountain").

The city's Turkish population plays an important role in the **Künstlerhaus Bethanien**. Turkish artists come and go in the former hospital on Mariannenplatz, which now houses print workshops, artists' studios, exhibition and theatre space, a Turkish lending library and the Kreuzberg Arts Office. Such successful cultural exchanges occur all over Kreuzberg.

In spite of the racist slogans daubed here and there on houses, the two communities live reasonably peaceably together. This can be seen at the Türkenmarkt (Turkish Market) held every Friday on **Maybachufer**. A bazaar atmosphere reigns until well into the afternoon and the riverside pavements are busy with women in veils and men with beards. Prices are haggled over, fruit and vegetables tested for their quality, and oriental delicacies and household goods from around the world are offered for sale. The smell of kebabs hangs in the air, mingling with the aroma of a mixture of oriental spices, which are slowly finding their way into the German cuisine.

On **Oranienstrasse** you can sample Kreuzberg's unique atmosphere in its undiluted form. Here Turkish cafés stand side by side with punk haunts, neon-lit bars and Berlin corner bars. Whenever one of the independent art galleries holds an open day, the Turkish residents will pop in, just as it's now taken for granted that long-established Kreuzbergers usually buy their vegetables from Turkish corner shops.

Left, U-Bahn line 1, immortalised in a musical.

TEMPODROM

Dressed inconspicuously in jeans and a sweater, Irene Mössinger, the director and boss of the Tempodrom, looks bored as she occasionally sits in the ticket office in front of the tent which serves as an arena for alternative functions. Nothing in her appearance would indicate that she has become a living legend on the fringe scene in Berlin – a sort of Cinderella whose childhood dream has come true.

The former nurse who used an inheritance to buy a circus tent has, through a colourfully varied programme and while periodically escaping bankruptcy by the skin of her teeth, made her Tempodrom into a Berlin institution.

Irene Mössinger maintains that dreams are the reason for her success. For her, the "alternative" circus is the realisation of such a vision. And yet, she finds it difficult to decide what her true aim in life really is. In retrospect she feels that she has always been searching for something. The daughter of wealthy parents who had fallen on hard times, as a child she lived in Spain for several years. Later she was a pupil at Salem, the exclusive boarding school, where her mother had found a position as teacher. Her father had settled in Italy some years previously. After matriculating, Irene Mössinger started to study journalism, changed to art and then finally trained as a nurse. She practised her new profession, from which she derived great satisfaction, for a total of six years.

The turning point in her life was the death of her father in Italy. To her great surprise, she inherited more than DM800,000 (US$ 470,000). For several years she was uncertain as to what to do with the money. Then, together with a handful of friends, she founded a circus company and erected her second-hand tent on the then unoccupied Potsdamer Platz. After the varied programme presented during the first year the Tempodrom, as the circus was called, went bankrupt. Irene Mössinger, however, had invested too many dreams to accept defeat without a struggle. And the Scene had no intention of allowing its newly acquired alternative mecca to disappear without demur.

The Senate provided funds for the undertaking, but the sum available was totally inadequate. Every year the spectre of bankruptcy haunted the green Big Top.

Finally, in 1985, the Tempodrom was allotted a new site at "In den Zelten" – *In the tents* – in the Tiergarten, near the Hall of Congress. Things slowly started to improve. The programme became more varied; in addition to the nostalgic circus there were traditional rock concerts, an open-air discothèque in summer, and a café. The mountain of debts became smaller and her love of the enterprise greater.

Irene Mössinger explains that things were by no means easy, and that there was no question of relaxation, let alone a holiday, during this period. She just had to keep going. Apart from the musical functions, which guaranteed income and thus formed the economic basis upon which the entire enterprise rested, Irene Mössinger was now prepared to extend the repertoire to include more risky undertakings. The esoteric fair "Consciousness '88", with discussions of the New Age brought in little money, but because of its unique character was worth the financial risk involved.

The Tempodrom was threatened again during the autumn of 1989, when the red-green Senate decided to enforce noise prevention regulations which would have meant that concerts could only take place once or twice a month. For the first time Irene Mössinger toyed with the idea of abandoning the entire project. She claimed that any reduction in the number of performances would have sounded the death knell of the Tempodrom. The storm of protest united the entire city.

The fall of the Wall only a few days later meant that the problem was temporarily shelved. The Tempodrom, now standing at the heart of a world metropolis, simply carries on. The peace and quiet of "Rest-Berlin" is a thing of the past, and this may result in a fairy-tale ending after all: Irene Mössinger's dream came true long ago. Now the entire city shares her vision. Persistent dreams of that kind are not so easy to erase.

PRENZLAUER BERG

What Kreuzberg was to West Germany in the 1980s, the "Prenzelberg" was to the GDR. A refuge for misfits unable to conform back home in the provinces; a playground for drop-outs wanting to try alternative ways of living; a meeting place for punks and gays and for opposition groups and artists from near and far; in short, a Mecca for the sub-culture of the whole country.

In Prenzlauer Berg it was possible to live largely beyond the control of the state and the norms of socialist society. The state housing department lacked on overall picture of the run-down workers' district, and it was thus possible to squat in empty apartments or to simply occupy them and thus circumvent the usual waiting list. Experts estimate that between 20 and 30 percent of the Prenzelberg population obtained their flats in this way.

Musicians, painters, theatre groups and political groups found space here, too, in order to work on their projects. Private galleries and bars sprang up. The "Scene", more a jumble of different sub-cultures than one distinctive social entity, flourished on the edge of legality – closely watched by the state, sometimes treated like a child, but by and large tolerated.

The "Scene" in revolt: No one can say how the Berlin "scene" will now develop or for how long it will continue to dictate the shape of the district. Since the Berlin Wall came down, a lot of west German squatters have come over. Support groups and local initiatives are going to the wall, because there's no money for projects aimed at cleaning up the streets and bringing some cultural life to the area.

All is now quiet again around the **Gethsemanekirche** (church), under cover of which the East German opposition came together and which became a symbol of the 1989 revolution. On 7 October 1989 the church opened its doors to give protection to protestors being beaten up by the Stasi and the police on the 40th anniversary of the founding of the GDR. It is possible that the character of Prenzlauer Berg will change completely in the coming years. In reunited Berlin, the "wild child" of the city's districts counts as a "prime city centre location" in property developer-speak. It would be easy for investors with plenty of capital to oust the incumbent impoverished population – students, artists and the elderly – from their homes.

Historical rapprochement: Prenzlauer Berg is within walking distance of the city centre. Head northeast from Alexanderplatz and you're in the thick of its historical past. Beyond Wilhelm-Pieck-Strasse, the southern boundary of the district, there is a marked incline – the old Windmühlenberg (Windmill Hill). This once lay beyond the city gates. At that time it was fields and meadows, and few people lived here.

The district's main traffic routes – Schönhauser Allee, Prenzlauer Allee and Greifswalder Strasse – were country roads, leading out from the city to the northeast. Along them are several old cemeteries, including (on Schönhauser Allee) what was the most fashionable Jewish cemetery in Berlin, where the painter Max Liebermann is buried.

After 1861, a whole town of tenements was blasted out of the ground on the outlying hill. By 1920, when the administrative district of Prenzlauer Berg came into being, 312,000 people were living here. There are very few individual attractions, but the district as a whole is of cultural and historical interest. It was largely spared during the air raids, and the few new buildings and redevelopment projects since 1945 haven't altered its essential face. Around 90 percent of the houses are five storeys high, set close together on absolutely straight streets. Gateways lead into a labyrinth of wings, side wings and narrow dark courtyards.

Behind the showy stucco facades, poverty escalated. Damp, dingy apartments, overcrowded rooms, inadequate sanitation, horrendously high rents – these were the social conditions which were to lead the painter Heinrich Zille to comment caustically that you can kill a man just as well with a flat as you can with an axe.

Today, the old houses mostly look better inside than they do from the outside. Fragments of stucco work cling to crumbling plaster and geraniums bloom on balconies in imminent danger of collapsing. Brickwork is exposed on many of the once so elegant facades. In the wide streets, once bordered by front gardens, residents have ripped up the surface and planted flowers. Above the basement stores, long since closed, faded inscriptions reveal the specialities of the former owners: Herrings and Potatoes; Soup; Cabbages.

Many of the old shops have since been rented out by new businesses. Residents are waiting with bated breath to **Spring fever can strike at any age...**

see what kind of premises will open here next.

Although the district's population has more than halved and hardly any tower blocks have been built, Prenzlauer Berg still has the same population density as all the other districts in what was East Berlin. Seventy per cent live in flats built before 1919; only 2.6 percent are in new dwellings. People have furnished the old buildings as well as they can and made the old houses habitable. But standards of housing are still low: many apartments still have no indoor toilet or bath, and often the rain comes in through the ceiling.

Around Kollwitzplatz: The emblem of Prenzlauer Berg, part of its coat of arms, is the **water tower** on Windmühlenberg (Knackstrasse), which was built in 1875. Several tenants still live there. Over the years the narrow tower next door has been used by various political parties as a flagpole. The last flag to flutter there, as on so many houses, was the black and red squatters' standard. This is one of

the city's oldest waterworks, erected in 1855–56 by an English firm at their own expense. Beneath are the old brick vaults, which are all that remains of the then open reservoir.

If the iron gates at the foot of the hill happen to be open, take a peek into the sinister place beyond. In 1933 the National Socialists set up a torture chamber here, to which communists were brought from the workers' district. A memorial stone remembers its victims. Children playing above the awful place are happy to tell you what it's like living around here.

Opposite the watertower, behind Rykestrasse 53, is the red-brick **Synagogue**, built, in simple classical style, in 1904. It was badly damaged by the Nazis in 1938, but because of the adjoining houses they didn't set fire to it, and between 1976 and 1978 it was restored as Germany's first synagogue. To the rear lie Kollwitzstrasse and **Kollwitzplatz**.

The artist and sculptor Käthe Kollwitz and her husband Karl, a doctor for the poor, lived here in the house on the corner of Knaackstrasse (formerly Weißenburger Strasse 25). In the grounds of the bombed out house, a statue based on one of Kollwitz' drawings, the "Schützende Mutter" (Guardian Mother), commemorates the artist. Käthe Kollwitz herself sits facing it, larger than life in bronze, and the children playing in Kollwitzplatz regularly leap onto her lap and climb up around her neck.

With the recent opening of several very popular bars and fringe theatres the area around Kollwitzplatz has become the centre of an exciting local *Szene*.

"Honnywood" is what the locals call **Husemannstrasse**, which leads off to the north from Kollwitzplatz. The shopping street was originally built around 1890 and was rebuilt, in 19th-century style, in 1987. Ornamental plasterwork, window frames, doorways, shop signs and signposts were painstakingly copied, with the result that the street now

..and any political persuasion.

resembles a film set. It is even possible to hire a horse and carriage from the stables here. More often than not you'll come across a real film crew here, shooting location shots for television and for the cinema.

However, it is still worth a visit, especially for the **Friseurmuseum** (Hairdressing Museum, with erratic opening hours) at No. 8. This has far more than mere curiosity value. Among the fascinating items on display are hairpins from the Bronze Age, a medieval bathroom, a wigmaker's workshop, old barbers' chairs and all sorts of tools of the trade. The witty tours led by Jürgen Platow, who looks after everything in his various guises as director, archivist, guardian and cleaner, really liven up weary groups of tourists.

A couple of houses further down at No. 12 in a restored tenement is the **Museum Berliner Arbeiterleben um 1900** (which translates as "Working-Class Life in Berlin Around 1900"). The exhibits show how a typical working class Berlin family lived at the turn of this century.

New centre in Thälmannpark: On the site of a former gasworks now stands **Thälmannpark**, a vast open space with an arts centre, playgrounds, a swimming pool and accommodation for 4,000 people. The massive Thälmann monument on Greifswalderstrasse was unveiled in 1986 to mark the centenary of the leader of the labour movement. Lengthy debate surrounded the Thälmann project, which was envisaged as giving the district a prestigious new centre. The end result looks very out of place standing in the midst of its 19th-century surroundings.

There are very few patches of green around here, but the locals have grown to like the new green-field site, which runs along the side of the S-Bahn as far as Prenzlauer Allee. On Prenzlauer Allee glistens the dome of the **Planetarium**, where you can embark on a journey through the solar system or be talked through the skies over Berlin.

At the principal entrance to the **Heimatmuseum Prenzlauer Berg** (Local Museum) a relief commemorates the head of the city planning department Hermann Blankenstein, under whose leadership the public building was erected between 1886 and 1889.

Schönhauser Allee: This loud, lively shopping street with lots of cafés is best reached by U-Bahn (Dimitroffstrasse station). The "Boulevard of the North" can't yet compare with similar shopping centres in the western districts. The junction of **Dimitroffstrasse and Kastanienallee** is one of the city's busiest for traffic. The **Berliner Prater** is also located here, an old-established assembly hall and function rooms. It's pleasant to stroll under the monorail, even in the rain. Since it was built in 1911–13, the locals have called it "the municipal umbrella". West of the railway begins the redevelopment zone around **Arnimplatz**, the socialist counterpart of Kreuzberg's "informed reconstruction".

Left, great, but who'll dispose of the bins of dog dirt? Right, "Honnywood" or Husemannstrasse, Honecker's show mile.

SELF-HELP ON THE KOLLWITZPLATZ

When Diana moved from Weimar to Berlin to write her dissertation about the Prenzlauer Berg, she acquired a flat in the customary manner. She broke into the uninhabited side wing of an disused tenement house and renovated a small two-room flat on the top floor. One day she found that her keys would no longer open the door. During her absence the communal housing authority had had the locks changed. A curt note attached to the door requested her to report to their offices immediately. After a series of discussions she was granted an official lease.

On her way to work, Diana passes Schönhauser Allee 20, a house which was occupied after November 1989. The ground floor of the five-story building has been barricaded up. Fine wire mesh protects the upper windows from stones. The squatters' banners flutter harmoniously alongside the flags of the former GDR. For former dissidents the latter have become their symbols of protest at the indecent haste with which the old system has been abandoned. Heavily disguised figures dressed in black stand on the balcony; punk music drones down onto the street below. The house looks as if a journey through time has

lifted it from the Kreuzberg of the 1980s into the next decade. And, as if it was already a museum piece, it has been placed under police protection.

Near the illegal area, in the former Jewish Old People's home, can be found the People's police station for the Prenzlauer Berg. On Saturday afternoons police vans with water cannon take up their positions to ensure that their illegal neighbours are not stoned by hundreds of right-wing extremists and skinheads.

Diana works in a tiny tenants' association office at the Kollwitzplatz, which also serves as editorial office for the local newspaper *Die Regionale*. Together with Lutz, a fellow student of architecture, Diana is developing a model for the meticulous renovation of the Prenzlauer Berg. The two students pore over their drawing boards as they translate into large-scale plans what they have managed to find out from the study of building schemes and countless investigative trips through the neighbourhood. In 1988, during a period of practical experience within the framework of his course, Lutz witnessed how, without studying the area at first hand, town planners decided on extensive demolition and rebuilding in the prefabricated concrete block idiom typical of the GDR. A citizens' initiative was formed to resist the execution of the project, and the district's countenance was preserved. The authorities demanded an alternative scheme – and Lutz and Diana were called upon to develop one.

Their plan for the rehabilitation of the area is based upon a painstakingly accurate presentation of the existing state of affairs, coupled with the wishes of the residents. They are trying to find an individual solution for each of the houses and back yards. They plan to demolish not more than a handful of houses in order to increase the light and space of those remaining. Spacious ateliers are planned for resident self-help groups, artists and the studio theatre of the Ernst Busch School of Drama. The students are aiming at a relatively modest standard of comfort in the renovated flats in order not to force sitting tenants to leave because of massive rent increases.

The results of the students' labours are greeted with considerable enthusiasm when they present their plans to a public residents' meeting. The subsequent discussion reveals, however, that there is little chance of the scheme being realised. In the new political situation it is unclear in many cases who actually owns the houses in question. This fact makes the residents unwilling to invest their meagre savings in renovation. The local community cannot help, for it has no money and is in no position to take out a loan. The few building contracts are awarded to West German firms which are forcing their way into the market by means of unrealistically low prices. There would be plenty to do, but the local building workers are unemployed because they are never awarded any contracts.

"The only thing we can do at present is refuse to grant planning permission", says the youthful housing representative on the district council whose participation in citizens' initiatives has fitted him for his present office. He is the one who has to face the wrath of the general public but his hands are tied. He would love to have Diana and Lutz work directly for the Town Planning Office but there are no funds available.

The only site where building is going ahead with any enthusiasm is behind the old Jewish cemetery on the Schönhauser Allee. Alongside the wall are a dozen or so crooked wooden huts, which a few children are attacking with hammers and saws.

The play building site for children was initiated in April 1990. The Parks Department made the land available and delivered the necessary building material. A van painted in gaudy colours is parked in front of the playground – a "play-mobile" full of toys. For 10 years now it has been doing the rounds on the Prenzlauer Berg. After the Wall fell the "play-mobile" served as the basis for the *Play Network*, a loose association of all amenities that were available for children in the district. It includes meeting places for schoolchildren, handicraft groups, children's libraries, a children's cinema and a theatre workshop.

A children's farm is being built on the former "death strip" on the edge of the district. The cheerful Network headquarters near the play building site is also the editorial office of a newspaper for the 20,000 children who live on the Prenzlauer Berg. The contributors are quite new to the art of writing and have great difficulty with the typewriter.

During the "Round Table" era, the transitional period immediately after the bloodless revolution in the GDR, projects like *Network* were given preferential treatment when it came to financial support. The association is one of the few dreams to bear fruit in the founding years of the GDR which matured sufficiently to survive German reunification. It is supported by various departments within the district council. Things are not likely to change much as long as the "Children's Council" meets regularly in the Town Hall with the authority to make binding decisions on behalf of the mayor in much the same way as the Round Tables did in their time.

The dilapidated facade of Rykestrasse 13 bears the message *Galerie ACUD* in white paint. An arrow directs the the visitor to the house across the back yard. All the lower storeys are uninhabited; the exhibition galleries - the bare rooms of two flats - occupy the light-filled top floor. There are attractive porcelain tiled stoves in the corners, and a small incinerator serves as a platform for sculptures.

Few visitors find their way to the gallery. The new exhibition of works by a Russian artist - collages of leather, wood, cardboard and string - does not deserve such neglect. Glancing from the muted colours of the pictures to the view from the window, the critical eye alights on the brown plaster of the front house, its crumbling walls and peeling window frames.

After studying the abstract pictures on view, one is better able to concentrate on the building itself. The ancient walls are a source of aesthetic pleasure. The exhibition, a melancholic improvisation of refuse, could find no better setting than this makeshift gallery.

Torsten, keeping an eye on the pictures, offers the only visitor on this particular afternoon a cup of coffee. He has been unemployed since 1990 but has plenty to do. After vain attempts with a group called "Megalomania", he has finally discovered an empty house for the alternative art association "ACUD", which fitted out the gallery. He is desperately negotiating with the authorities to obtain a proper lease before all traces of the GDR have disappeared. The gallery is to move to its new premises in a couple of years. The renovation may be financed by a Berlin Senate fund for self-help projects.

The artists dream of a multi-cultural centre with a solar roof, ecological advisory centre and screen printing workshop, plus a café and theatre.

There is certainly no shortage of ideas, of realisable dreams and projects on the Prenzlauer Berg – even if the initial enthusiasm which erupted immediately after the SED was stripped of office has diminished somewhat. Unfortunately, the children of the Kollwitzplatz are not the only ones who will be in a position to decide how much of it can be saved in the future.

WEDDING

Red Wedding,
welcome your comrades,
hold your clenched fists high.
Keep your ranks unwavering,
for our day draws nigh...

Erich Weinert's proletarian battle song from the late 1920s was once typical of the district's reputation. It was already a stronghold of the socialist labour movement at the time of Germany's industrial expansion in the late 19th century. On 9 November 1918 workers at the AEG and Schwarzkopff plants marched on the government quarter with their revolutionary red flag.

Faced with rising unemployment towards the end of the Weimar Republic, the communists held more and more sway in Wedding. At the parliamentary elections held in 1928, they gained more votes than the Social Democrats and, for the first time, became the strongest party.

When the engineering and electrical industries moved in to north Berlin towards the end of the 19th century, thousands of workers were attracted to Gesundbrunnen and Wedding. Both districts had been part of Berlin since 1861, but now building land was in short supply. Five-storey tenement blocks with dark inner courtyards shot up out of the ground, unbearably close to each other.

In the 1920s over 250,000 people, more than double the present number, lived packed together in the district's 15 sq. km (6 sq. miles), most in damp, dingy apartments. Mass poverty and factory work – if you were lucky enough to have a job at all – characterised the daily round in proletarian Wedding.

Modern Wedding: Today, the population of Wedding numbers only 155,000 people. A good one-fifth of the district, just over 297 hectares (734 acres), is parkland, located mainly around the man-made hill (87 metres/285 ft) at

Humboldthain, the Schillerpark and Volkspark Rehberge. The last named is famous for its open-air summer theatre. Both banks of the river Panke, which rises in Pankow and flows through the district into the North Harbour, have been planted with trees and bushes to create an attractive riverside walk.

At the same time the population density in the district (approximately 10,000 per sq. km/25,000 per sq. mile), is at least twice the average in West Berlin. Wedding, like its eastern neighbour Prenzlauer Berg, is a district of the common man, where you'll hear the thickest Berlin accents.

To appreciate how much the face of the district has changed since the war, take a walk through the redevelopment area on Brunnenstrasse, south of Gesundbrunnen S-Bahn station. The large area of new buildings was once a deplorable poverty stricken slum. One of the grossest examples was Meyer's Hof at Ackerstrasse 132–3, a run-down tenement with six courtyards. At one

point up to 2,000 people lived here in 230 tiny apartments with only outdoor toilets.

In an attempt to rid itself once and for all of its grey stone boxes and squalid image, the district went in for demolition in a big way in the 1960s. The proletarian areas of old buildings on either side of Brunnenstrasse and Badstrasse were cleared away, together with their tenants, and the whole social and economic structure of the surrounding area changed.

Computers, not turbines: The industrial face of Wedding has changed, too. Nothing demonstrates this more clearly than the deserted **AEG entrance** in Brunnenstrasse, dating from 1891. One hundred years of Berlin industrial history came to an end when the electrical firm founded by Emil Rathenau in 1883 had to close its last production plant at Wedding in 1984.

Now the former "white-collar gate", a decorative neo-Gothic brick gateway, is reflected in the tinted glass of a state-of-the art office block. The computer firm **Siemens-Nixdorf** built a factory for 1,200 employees on the same site (No. 111). All around are the old AEG buildings, stretching as far as **Ackerstrasse**. The former light motor plant on Voltastrasse and the heavy machine plant on Hussitenstrasse, also known as the "cathedral of work", stand out as pioneering examples of industrial architecture. They were designed by Peter Behrens.

Today, the locality is known as Silicone Wedding and the microchip age has taken over the AEG complex. The offices of the **Berliner Innovations- und Gründerzentrum** (BIG) (Centre of Innovation and Invention) are on Ackerstrasse. The **Kunstquartier Ackerstrasse** has established a new arts exhibition centre in one of the old factories. The environmental artist Ben Wargin uses the inner courtyard to show his highly original creations.

On Millerstrasse: Wedding's largest employer is now **Schering AG**. About 500 people are employed at the extensive works on **Weddingplatz**. The chemical and pharmaceutical company employs 20,000 people worldwide, a fact it boasts with a 14-storey aluminium-clad headquarters. Together with the research centre, which is almost as high, it towers over the south-west corner of Wedding. Mainly known for the contraceptive pill and other special pharmaceutical products, Schering is the only international company to have retained its head office in west Berlin. The company grew out of Ernst Schering's "Green Chemist" on **Müllerstrasse**, now the main shopping street and the centre of the Wedding community.

The Rathaus (town hall) near Leopoldplatz U-Bahn station consists of a 49-metres (163-ft) high administration block, connected by a glass corridor to the original 1920s town hall. Also on Müllerstrasse (No. 163) are the headquarters of the regional branch of the SPD in **Kurt-Schumacher-Haus**.

From the very beginning, Social

Redevelop–ment instead of the demolition ball.

Democrats led the way in local politics. Wedding's first welfare housing estates date from the period of office of the first SPD mayor, Carl Leid. The Afrikanisches Viertel (African Quarter) with its "living cubes" designed by Mies van der Rohe, is one example. Other famous Weimar architects such as Bruno Taut, Paul Emmerich and Paul Mebes responded to the degrading 19th-century tenements with their apartments on the **Friedrich-Ebert-Siedlung** (estate) between Müllerstrasse and Rehberge.

Two neo-classical churches, the **Alte Nazareth Kirche** on Leopoldplatz and **St. Pauls Kirche** at the corner of Bad Strasse and Pank Strasse in the Gesundbrunnen quarter are based on K.F. Schinkel's design and are among the oldest buildings in the district.

Teaching and research: The district owes its name to the village and later the estate of Wedding, whose boundaries once included the traffic-bound **Nettelbackplatz**. **Gesundbrunnen** developed from a second settlement around **Bad-strasse**, named after one of the sources of the Panke. That source was destroyed in 1882, when the Panke was turned into a canal. Shortly afterwards, the industrialisation of the neighbourhood, popularly known as "Plumpe", began.

The Rudolf Virchow hospital, named after its founder, stretches to the northern bank of the Berlin-Spandau Ship Canal. As a doctor and Progress Party member of the Reichstag, Virchow was committed to the building of a modern hospital in overpopulated North Berlin. It was opened in 1906 as a "garden city for the sick" with 57 pavilions, revolutionary for those times. Nature was to help heal the patients.

Nobel Prize winner Robert Koch (1843–1920), who discovered the cholera and tuberculosis bacilli, moved his Institute for Infectious Diseases from Charité to Wedding's north bank in 1900. Today, members of the **Robert Koch Institute** and their colleagues in the Federal Health Department are playing a key role in AIDS research.

Some tenements have not changed since the last century.

PANKOW

"Bolle went away for Whitsun, Pankow was his goal," goes an old Berlin melody about the alcoholic adventures of a man from Berlin. People were already going to Pankow to enjoy themselves at the turn of this century, either in the open-air pool in the Bürgerpark or on the Schönholzer Heath.

But excesses like Herr Bolle's are rather the exception these days. Upper-class Pankow with around 140,000 inhabitants is Berlin's northernmost district, and has always been a bit grander than its proletarian neighbours the districts of Wedding and Prenzlauer Berg. Its villa district in Niederschönhausen emerged between about 1880 and 1900, as rich Berliners moved out beyond the boundaries of the city.

Nowadays, former SED bigwigs still live in this pleasant neighbourhood, and the diplomatic representatives of many countries have settled here, too. The East German government was even based for a time in **Pankow Castle**. For reasons of wealth and of prestige, therefore, the villas in Pankow are noticeably better maintained than they are in other parts of the city. Town houses are more frequent here than are tenements. Among the suburbs on the district's outskirts and their typical wooden houses, there is still the occasional flash of village character. Fields and allotments characterise the area.

History: Pankow owes its name from the little river Panke which rises at Bernau and which winds its way largely underground through Wedding and joins the Spree at Schiffbauerdamm in Berlin Mitte. Formerly a farming village, probably a Slavic settlement, it is officially mentioned for the first time in 1230. At that time there were only a couple of huts on the village green, which was later renamed Breite Strasse.

Around 1800, Pankow had only 286 inhabitants. In 1920, it was incorpo-rated into Greater Berlin along with many other districts and combined with the outlying villages of Niederschön-hausen, Buchholz, Rosenthal, Blanken-felde, Buch, Wilhelmsruh, Karow, Blankenburg and Heinersdorf. Together, these had a total population of around 93,000 people. The latter three villages were incorporated into the neighbour-ing district of Weissensee in 1985, but will possibly revert to Pankow now that Berlin has been reunited.

Old Breitstrasse is now known as **Johannes-R.-Becher-Strasse**, after the 1920s' Expressionist poet who was later the GDR's first Minister for Culture. He was a Pankow man. It starts at the red-brick **Rathaus** (town hall), which was built in 1903 in art nouveau style with fanciful cupolas, gables and towers.

It then passes on either side of the old village green on which stands a fountain and the **Alte Pfarrkirche** or old parish church. This is invariably called the "Church of the Four Evangelists" and is the oldest building in the district. The

eastern part was built in the 14th century from grey brick and the red tower on the west side was added at the turn of the last century, which accounts for its rather uneven appearance.

Among the points of interest are the altar window, which depicts the four evangelists, the ancient altar cross and the Coventry cross, raised in 1965 to commemorate the English town bombed by German planes.

Niederschönhausen Castle: Pankow's reputation, however, was not founded on sacred buildings. Schloß Nieder–schönhausen (castle) was where the first president of the GDR, Wilhelm Pieck, held office from 1949 until 1960. The SED government therefore became commonly known, rather arbitrarily, as the "Pankow regime".

Until 1964, the castle was the seat of the Council of State and before the changes of November 1989 was used by the East German government to accommodate guests. The "Fast Train to Pankow", which singer Udo Linden–berg was so keen to board, was a reference to this. Now "Our Udo" can travel there whenever he likes, although his friend of the song, Honecker ("Honi"), is unlikely to be there to greet him. The "Pankow Round Table", the city committee that made political decisions in the district between November 1989 and the parliamentary elections in 1990, also met here. Pankow Council hopes to open the Niederschönhausen castle to the public soon.

The castle is reached from Pankow S-Bahn station or Vinetasstrasse U-Bahn by tram in the diretion of Blankenfelde. It was built in 1664 as a country house for Countess Dohna of the house of Holland-Brederode. It was subsequently altered a number of times, until barely anything of the old building remained, first by Johann Arnold Nering, then again around 1704 by Johann Friederich Eosander, and 60 years later Johann Boumann set to work on it.

At the end of the 18th century the castle was inhabited by Queen Elisabeth **The Soviet memorial.**

Christine, the unloved wife of Frederick the Great. He was ordered to marry her by his father, the Soldier King, but the minute he ascended to the throne he banished her to Pankow. Elisabeth Christine was very fond of her misogynist husband, in spite of – or perhaps precisely because of – the lack of a married life.

The **Schloßpark** (castle grounds), which is open to the public, was laid out as a French-style rococo pleasure garden in 1764. In the mid-19th century it was restyled into an English landscape park, with sweeping lawns. The Panke river flows through the park, crossed by several small bridges. Among the oaks and plane trees, rare specimens such as hickories, yews and tulip trees, give the park an exotic air.

On the other side of the street Am Schloßpark is the local landmark, Pankow open-air swimming pool, which was opened in 1960 and is the district's pride and joy. As the newspapers reported at the time, "numerous local men

and women voluntarily gave up their time to help with its construction".

Prominent small towns: Bourgeois Pankow was not only the SED seat of government. The district is also extremely popular with prominent politicians as a private residence. Walther Ulbricht used to live with his wife Lotte on nearby Majakowskiring, alongside Wilhelm Pieck at No 29 and the President of the Volkskammer Otto Grotewald at No 46. Majakowskiring was then known as "small town" by the local people. It was a no-go area, sealed off by barriers and security guards, until the early 1960s when the old boys and their families moved to exclusive Wandlitz.

North of Majakowskiring in Niederschönhausen countless foreign embassies moved into the buildings on Kuckhoffstrasse, Tschaikowskystrasse and Heinrich-Mann-Strasse, among them those of the US, Switzerland, Iran, Cuba, Nicaragua and China. The West German representative and office was in residence for a while on Kuckhoff-

Pankow's
district
chronicler:
Rudolf
Dörrier.

strasse, before moving to Hanoversche Strasse in Berlin Mitte.

Songwriters and poets: In the 1920s many artists and literary figures such as Heinz Knobloch, Hans Fallach, Willy Bredel and Arno Holz lived around **Majakowskiring**. Johannes R. Becher, who wrote the lyrics of the East German anthem *Auferstanden aus Ruinen* ("Risen from Ruins") lived at No. 34. His house is now home to the Johannes R. Becher-Archiv, a small museum exhibiting some of the poet's belongings. A short walk away, at Homeyerstrasse 13, you can visit the former apartment of writer Arnold Zweig.

If you then cross the quiet, tree-lined Heinrich-Mann-Platz, you will arrive at Leonhard-Frank-Strasse 11, once the home of Ernst Busch. Busch was one of the many writers and artists who volunteered to fight against the fascists in the Spanish Civil War, but is today better known as a political songwriter. He toured Berlin's theatres giving emotional performances of his own work, to the delight of the communist workers and the dismay of the Nazis.

Carl Ossietzky, a winner of the Nobel Peace Prize and the publisher of the magazine *Weltbühne*, also lived in Pankow at around this time, in what is now designated Ossietzky-Strasse 24-6. Ossietzky was arrested by the Nazis in 1938 and tortured to death. His grave is in Niederschönhausen cemetery on Buchholzer Strasse, alongside that of his wife Maud, who refounded *Weltbühne* in East Berlin in 1946.

The magazine itself was still running at the end of 1990. Having been subordinate to the SED for so long, the editorial team is now looking for a new political direction for the publication. Ossietzky's home was destroyed in the war. Today, a new building stands in its place, in front of which is a bronze statue of the man himself.

Not far away is **Pankow Bürgerpark**, a favourite with day-trippers from Berlin. Entering through the high gateway, ornamented with figures like an Italian triumphal arch, you find yourself unexpectedly in the midst of the most romantic surroundings: well-kept gardens, flower beds, fountains, statues of animals and outdoor cafés, ideal for relaxed coffee-drinking and idle people-watching. The park radiates a peaceful stillness, regrettably disturbed by the frequent aircraft coming in to land at nearby Tegel airport. The old open-air pool on the Panke, also known as the "Bürgerbad", closed when the Wall was built in 1961.

Park and heath: The Bürgerpark merges with the Pankow Cemetery and another park, the Waldfriedhof, and eventually runs on to the **Schönholzer Heide** (heath). The heath can be reached from the Bürgerpark via the quiet Bahnhofstrasse between the S-Bahn platforms and the cemetery, where the Wall used to run.

Schönholzer Heath is wilder and more overgrown than the Bürgerpark, in places even quite untidily kept, with the exception of the **Soviet Memorial** in the northwestern part.

Of the 30,000 Soviet soldiers who were killed in battle, 13,200 are buried here in dozens of communal graves. The bronze slabs listing the many Russian names are separated by flower borders, laid out in a strict geometric pattern. The memorial is dominated by an obelisk, in front of which stands a statue of a symbolic Russian mother, her dead son at her feet.

Industry: Pankow does not only consist of town houses. Some industry has also settled here, such as VEB Bergmann-Borsig, the largest engineering company in what was formerly East Germany, and the Berlin cigarette factory, whose products include the famous brand "Karo", known as the "workers' cigarette" because of its pungent, herby flavour.

The first cinema film: You can find out more about the history of Pankow in the **Stadtbezirkschronik** (district museum) at Heyerstrasse 8, near Wollankstrasse. For example, housed here there is Max

Skladanowsky's invention, the first cinema film, a piece of technology which was to revolutionise the 20th century. The Lumière brothers in Paris were also working on moving film at the same time, and it was they who did the better marketing of their product and who therefore have the most credit for it in history. Skladanowsky himself organised the first Berlin film show in the Berlin Winter Gardens in Pankow in November 1895.

Historical monuments: Pankow has all sorts of fascinating historical monuments in all sorts of unlikely corners, such as the Hartmann bakery at Wollankstrasse 130, which has a shop counter dating from the turn of the century. The *Schippen* rolls there are somewhat more recent, even if they're not quite as fresh or tasty as the crisp little *Brötchen* (bread rolls) from the DDR days.

The old village smithy which is on Dietzgenstrasse in Niederschönhausen was built in 1757. It is under a preservation order, but is so badly dilapidated that it might possibly have to be pulled down. The Holländerhaus (Dutch House), a two-storey patrician house on the junction of Dietzgenstrasse and Platanenstrasse, dates from the same period. "If you want everything to go well, build to God in all things," is engraved into the wood-carved balcony.

At the end of Dietzgenstrasse is the Pankow tram depot, dating from the early years of this century. Berlin's first tram travelled back and forth from the Rathaus to Gesundbrunnen S-Bahn station around 1895, at that time still drawn by horses.

The village churches in Buch and Blankenfelde are 13th-century granite constructions, extended in the 19th century, as is the church at Buchholz, which became known as "French Buchholz" after a group of Huguenots established themselves there in 1688. Between Rosenthal and Blankenfelde there is a botanical garden currently under construction, with a tropical greenhouse and a palm house.

iberty, quality, raternity.

WEISSENSEE

On the northeastern edge of the city is the district of Weissensee, hemmed in by Pankow to the west, Prenzlauer Berg to the south, Marzahn to the east and Lichtenberg to the southeast. Visitors without cars should take the S-Bahn to Ernst-Thälmann-Park and then the red Tatra tram trains 24 or 28, which rumble out from the city centre every five minutes heading for Klement-Gottwald-Allee. Routes 3, 20, 70 and 72 go via Antonplatz straight to the small-town dream-world of Weissensee.

On 1 November 1873 the first horse-drawn omnibus left Alexanderplatz, transporting passengers efficiently to Weissensee. In 1877 these were replaced by the horse-drawn trams of the "New Berlin Tram Company". Since 1901 the trams have run on electricity.

The low rows of houses which line the main roads are relieved now and then by four- or five-storey buildings. In spite of the many colourful window displays in the shops, slowly adjusting to a market economy, and the bright signs luring customers to restaurants and little cafés, the facades arouse little interest. Weissensee was viewed as a suburb by the old city fathers, and had no significance either as a showcase or as a prestige district.

History: There are several explanations for the origin of the name Weissensee. In Low German it means something like "Wittense" (bright sea). The name crops up repeatedly in subsequent years in modified form as Wittensey, Wittenssehen, Weydtensehe, Weissensee.

The little Brandenburg village is mentioned for the first time in 1313. In the late-Middle Ages three manors emerged from the settlement. In 1745, von Nüssler, the head of the area, united these manors under his control. After its sale in 1872 the estate of Weissensee came into the possession of the power-

ful merchant Adolf Schön, who speculated with the land during the industrial boom, in order to build tenements. In 1872 the settlement of Neu Weissensee was founded to the southwest of the old village. This became an independent district in 1880 and was united with Weissensee in 1905. The extended district was chiefly populated by workers. The amalgamation of the villages of Weissensee, Hohenschönhausen, Malchow, Wartenberg and Fahenberg followed in 1920.

Currently the district covers an area of 40 sq. km (15 sq. miles) and is home to 98,000 people, a number which will increase with the completion of an extensive new housing estate.

Lakeside recreation: Weissensee offers plenty of contrasts: factories and commercial concerns, workshops, nurseries, small farms, quiet leafy residential streets, allotment gardens, picturesque parks, lakes and ponds. The most important stretch of water is the "**Weissen See**", originally the Grossen See, which covers 10 hectares (25 acres) to the west of Klement-Gottwald-Allee.

At first sight it takes you by surprise: a floating classical fountain in the midst of fields, poplars and robinias, a popular recreation area. The park was founded in 1859, together with a country house which in 1874 was to become the venue for what would become the famous "Sternecker Fireworks". On the eastern side of the lake there is an inviting open-air swimming pool with a man-made sandy beach beside it. Boats for hire, rose gardens, an open-air stage, an animal enclosure, a large playground, a paddling pool and a sun-bathing area: here is what all the visitor could possibly need in order to unwind.

On the western bank are two observation terraces, bordered by two groups of sandstone tritons, men and women with the bodies of fish (Hans Schellhorn, 1908). The statues reflect the wealth of fish in the Weissen See. From here you can look out over the land around the lake, which has no natural tributaries. In winter it makes a brilliant ice-skating rink.

A few minutes' away, at Parkstrasse 82, is the Rathaus (town hall). Immediately outside the mayor's front door is another picturesque pond in a parkland setting. The district council buildings were built by Mettmann in 1929 as a school and are a classic example of the architectural style known as "New Objectivity".

In Pistorius-Strasse is the **Kreuzpfuhl**, a park with a pond, surrounded by four-storey red brick buildings with ornamental gables, curved balconies, decorative brickwork and large leafy courtyards. The estate, built between 1908 and 1910 as part of a communal "forum" but never finished, was set out by architect Karl James Bühring. Structurally interesting, it is a valuable document of social history and a pleasant contrast to the usual city tenements. North of the complex on Schönstrasse is Weissensee City Hospital.

Nearby on Mirbachplatz is the high tower of **Bethanienkirche**. The church was built to plans by Ludwig von Tiedemann and Robert Leinitz and has some interesting features, but was badly damaged in World War II.

The Jewish cemetery: In the past, the Berlin authorities removed the city's cemeteries out to Weissenhof. One of the most important from a cultural and historical perspective is the Jewish Cemetery (Jüdischer Friedhof).

"The clock ticks.
Your grave awaits,
three metres long,
a metre wide.
You may see four more
foreign places,
you'll see another naked girl
and twenty, twenty time more
snow –
and then: P field –
in Weissensee – in Weissensee."

When he wrote those lines, Kurt Tucholsky had in mind the Jewish Cem-

Western films were shown in Weissensee as soon as the transition came.

etery south of Klement-Gottwald-Allee. The final resting place of over 115,000 souls, it is the largest cemetery of its kind in Europe. The grave of Tucholsky's father Alex (1855–1905) lies in this "God's acre". The writer's mother Doris (1869–1943) died in Theresienstadt.

Berlin's Jewish community, which by 1880 had reached over 65,000, bought the 40-hectare (100-acre) plot because they were running out of space in the old cemetery on what is now Schönhauser Allee. At that time it would have been far away from the city gates. The architect Hugo von Licht was responsible for the design of the yellow brick entrance, which still survives in more or less its original state.

In the forecourt is a simple memorial stone in form of a tablet set in a circle and bearing the names of all the large concentration camps. It bears the inscription: "Dedicated to the memory of our murdered brothers and sisters of 1933–45, and to the living who should

fulfil the legacy of the dead". Near the main entrance is the grave of the Jewish resistance fighter Herbert Baum (d. 1943) who in 1942 organised an arson attack on an exhibition of anti-Soviet propaganda in the Lustgarten. Baum was tortured, then killed in custody.

The famous names on the family graves give an indication of the Jewish contribution to the economic, scientific, spiritual and artistic might of Berlin. (Actually, the more prominent members of the Jewish community were usually buried in the smaller cemetery on Schönhauser Allee in Prenzlauer Berg.) Sadly, time is wearing away all the old gravestones, and the lack of cemetery caretakers is also playing its part in the slow decay.

Among those buried here are: Hermann Cohen (d. 1918, philosopher); Eugen Goldstein (d. 1930, physicist); Lesser Ury (d. 1931, artist, impressionist and member of the Berlin secession); Rudolf Mosse (d. 1920, newspaper advertiser and publisher of the *Berliner*

Women drivers – nothing unusual in that.

Tageblatt); Samuel Fischer (d. 1934, publisher and founder of S. Fischer Verlag); Lina Morgenstern (d. 1909, women's rights campaigner and a socially committed writer who founded the first Women Workers' Educational Society and was on the committee of the German Peace Group); and last but not least the founders of the two large and well-known Berlin department stores, Adolph Jandorff (d. 1931, KaDeWe) and Hermann Tietz (d. 1907, father of the Her-Tie group).

Near the administrative buildings are several well-tended postwar graves indicative of the fact that a few thousand Berlin Jews survived the Holocaust (not necessarily in Germany) and that the city still has a small Jewish community of fewer than 7,000 persons.

Here, too, are interred the ashes of 809 Jews murdered in the concentration camps, as well as the bodies of around 3,000 people who chose to take their own lives rather than be executed during the Nazi era. Near the main entrance is the grave of the Jewish resistance fighter Herbert Baum (d. 1943).

Another Jewish cemetery can be found to the east on Wittlicher Strasse. This belongs to the orthodox Jewish community Adass Jisroel, and was closed by the East Berlin authorities in the mid-1970s. It subsequently fell into disrepair and has only recently been restored.

Where Falkenberg Strasse joins Klement-Gottwald-Allee lies the original site of the village meadow of Weissensee. Here stands the largely medieval church, which was extended to its present size in 1863 and 1899. The architect Bruno Taut left his legacy in **Busch-Allee**. He designed the row of houses, around half-a-mile (one kilometre) long, which were built between 1926 and 1930 and stretch almost to Hohenschönhausen.

Taut's functional style can also be found north of Trierer Strasse. The artist Karl Schmitt-Rottlauf undertook the colourful decoration on the facades, decoration which has led to this area

At leisure: elderly Germans on their allotments...

being called the "parrot estate". Weissensee has its own art college in Strasse 203, which can be reached via Gustav-Adolf-Strasse.

Sports and music: Sports enthusiasts also flock to Weissensee. Indira-Gandhi-Strasse (formerly Lichtenberger Strasse, but it may revert to its original name, as many streets are) branches off to the south over Ho-Chi-Minh Strasse to the Berlin Sportforum, which covers an area of 45 hectares (110 acres). The Dynamo sports hall, together with the swimming centre and the ice stadium, are used for national and international competitions.

North of the Weissensee, off Radrennbahnstrasse, in the **Radrennbahn Weissensee**, is an open-air cycle racing track which can seat 9,000 spectators. It was built in 1954 on the site of the old racecourse, where carriage races used to be held and, in this century, motorcycle racing. The area around the racecourse has meanwhile become a home for bike enthusiasts, and also a venue for various rock extravaganzas – the Rolling Stones, Joe Cocker, Tina Turner and Simple Minds. Bird-watchers and nature-lovers disapprove of the concerts because of the decibel count.

Rural idyll: While Weissensee itself is an industrial and residential area, **Falkenberg**, **Malchow** and **Wartenberg** are more rural. One-third of East Berlin's farming land is centred here, and is used mainly for vegetables.

Klement-Gottwald-Allee leads north to Malchow. The former landmark of the town, the imposing tower of the 13th-century church, was blown up in the last days of the war. Only a few segments of wall betray the existence of the sacred building. The late Romantic 13th-century church in nearby Wartenberg met a similar fate. It was destroyed in an air raid in 1945. Even less remains of the church in Falkenberg. The mother of Alexander and Wilhelm von Humboldt had the tower erected in 1795 and a family vault built for herself and her two husbands.

...and young Germans in the stadium on Weissen See.

LICHTENBERG

Lichtenberg, situated in the east of Berlin, is an industrial and working-class district, and with 177,000 inhabitants, one of the most densely populated of the eastern districts. There are hardly any prestigious buildings – wealthy folk have settled elsewhere. Nor does Lichtenberg have the united, communal feel of Prenzlauer Berg. Somehow this part of town lacks cohesion. It is characterised by the grey tenements of the expansion era, industrial estates and boring modern tower blocks.

This eastern part of the city was badly damaged in World War II. In 1945 the Soviet artillery shot their way into the city centre along Frankfurter Allee. The eastern section of the street, which for that reason has been called "the street of liberation" since 1945, was completely rebuilt in the 1970s. Until only a few years ago, every third or fourth house along Frankfurter Allee was followed by a gaping hole where an Allied bomb had fallen.

Older history: There is a place in Lichtenberg which local historians credit as being the "cradle of the district". This is Loeperplatz, on what is now Jacques-Duclos-Strasse, where there's an early Gothic, stone-built church on the former village green. The church is well preserved and the square around it well cared for. But in the rush hour the green is little more than a forlorn island in a sea of traffic.

The village is officially mentioned for the first time in 1288. It received a town charter in 1907. The imposing brick Rathaus (town hall) was built a few years before, also on Jacques-Duclos-Strasse. In 1920 Lichtenburg became part of Berlin. The marshes land, fields, coniferous and deciduous forests had long since given way to tenements and smoking chimneys. Only Friedrichsfelde and Karlshorst retained their village character. Since the beginning of this century, Lichtenberg has been home to the little man, the workers and the poor.

Tenement misery: The closest you'll probably get to the atmosphere of those long ago years is the area around Tuchollaplatz (between Rummelsberg and Nöldenerplatz S-Bahn stations), which was spared in the war. The painter and artist Heinrich Zille lived here for almost 20 years. Many of his drawings are rooted in this neighbourhood, in the plight of the poor, the grimy streets and the grey treeless world of children. In recent years part of this area has been renovated.

The new zoo: Probably the best known of the district's attractions is the zoo. It was founded in the 1950s in Friedrichsfelde Schloßpark (castle grounds), to replace the old Berlin Zoo in the western half of the city. At the entrance to the park stands Schloß Friedrichsfelde, built in the late 17th century in the style of a Dutch country house. The last owners of the castle and park were the lords of

ichtenberg
festyles:
eft, historic
nd
xclusive in
chloß
riedrichs-
elde and...
ight, ...in a
/FS
Werktätigen-
eierabend-
chublade).

Treskow. Incidentally, a member of this family was among the officers who waged the attempt on Hitler's life on 20 July 1944 and who were later sentenced to death.

The castle was restored in the 1960s and the early 1970s. The rooms are now used as a wallpaper museum, and chamber concerts are sometimes held in them in the evenings. Behind the castle begins the actual zoo, which covers a vast and varied terrain and which is one of Europe's largest.

Paths lead across large meadows, between oaks centuries old and through thick undergrowth. In many cases little moats provide a natural boundary between the animal enclosures and visitors. Nine hundred different species of animal live here. Many of them, for example the bears, llamas, giraffes and zebras, enjoy pleasant open enclosures. The elephants, reptiles and great cats are kept in huge houses where exotic plants grow and where a tropical climate is maintained.

The zoo is a favourite attraction for locals and tourists alike, especially in the warm summer months and at weekends. Lying in the middle of a built-up area, it is also simply a place to which to come and to relax and enjoy long walks. The area is so vast that it still hasn't been entirely developed. Every so often you come across building work in progress or a neglected corner. As soon as the rear part of the park has been tidied up, there is still much more work to be done in the front.

Horses and soldiers: Not far from the zoo, in Karlshorst, the racecourse was built. Bets were being taken here back in the days of the German Empire. Diagonally opposite the entrance to the racecourse you can see a large, rather dilapidated wooden building. Older citizens know this as "Rennbahn Station" and recall how the Emperor always used to alight here whenever he came to the race meetings.

The stand, betting hall and bars must have looked somewhat smarter in those days than they do now. Although they were renovated in 1984, the plastic seats and concrete flower beds scarcely do justice to the course's glorious past. But in the betting hall if nowhere else the timeless, feverish excitement still reigns. (Race meets, which are not especially elegant, are held on Wednesdays, Saturdays and Sundays, starting at 3 p.m.)

With the advent of the market economy, the future of the until now state-subsidised racecourse is uncertain. Apparently it is not profitable, and it's also said that one racecourse – namely the one in Mariendorf – is enough for the whole of Berlin.

In that part of Karlshorst which borders the racecourse you are as likely to hear Russian spoken as you are German. For here are the vast grounds of the Soviet barracks. A section of the Soviet command force has been stationed in Karlshorst since May 1945. The peaceful villa neighbourhood which ultimately became an exclusive enclave for GDR bigwigs and foreign embassy residents

Young families need space to live...

was barely touched in the war. On 9 May 1945 the notice of surrender was signed in a building at the end of Fritz-Schmenckel-Strasse. For many years this house where the Wehrmacht surrendered has been open to visitors as a museum which is officially called the "Museum of the Unconditional Surrender of Fascist Germany in the Great Patriotic War of 1941-45".

The museum, which has 14 rooms, is run by the Soviet Army and contains dioramas and battle reconstructions. In addition there is also a brief history of the Soviet Union in photographs and text. The spirit of perestroika doesn't seem to have reached this far, for the exhibition is a mixture of boring propaganda, revolutionary kitsch and deliberate omissions.

..and a egister ffice, the own's only riginal uilding.

At the corner of Hermann Duncker Strasse and Fritz-Schmenkel Strasse stands the Haus der Offiziere (Officer's Club) with facilities for those Soviet soldiers and their families who live in the neighbourhood. In this neighbour-

hood stores sell Russian food, papers and books.

Socialist memories: The Socialists' Cemetery (**Gedenkstätte der Sozialisten**) is another memorial with links to the city's political history. It's located within the main cemetery, a 10-minute walk to the northeast from Lichtenberg S-Bahn station. Rosa Luxemburg and Karl Liebknecht were buried here in January 1919, having been murdered by officers of the Reichswehr.

Several years later, the German Communist Party had a memorial built on this spot. The simple structure is the creation of the architect Mies van der Rohe, and consists of a circular wall around a 4-metres (17-ft) high porphyritic stone, bearing the inscription "*Die Toten mahnen uns*" (The dead remind us). The monument was ceremonially unveiled in 1926.

Alongside the memorials to the famous leaders of the labour movement were added plaques to those who died in

the Hamburg Uprising, the Bavarian soviet republic of 1919 and the Red Army of the Ruhr. Every year the left assembles here to remember their heroes. Even in 1991, around 100,000 people turned out.

The Nazis destroyed the memorial but after the war it was rebuilt true to the original. Numerous tablets were added to commemorate murdered anti-fascists and victims of the Spanish Civil War. Over the years, as the SED leadership aged, the "Socialists' Memorial" became the burial ground of the party elite. Wilhelm Pieck, Otto Grotewohl and Walter Ulbricht are all buried here. There were strict rules as to who was allowed to be laid to rest within the enclosure and who was honoured with a simple stone outside it on the main burial ground. The bureaucratic hierarchy continues even after death.

SED rituals and resistance: Increasingly, the Berliners' traditional January demonstration became a fixed ritual, where the Politbüro basked in their own glory and used the names of Karl Liebknecht and Rosa Luxemburg to legitimise their own regime.

This became startlingly apparent on 17 January 1988, when members of the church-led opposition wanted to take part in the march with banners, including some with a quotation from Rosa Luxemburg: "Freedom is also the freedom to think otherwise." However, they were arrested even before they reached the demonstration, and received steep prison sentences for "activities hostile to the state". Those arrested included Vera Wollenberger, Bärbel Bohley, Wolfgang Templin and Werner Fischer, who were later among those to initiate the events of autumn 1989.

This act of state despotism in January 1988 triggered a wave of protest and show of solidarity in Berlin and other cities. Every evening, a rogation service was held in one Berlin church – a religious front for a protest rally. Several thousands of people also used to gather in the Erlöserkirche near Rummelsburg

Street festival in Fennpfuhl.

S-Bahn station, to demand the release of those who had been arrested. This church played a role in the founding of the opposition movement, notably during the annual "Peace Workshop", where Christians and Marxists got together to analyse the situation and to discuss new alternatives.

Stasi centre: Those who took part in the Peace Workshops were accustomed to seeing Stasi men posted all around the area and cars with big aerials in the parks. That was everyday surveillance. The main centre for spying on the East German population, the Ministry of State Security, was also based in Lichtenberg. On Strasse der Befreiung a huge complex was built in the 1970s. The high wall around it, the spotlights, cameras and military guards made it only too obvious to passers-by who had moved in. Like a spider in its web, the Stasi sat in their stronghold and continually extended their powers.

When in January 1990 incensed demonstrators stormed the ministry to put an end to its activities once and for all, they were flabbergasted by the size of the sprawling complex. They found a kind of state within a state, with dozens of offices, clinics, savings banks, sports facilities, barbers, workshops and the like. A citizens' committee was formed that night, which occupied all the buildings and exits and attempted the painstaking task of halting this giant machine and dismantling its various components. In June 1990 they were disbanded by a government commission.

What happened to the mountain of files that were stored in the ministry remains unclear. In these the Stasi had accumulated information about millions of East German citizens. Debate continues and the trauma of the Stasi is far from over.

Meanwhile, plenty of innocuous organisations have moved into their buildings to provide information on the history of the State Security Service and to ensure that the memory of its victims is kept alive.

arlshorst
acecourse.

TREPTOW

In the district of Treptow, economic prosperity, pleasure and leisure are interwoven with the more sorry aspects of the city of Berlin. Spacious parks on the banks of the Spree, heavily built-up industry along the Landwehr canal and, as a historical reminder, the Soviet memorial. The town of Treptow grew up in the southwest of the city, on the large heath, the *merica*, at the mouth of the old Floßgraben.

In 1261, Margrave Otto III donated the heath to the town of Cölln and in 1435 it was extended to become the great 3,000-acre Cölln Heath, by the purchase of lands belonging to the Tempelhof order. In 1568 the fishing community of "Trepkow" is officially mentioned for the first time. It first appears as "Treptow" in 1740.

The Spree's supplies of fish, naturally good lines of communication, the man-made waterways of the Landwehr, Spree and Teltow canals, as well as the forest, provided a variety of commercial opportunities. At the beginning of the century and in the years of industrialisation, they contributed to Treptow's economic growth.

The timber, chemical and metal industries continue to dominate the economic face and the infrastructure of the district. Industrial development along the Landwehr canal, the Wiener and the Schlesische Brücke began as early as 1750, with the construction of the "Lohmühlen" (tanneries).

After 1871, Dr Max Jordan, Beermann and Graetz established industrial enterprises. The "Elektro-Apparat-Werke" site north of Treptower Park S-Bahn which was later extended to become an electrical appliance factory for AEG was one of East Berlin's largest concerns, employing 10,000 people.

That area of Treptow known as Baumschulenweg developed comparatively independently, thanks to a forester's lodge, which gave rise to the estate of Marienthal. The nursery founded in 1720 by Christian Späth was transferred to Baumschulenweg by Franz Späth in 1864. In Späthstrasse the late classical villa belonging to the former tree nursery, in the headquarters of the 3.5-hectare (8-acre) arboretum of the Natural Science Museum which is well worth seeing. It is open from May to October.

The Frederican settlements of Niederschönweide, Johannisthal and Adlershof also belong to Treptow. Altglienicke and Bohnsdorf originate from the colonial period of the 13th century. A multiple railway line, along which passenger and goods trains shunt to and fro between Berlin and the cities in the south divides the district. During the rush hour, most of East Berlin's traffic races along three main thoroughfares – Adlergestell, Köpernicker Landstrasse and Puschkin-Allee.

Plänterwald playground: Treptow's popularity with Berliners and tourists alike is based mainly on its spacious

THE OPPOSITION LINES UP

It must be the most self-effacing place of worship in the city. The Church of the Confession lies in the middle of a row of houses on Plesser Strasse in Treptow. A half-flight of steps leads down to the meeting room. Having heard the news on the bush telegraph, 400 people gathered here on 13 August 1989, 28 years after the construction of the still-impregnable Wall. They did not intend to leave the country, nor did they wish to be placed in the same category as the 1–2 million others who would leave if they could; they wanted to change the GDR. On that particular evening the church was, for once, easy to find. The inconspicuously conspicuous gentlemen from the Department of National Security stood like signposts at each end of the street.

In West Berlin, the anniversary was marked as always with unrest. At Checkpoint Charlie an American lay down and prayed for German unity. Drunkards threw beer cans at the East German frontier guards as they approached. "Get back over there, you swine!" one of them called. "What did he say?" asked a Canadian tourist. Nobody translated for her.

The critical comments about the Wall were expressed differently in the Church of the Confession. There, a songster mocked "Throughout the world the Wall stands for the superiority of our system, for the creative power of socialism." As on any other evening, a trip from West to East Berlin cost DM30, with the customary compulsory exchange of currency and visa requirement. "Put the contents of your pockets on the table!" the frontier guard demanded curtly. A few weeks later, photographs of cheerful, reformed border guards would be wired around the world.

Since 2 May 1989 hundreds of East German citizens had taken refuge in the West German embassies in East Berlin, Budapest and Prague and thousands had fled to the West across the open Hungarian border. But this exodus also spelled danger for the opposition who wished to remain in the country. "If everybody tries to squash through a narrow opening, they cut off the air supply to the

others." The opposition was underdeveloped, badly organised and illegal. That particular evening was their first public appearance. "We no longer wish to exist as secret cells scattered across the country. We want to show that there are those here who have plans for changing the system and who are prepared to talk about them" declared Dr Hans-Jürgen Fischbeck, a grey-haired physicist, one of the brains behind the 500 or so opposition groups throughout the GDR.

The goal of the unified movement was representation in the next elections to the People's Chamber in two years' time. In Poland, the opposition movement had achieved the passage from military law to Round Table government within only a few years. On that evening nobody could have imagined that German reunification would take place the very next year. Some of those present spoke up against the suggestion that the group form itself into a legal opposition party. "You can't strike up a dialogue with criminals", was the comment from the radicals. Others were influenced by a fear of reprisals similar to the Chinese solution. Only a few days previously, the SED party newspaper, *Neues Deutschland*, had justified the blood bath on Tiananmen Square: it had been an answer "to the counter-revolutionary uprising of an extremist minority". In reply to a question posed by several of the younger participants in the discussion as to why he had

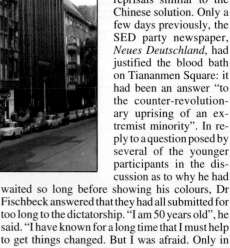

waited so long before showing his colours, Dr Fischbeck answered that they had all submitted for too long to the dictatorship. "I am 50 years old", he said. "I have known for a long time that I must help to get things changed. But I was afraid. Only in recent years have I had the courage to express my opinions in public. The changes taking place amongst our socialist neighbours mean that for us, too, the fringe conditions have changed."

One man refused to believe that this was true - Erich Honecker. The very next day he explained his view of the system to workers in Erfurth: "Neither ox nor ass can hold up the progress of socialism." Shortly afterwards, the opposition groups *Democracy Now*, *Emergence '89* and *New Forum* were founded – the precursors of a democratic, united Germany.

**eft, on 13
ugust 1989
ie first
emand for
n opposition
ovement
as voiced in
ie unlikely
etting of the
ekenntnis-
rche.
elow,
reptow's
oviet
emorial.**

parks. **Treptow Park**, which covers 230 hectares (570 acres), stretches northwards from Bulgarische Strasse on either side of the plantane-lined Puschkin-Allee. Plänterwald lies between Neuer Krugallee and the Spree. Whereas in the past, summer holidaymakers and those in search of recreation would be driven in their horse-drawn carriages out beyond the city gates to Treptow, now the S-Bahn (Treptower Park station) is the simplest way to reach the green lung on the banks of the Spree and the Berlin stop of the Weiße Flotte (White Fleet). To the left of the S-Bahn station are the jetties, from where passenger "steamers" chug up and down the Spree.

You can walk upriver along the airy, wide promenades to the **Rosengarten** (Rose Garden). The lawns, red beeches, chestnuts and plantanes, along with the immaculate gardens, provide landscape designers and sculptors with an inspirational backdrop for the regular summer and autumn exhibitions of flowers and sculpture. People stroll, amble, jog and skateboard through the grounds. In spite of its neat, "cultivated" air, this green corner provides space for the widest possible variety of plants and trees, to the joy of conservationists and ornithologists. The very English lawns and benches invite you to sit and linger. Don't be tempted into a dip in the Spree!

Thanks to the liberal inclinations of the municipal authorities, the 109 hectares (270 acres) of land on the outskirts of the Tiergarten, Friedrichshain and Humboldthain were turned into the city's fourth largest park in 1861. In 1876 the public health officer Rudolf Virchow commissioned landscape designer Gustav Meyer for the project. The city fathers intended that the trades fair held in the park in 1896 would expand into a world fair. However, this may not have suited the Emperor who was always rather strapped for money and his excellency forbade the ambitious project. Nevertheless the exhibition improved communications and public amenities for the people of Treptow.

Leaning Tower of Stralau: Pisa is not the only place with a leaning tower. It may be the most famous, but it you look out over the Spree from the Rosengarten, you'll see on the opposite bank behind the trees, the tower of the 15th-century **Alt-Stralau (Old Stralau)** village church. It was displaced in an air raid in 1945 and has visibly tilted ever since. Further along the river bank on the site of the old outworks is the Zenner restaurant, a popular place to drive out to for a meal. In 1602 the local authority bought a fishing hut on this spot for an incredible 100 Thaler. The occupants ran a bar. In 1702 a brewery was added, and then a century later Carl Ferdinand Langhans built the "Neue Gasthaus an der Spree" in place of the "Spreebudike". The "elegant" inn opened its doors on 11 June 1822 and was later given the name Zenner after a landlord.

This is an excellent place to watch the annual firework display **"Treptow in Flames"**, which has been held since 1825. A swing bridge with a span of 76 metres (250 ft) links the bank with the Abteiinsel (Abbey Island), which has been taken over as an activities centre for youngsters. Among its attractions are an open-air theatre and a large bathing beach (for those who don't mind risking the pollution), as well as boats for hire.

Past Bulgarische Strasse you come to the old Kaiserbad and the terraces of the Spree. There's a lovely view from here over Stralau, Abtei and the little islands in the Spree.

From here it's not far to the 12-hectare (30-acre) **Berliner Kulturpark**, stretching to the north of the Plänterwald. In the past this was where the Berliners' "Rummel" or annual fair was held. Nowadays, bumper cars, waltzers and colourful carousels spin non-stop from spring to autumn. The landmark of the Kulturpark is a 45-metre (150-ft) giant ferris wheel, with 40 cars. Over a million visitors flock here every year. Further south is an open-air stage and various sports pitches.

An elaborate system of canals connects the industrial quarter of Treptow with Berlin's waterways – here, the Kabelwerk Oberspree (KWO) cable factory.

In the part of Treptower Park away from the Spree, to the right of Puschkin-Allee, is the imposing and moving **Soviet Memorial**, erected between 1946 and 1949. This is the major monument in Berlin to the 5,000 Red Army soldiers who fell in the Battle for Berlin in 1945. In the avenue leading to the entrance stands a female figure, "Mother Russia", carved from a 50-tonne granite block. A broad path lined with silver birche trees leads to the "Grave of Honour" with two walls of red granite symbolising Soviet flags lowered in mourning and at the ends of which are figures of kneeling Red Army men.

Beyond this a series of white tombs stretch to the centrepiece of the memorial, the "Hill of Honour", on which stands a cylindrical mausoleum carrying an 11-metre (43-ft) high bronze figure of a soldier clutching a child to his breast with one hand and shattering a swastika with a mighty sword held in his other hand.

Further north, past the picturesque **Karpfenteich (Carp Pond)** ringed with ancient trees, you come to **Archenhold-Sternwarte** which is open to the public. The state observatory, which opened in 1896, owes its existence not to the trades fair mentioned previously but rather to the financial generosity of the people of Berlin, and the enthusiasm of its founder, the astronomer Friedrich Simon Archenhold. The 21-metres (68-ft) long, 130-tonne giant outdoor telescope, claimed to be the longest refracting telescope in the world, is no longer in use.

In 1959 the observatory was expanded to include a Zeiss planetarium, which can project the movement of around 5,000 stars on its heavenly dome of 6 metres (20 ft) diameter. In addition, the observatory also possesses a reflector telescope and a code-refractor. Since 1970 it has also housed a research department for history and astronomy.

Near the observatory is the **Hain der Kosmonauten** with busts of Yuri Gagarin, the first man in space, and the GDR's own cosmonaut, Sigmund Jähn.

NEUKÖLLN

With 300,000 inhabitants, Neukölln, in the southeast of the city, has the largest population of all the Berlin districts. It is part of that ring of concrete suburbs that encircled the German capital in the 1870s. Berlin grew at an astonishing rate. Hundreds of thousands of people, especially from the eastern provinces, were lured to the new metropolis during the industrial boom years. Property speculators hurriedly erected the notorious tenements that were to prompt the graphic artist Heinrich Zille's comment that you can "kill a man as well with an apartment as with an axe."

Nowadays most tourist routes tend to by-pass this traditional working-class district, although there is more of historical interest here than in Kreuzberg – for example the Britzer Dorfmühle (windmill) in Buga-Park, Berlin's first Muslim cemetery on Columbiadamm

and "Bohemian Rixdorf", which Egon Erwin Kisch once considered worth writing about. Unlike Kreuzberg, whose boundaries follow the line of Südstern, Hermannplatz and Kottbusser Damm, the visitor has no high expectations of Neukölln, and it is therefore free to weave its unsophisticated charm without prejudice. When you alight from the U-Bahn or the 29 bus at **Hermannplatz**, the "gateway to Neukölln", expect to encounter a genuine piece of Berlin.

Hermannplatz was restored for Berlin's 750th anniversary celebrations. In the centre glitters the *Tanzendes Paar* (*Dancing Couple*), a bronze by the Berlin sculptor Joachim Schmettau, who was also responsible for the popular "Wasserklops" in the inner city centre. The sculpture is ringed by old Berlin apartment buildings and offices with renovated facades.

Rixdorf traditions: Hermannplatz is an ideal starting point for exploring Neukölln for the first time. The district's three most important roads and shopping streets start here: **Sonnenallee**, **Karl-Marx-Strasse** and **Hermannstrasse**. In addition, two of the locals' favourite outing places – Neue Welt and the Hasenheide – are close by. In the past, the **Neue Welt** was a venue for evening dances, bock beer festivals and political gatherings. Since being restored, it has become a shopping centre and roller-skating park.

Adjacent to the Neue Welt is the **Hasenheide**, a public park with very old trees, meadows for sunbathing and an open-air stage. In this old hare reserve – hence the name, which means "hare heath" – Friedrich Ludwig Jahn established the first German gymnasium in 1811. The **Jahn Monument** recalls the bearded forefather of national gymnastics, and gym clubs from around the world have added inscriptions and commemorative plaques to the plinth.

Around Richardplatz: Even from a distance Neukölln Rathaus and its 65-metres (213-ft) high tower dominate Karl-

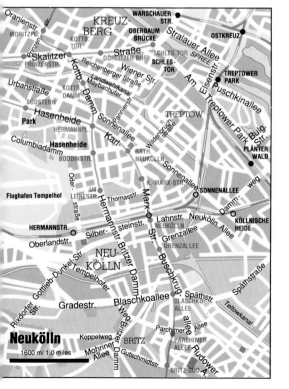

The "Dancing Couple" on Hermannplatz.

Marx-Strasse, the district's main "boulevard". **Richardplatz** U-Bahn station brings you out at Richardplatz, the historic heart of what would become the town of Neukölln. The town was originally called "Richardsdorp", then Rixdorf, and was first officially mentioned in 1360. Richardsdorp stood on the road from Cölln to Köpenick and consisted of farmhouses clustered around an elongated village square. The 15th-century Bohemian-Lutheran **Bethlehems-Kirche** (church) still survives from those times, along with Berlin's oldest **village smithy**.

Kutschen Schöne, a carriage business founded in 1894, has also survived. Twelve of its 153 carriages are white wedding coaches still hired to take couples to the church or registrar's office.

Some 400 Protestant refugees from Bohemia, almost all from the same village, set up a new home in Rixdorf in 1737. Thus Richardstrasse and the area around Kirchgasse became the Böhmisches Dorf ("Bohemian Village"). With its own assembly room, squat farmhouses and starkly simple Herrnhuter brotherhood, it stood on its own as an "almost misplaced idyll" (Egon Erwin Kisch), a mere stone's throw from the urban hurly-burly of Neukölln.

To distinguish their settlement from old Richardsdorp, it was called Böhmisch-Rixdorf. The two were merged in 1874, and in 1899 Rixdorf received its town charter. In 1912, the town authorities decided to revive the name of Berlin's old sister town and renamed the district Neukölln.

In the reforms of 1920, Neukölln was united with the villages of Britz, Buckow and Rudow to the south, to become Berlin's 14th administrative district. All three places retain their rural character to this day.

Buga: The Federal Garden Show (BUGA), held in Berlin in 1985, presented forest-poor Neukölln with a beautiful recreation area. The 100-hectare (247-acre) terrain, with forest and meadows, streams, flower beds, and a large

A card drive at Hasenheide.

man-made lake attracts regular visitors from all over the city.

Two experiments: In the past the oppressive living conditions in the proletarian quarter of Neukölln became a powder keg. The problem was exacerbated by the building of a massive estate with 2,500 flats in the grounds of the Britz estate between 1925 and 1931. Part of it, the **Hufeisensiedlung** (horseshoe block) designed by architects Martin Wagner and Bruno Taut, is a perfect illustration of the way in which progressive engineering techniques can be used to realise the concept of social housing. These revolutionary Weimar apartments are still regarded as exemplary throughout the world, in stark contrast to the **Gropiusstadt**, Neukölln's second major experiment in town planning.

The foundation stone for this satellite town was laid in 1962. The founder of the Bauhaus school of architecture, Walter Gropius, designed the ground plans for the modern complex, which today houses over 60,000 people. One of Gropius' own tower blocks dominates the skyline. Thirty-one storeys high, this is the highest residential block in Berlin and is surrounded by buildings that vary in height from one to 16-storeys, forming a semi-circle open towards the south.

Even at the planning stage, the architects had an eye on the location of playgrounds and open spaces. Of central importance in this respect is the sickle-shaped flash of green which encloses four U-Bahn stations. In spite of these seemingly well-intentioned facilities, living conditions in Gropiusstadt are disastrous. Drug-dealing, racism and right-wing extremism are the morbid consequences of a hostile living environment. It is far from coincidental that this was the stronghold of the REPs, the extreme right-wing Republicans, during the 1989 elections.

Around the "Kiez": Meanwhile, the Neuköllners can be satisfied, indeed proud, of the cultural range on offer in their part of the city. The **Neukölln Opera**, an independent musical theatre group, has long established a reputation outside the district. And the days are long gone when Neukölln artists had to draw attention to themselves with the battle cry: "There's life in the desert."

Today they've found an ideal exhibition space in the **Galerie im Körnerpark**, where their work is shown to best advantage. Lying in the heart of Neukölln, between Hermannstrasse and Karl-Marx-Strasse, the Körnerpark is a horticultural gem, with sweeping flights of steps, water fountains and ornamental flower beds. Visitors don't expect to find such a refuge here, for Neukölln is not only densely populated but it also has much industry, including a film processing plant, a cement works, the Berlin Kindl brewery and the Trumpf chocolate factory.

In Neukölln, tradition rubs shoulders with the present day, city bustle contrasts with village quiet. Here, it's possible to experience "Berlin Kiez" (local Berlin) still largely unchanged.

Father of gymnastics, Friedrich Ludwig Jahn.

Friedrich Ludwig Jahn.

TEMPELHOF

The name Tempelhof is automatically associated with the airport, which has brought worldwide fame to this part of the city. The birth of commercial flights, the early days with the "Aunt Ju S2", the rapid increase in air traffic after the Blockade, through to the age of the jet engine – all this has been witnessed at close hand by the people of Tempelhof.

The town of Tempelhof is very much older. It was founded in the 13th century by the Knights Templar, as too were the southwest districts of Maiendorf, Marienfelde and Lichtenrade. Like Tempelhof, all three were once simple Brandenburg farming communities. Friedrich Wilhelm I turned the fields and meadows north of Tempelhof into an exercise and parade ground for his troops in 1722. As Tempelhofer Feld, it became a recognised showground for numerous military events outside the gates of Berlin.

The first world airport: Other aeronautical spectacles were offered after 1883 when the new airship troops of the imperial army were installed on Tempelhofer Feld. In 1909 Orville Wright, one of the famous American flying brothers, rattled across the airfield on a bold test flight. The era of mechanised flight had just begun.

On 23 October 1923, Berlin Airport was officially opened in the eastern part of the former parade ground. To start with, there was very little to see beyond the signpost, a few aircraft hangars and a customs shed. Planes took off and landed on open grass runways. Not until at least five years later did the huts and sheds give way to a respectable terminal with a hotel, restaurants and concrete airfield.

From 1936 to 1939 this terminal became the centre of the massive present complex at the Platz der Luftbrücke. The war interrupted its completion and not until the 1950s was Tempelhof Central Airport finally opened to civilian traffic. When the large commercial airlines rerouted their flights to Tegel in 1975, Tempelhof became quieter. In the 50 years until then, 60 million passengers had flown in and out of Tempelhof without any serious accidents. In spite of its location on the outskirts of a heavily built-up city Tempelhof had proven that it was one of the safest of the world's major airports.

Memories of the Airlift: Compared with its original importance Tempelhof airport is today but a shadow of its former self. Some of the administrative offices and maintenance sheds have been rented to outside firms and authorities. The arrivals building on Platz der Luftbrücke is part of the military airfield, from where the Americans run their Tempelhof Air Base.

Further east at **Gate 5**, as a reminder of the Blockade, they have preserved a four-engine DC-54, one of the "raisin bombers" that delivered food parcels in 1948. Now over 40 years old, the vet-

Preceding pages: facing at Mariendorf. Left, American and British "raisin bombers" made 277,264 flights over Berlin. Right, the "hunger claw" on Platz der Luftbrücke.

AIR CROSSROADS BERLIN

West Berlin must be the only city in the world to erect a monument to its own air traffic. The "Air Bridge Memorial" in front of the former central airport at Tempelhof is intended to recall the weeks of the Blockade in 1948–49, when up to 1,300 aircraft landed at West Berlin's airport every day carrying food and other supplies and, at peak hours, a four-engined *Skymaster* either took off or touched down every 90 seconds. Until very recently the air corridors, the only truly "free and uncontrolled access to West Berlin", were elevated to the rank of myth.

The Allies remained the uncontested rulers of the air space. During the years of the Cold War, air traffic kept alive the only shared institution of the Western Powers and the Soviet Union. Representatives of the joint forces of occupation kept guard in the air safety control building in the Allied Supreme Command Headquarters, ensuring that aircraft flying outside scheduled times did not wander into the sights of the opposing air force.

It will be difficult for the airlines of the allied nations, especially Pan Am, British Airways and Air France, to relinquish their Berlin routes. Lufthansa has returned to Berlin and therefore to its birthplace. The American, British and French companies will only be allowed to continue to provide links between Berlin and the cities of what was once West Germany for a further 2–3 years. Thanks to the Allied air supremacy over Berlin, they previously held the monopoly. When the Transit Agreement of 1971 was signed, many visitors to Berlin drove rather than flew. The airlines shared out the market proportionately. Lack of competition meant that some companies, such as Pan Am, were noticeable not only for their mediocre service but also for their large profits, which were further increased by subsidies from the Bonn domestic budget.

The rulers of the air had all lost their haloes by 1988, when Berlin air traffic was liberalised once more under the slogan "Air Crossroads Berlin", invented by the President of the United States, at the time, Ronald Reagan. The Allied Powers haggled shamelessly amongst themselves to gain the best take-off slots for their respective national carriers. Faced with the increasingly frequent take-offs and landings, the local residents took to the barricades.

Their protest had virtually no effect, although the red-green Senate was able to persuade the airlines to increase their use of reduced-noise aircraft. Since the opening of the Wall, Berlin – with its airports at Tempelhof and Tegel in the West and Schönefeld in the former GDR – is well on the way to becoming once more the air crossroads it was back in the 1920s. Schönefeld Airport is already overloaded. The air traffic control tower at Tegel alone supervises some 300 take-offs and landings every day. At the latter airport the total number of passengers rose to a total of more than 7 million by the end of 1990.

In spite of the boom, Tegel and Tempelhof share a joint burden from the era of the divided city. They lie within the city limits, and hence in the middle of a built-up area. Even Schönefeld, the former hub airport of the GDR, is faced with problems stemming from this period. In recent years, the old regime had begun to construct an entire new suburb at Alt-Glienicke, not far from the airport.

Berlin politicians and airlines alike are therefore obsessed with the idea of building a large new joint airport for all traffic, far from the city centre – if possible, on the military airfield at present occupied by the Soviet air force in Sperenberg, which is a good 25 km (16 miles) south of the city.

Fifteen to 20 years are likely to elapse before the first civil aircraft are able to land at the hoped-for Berlin International airport. In the meantime, the new promise that Tegel and Schönefeld will then be closed provides scant comfort for the nearby residents. Only at Tempelhof is there any chance of things becoming quiet before that. More voices are demanding that the site be used for the construction of flats or an Olympic Village. The Air Lift Memorial, which stands in front of the National Socialist-style administrative buildings and departure terminal, would then really become just another piece of history.

eran of the airlift stands alongside the fence.

The Luftbrücke Denkmal (memorial) on the airport forecourt is also dedicated to the Airlift. The concrete sculpture by Eduard Ludwig represents the arch of a bridge, while the prongs at the top symbolise the three air corridors to the west, which kept West Berlin alive with food supplies during that period. Listed in bronze on the base of the memorial are the names of 70 Allied pilots, as well as four German assistants who gave their lives in the airlift.

Barely was the memorial inaugurated in 1951, before the locals had already given it an appropriate nickname: with grim humour the work of art was christened "the hunger claw", in memory of the meagre rations of the Blockade. Its twin, although smaller in size and with the three spikes aiming north, stands alongside the Frankfurt-Darmstadt Autobahn on the American Rhein-Main Air Base at Frankfurt's international airport. It was from there and from Wiesbaden that flights took off for Tempelhof during the blockade.

Not far from Platz der Luftbrücke between **Bayernring** and **Dudenstrasse**, which runs from Schöneberg, is a five-storey house painted in green, dating from 1912, and typical of the neighbourhood. An inconspicuous plaque at the entrance recalls that world history was made in the first two storeys of this house – **Schulenbergring 2** – in May 1945. During the fighting, the head of the 8th Soviet Guards, General Wassili I. Tschuikov, had his command post on the ground floor. One floor up, General Katukov and the staff of the 1st Armoured Division directed the operation to take Hitler's chancellery and the Reichstag.

On the morning of 2 May 1945, on the ground floor of this building, General Helmuth Weidling, Berlin's last commander, signed the order to his troops to surrender. For the long-suffering population of Berlin, the war was finally at an end. The oak table, on which Weidling signed the historic papers, now stands in Tempelhof local museum.

Leading from the Platz der Luftbrücke which is directly opposite is the old Reichsstrasse 96 to Zossen, which runs through the district. Up here on the border with Schöneberg and Kreuzberg it's called Tempelhofer Damm, but it assumes the secondary names of **Maßendorf** and **Lichtenrade** as it runs through these districts. Together with Mariendorf, Lichtenrade and **Marienfelde**, Tempelhof became part of the 13th administrative district of Greater Berlin following the reforms of 1920. At that time it had 61,000 inhabitants. The number has now trebled to around 185,000.

On Alt-Tempelhof street, to the right and left of Tempelhofer Damm, you'll find the old town centre with its village green and the last remaining farmhouses. Opposite the Rathaus (town hall), built in the 1930s, the half-timbered tower of a 13th-century fortified church peeks out from a little park. It was rebuilt in

1956 after having been badly damaged in the war. The old school on the village green in **Alt-Mariendorf** now houses the **Heimatmuseum und Archiv Tempelhof** (Local Museum and Archives), displaying furniture, folk art and old documents from the past. In the former estate of **Alt-Lichtenrade**, weeping willows ring the village pond. The surroundings are idyllic, and the traditional village inn and fire station have been preserved. The village church at **Alt-Marienfelde**, in granite late Romanesque, dates from 1220 and is the oldest building on Berlin soil.

About 800 horses are stabled in Tempelhof – no longer on farms, but in the stalls of the **Trabrennbahn Mariendorf** (racecourse). The country racecourse was opened in 1913 and with its new grandstand is one of southern Berlin's major attractions. The five-storey building is well equipped with restaurants and bars. Gambling fever is rife on Wednesdays and Sundays.

Industry on the water: Tempelhof plays a vital role in the economy of the capital as the largest industrial district after Spandau. The building of the Teltow canal at the beginning of the century fostered industrialisation in the south. Tempelhof's industrial area also follows the canal in part. From **Stubenrauchbrücke** (bridge) on Tempelhofer Damm, you can look out over the cranes and warehouses of Tempelhof harbour.

Tempelhof's most striking piece of industrial architectural design is the expressionist facade of the **Druckhaus Tempelhof** (printworks) at Ullsteinstrasse U-Bahn station. The plant was built in 1925–26 by Eugen Schmohl and was Berlin's first reinforced concrete tower block.

Under the name **Ullsteinhaus** the works on Mariendorfer Damm housed the editorial staff, printworks and administration of the Ullstein Brothers' enormous newspaper and magazine publishing company. Since the final closure of the main printing works, the publishing house, which is itself a listed **Sunday races in Mariendorf.**

building, has been leased out to smaller businesses.

UFA's second wind: "Three things have come into the world from Tempelhof: films, planes and the Knights Templar," proclaimed the district authorities proudly on the occasion of their 750th anniversary celebrations. Tempelhof was UFA's largest production centre after the "film city" of Babelsberg. Countless cinema classics were made at the studios at **Oberlandstrasse 26**. The first silent movie studio was operating here as early as 1909. In April 1945 Herta Feiler and Heinz Rühmann, the super-stars of German cinema, went in front of the cameras for *Sag die Wahrheit* (Tell the Truth). In the 1950s, however, Berlin's film industry enjoyed its last commercial success.

Now German TV's "Second Programme" (ZDF) rents the Union-Film studios as its main production centre. Around 70 percent of all mid- and long-term projects like series and television films are made in the **ZDF studios** at Tempelhof. Programmes such as *Hitparade*, the popular quiz-show *Der Große Preise* and the magazine programme *Kennzeichen D* also originate from the Tempelhof studios.

In **Viktoriastrasse**, not far from the printworks, dreams of a "great Germany" were filmed at the time of the Third Reich, as were socially critical films such as *Mutter Krausens Fahrt ins Glück*. In 1976 the print laboratory occupying the former UFA site was declared bankrupt, and the old production halls fell into disuse.

In June 1979 a crowd of activists occupied the run-down dream factory. Under the slogan "The second wind of the UFA", they transformed the empty complex into a self-governing multifunctional centre, catering for everyday needs. Since then, the new **UFA-Fabrik**, with its circus, Tempelhof's only cinema ("Ufer-Palast"), bar, cabaret stage and the café Olé, has become a lively splash of colour in a district otherwise notorious as a "cultural desert".

STEGLITZ

"Life is peaceful here in Steglitz, the children look healthy, the beggars don't press you too hard," wrote Franz Kafka to a friend in 1923.

Apart from the bustle of shoppers on Schloßstrasse, it is still very peaceful in Steglitz. Today, a district with a population of 170,000, it has retained its traditional bourgeois atmosphere. New housing and industrial estates may have appeared, but the quiet alleys about which Kafka enthused in his letters, can still be visited.

People come to this highly respectable neighbourhood to marvel at the marvellous orchids in the Botanical Gardens, or for some high-brow entertainment in the Schloßparktheater, or if they're unlucky for treatment at the university clinic.

Southern shopping paradise: Above all, though, Steglitz is famous for its **Schloßstrasse**. There are four of that name in Berlin, but usually those who use the name are referring to the main shopping street in Steglitz, which starts at the U-Bahn station on Walter-Schreiber-Platz as a continuation of Rheinstrasse heading south. A shopping mall which runs all the way from Steglitz Forum, a five-storey "multi-centre", to the Rathaus (town hall), was built for southern Berliners after the war.

While the **Titania-Palast** remained open, people also flocked to Schloßstrasse in the evenings to enjoy all sorts of artistic events: cinema, concerts, ballet, operetta and variety. Since the 1970s its glittering past as a palace of culture can no longer be detected from the outside and the building is under a preservation order as an example of 1920s' architecture. Meanwhile, the town's theatre uses a part of the premises as a rehearsal studio.

Since 1976 Schloßstrasse has gained one landmark. On the corner of Schildhornstrasse, immediately beside the motorway flyover, is the Turmrestaurant Steglitz. A lift takes you up to the three restaurant levels, where diners can enjoy a magnificent view from the picture windows. At the bottom end of Schloßstrasse you'll find Steglitz Rathaus (town hall), built in 1896–97 in Brandenburg brick Gothic. In the cellars, which no longer exist, the founders of the "Wandervogel" met in 1901, the New Romantic youth movement which began in Steglitz high school and caught the imagination of hundreds of thousands of young people before it was disbanded by the National Socialists.

Diagonally opposite on the corner of Albrechtstrasse, Berlin's highest office block towers over the town. Like so many other concrete blocks, the 130-metres (425-ft) **Steglitzer Kreisel** is a product of the frantic building boom in the late 1960s. Tax concessions as part of the "Berlin promotion" attracted a lot of capital into the city. But in the 1970s the tower block was seen primarily as a scandalous indictment of the policy of "write-offs" and was put up for auction. After a new investor had been found and the Kreisel completed, a hotel moved in here, together with the office of the mayor of Steglitz and several of his administrative departments.

Papa Wrangel's castle: The old farming village of Steglitz was conveniently situated on the road to Potsdam. In 1375 it was offically mentioned for the first time as the seat of a Lord von Torgow zu Zossen. In 1920, when it was the largest village in Prussia with 84,000 inhabitants, it became part of the 12th administrative district of Greater Berlin, along with the rural communities of Lichterfelde, Südende and Lankwitz.

On the corner of Wrangelstrasse an old Prussian manor house has been preserved from the days of the lord of Steglitz manor, Karl Friedrich von Beyme. The house is now a restaurant and wine bar. Built in 1804, it was named Wrangel Schlößchen ("Wrangel Castle") after its most popular resident. Field Marshall the Count von Wrangel was known as "Papa Wrangel" by young and old alike.

In 1921 the actor Paul Henckels opened a theatre, which was later converted to a cinema, next door to the manor house. Badly damaged in the air raids, it was opened again in November 1945 before all the rebuilding work had been completed, as the first functioning theatre in the American Sector, under the directorship of Boleslaw Barlog. The repertoire included *Hokuspokus* by Curt Goetz, bringing to the stage an up-and-coming young star, whom Barlog "discovered" for this production: Hildegard Knef.

The **Schloßparktheater**, which has a small auditorium seating only 478, attracts large enthusiastic audiences every night with its reputation for staging first-class plays, mostly light works and comedies, by leading playwrights.

Meteorologists and medics: Berlin's often deplorable weather may not come from Steglitz, but it is forecast there hour by hour. Since 1983 the **Meteorological Institute of the Free University** has been based in the old **Wasserturm am Fichteberg** (water tower), remodelled for its new function at a cost of millions. The technological heart of the water tower lies on the 6th floor. Teleprinters spew out an unceasing stream of numbers; a screen relays the radar picture from the weather fronts within a 200 km (125 mile) radius; 40 metres (133 ft) up, on the roof of the tower, an aerial receives data from weather satellites. The tower also has its own studio for telephone weather reports. Four to five million calls are logged annually.

In Klingsorstrasse, near the Teltow canal, the **Klinikum Steglitz der Freier Universität** was erected in 1961–69, with the support of the Bejamin Franklin Foundation of America. The 1,400-bed clinic is Europe's most modern centre in the field of medical research and teaching.

Botanical world tour: Another natural scientific institution which is a favour-ite with daytrippers is **the Botanical Gardens**. The Steglitz entrance lies at the bottom end of Schloßstrasse, which joins the widened Fernstrasse **Unter den Eichen** south of Hermann-Ehlers-Platz. An avenue leads to the 16 filigree greenhouses on a hill, which look out over the 42 hectare (116 acre) site. The most eye-catching is the large **Tropenhaus** (Tropical House), a palace of glass, 25 metres (83 ft) high.

Altogether there are around 18,000 different types of trees and plants in the Botanical Gardens. In the Freigelände (open-air gardens) you can wander along winding, marked trails, all beautifully laid out, through the flora of the earth's temperate zones. To the north, the garden borders on Königin-Luise-Platz in Dahlem. At the entrance is the **Botanisches Museum** – the only one of its kind in Germany – with a specialist library of over 60,000 volumes.

On what is now **Finckensteinallee**, the "Napoleon of land speculators", Wilhelm Carsten, endowed the Prus-

One of Berlin's "secret sights" – Lankwitz animal cemetery.

242

sian military with a tract of land, on which the **Hauptkadettenanstalt** (Main Cadet School) was built in 1878. In 1934 the SS – "Hitler's bodyguard" – took up station here. In the cellar of the Lichterfelde college, death squads killed around 40 Berlin SA-leaders who were involved in Röhm's alleged putsch on 30 June 1934. Since the end of the war, the buildings have been used by the US army as Andrews Barracks.

Berlin would never have developed into a metropolis so quickly without modern transport. In Lichterfelde in 1881, the inventor Werner von Siemens made a name for himself with a world first, the "Electric". On 16 May, on a test ground that stretched from the cadet school to Lichterfelde-Ost station, he started up the first electric tram for public passenger service: a converted horse-drawn tram with an electric motor under the floor.

The Father of Aviation: Lichterfelde is also the cradle of German aeronautics. Otto Lilienthal who, it is claimed, was the "first flying man" lived on Booth Strasse. In 1894 he built a 15-metre (50-ft) hill near his house from where he tested his machines and glided through the air for as far as hundred yards. Today a staircase leads to the top of this grassy mound where a stone globe, surrounded by a circular observatory pavilion, open to the sky, symbolises man's conquest of the air.

Compassion for animals: To the north, Lichterfelde crosses into the district of Lankwitz. The **Tierheim Lankwitz** (animal sanctuary) at Dessauer Strasse 21–27 is famous throughout Berlin and beyond. Here, surrounded by her charges, resides animal protection president Erna Graf, a determined elderly lady who has dedicated her life and personal fortune to "protecting tormented creatures".

In a city of 100,000 dogs and at least as many cats, not to mention all the other animals, saving homeless pets is a major enterprise. The home employs about 50 workers. It includes an emergency veterinary practice and boarding kennels. At any one time there are several hundred cats and dogs in the two-storey building, waiting for a caring home. There is also a sanctuary for unwanted horses and donkeys.

The **Tierfriedhof** (animal cemetery) in front of the main building is included as one of "Berlin's secret sights" in a pocket guide of that name. Here, under birches and pines, rest Harro and Waldo, two police dogs killed in the line of duty; Bimbo the circus monkey, and four-legged stars of the small and large screens.

Altogether, some 2,000 pets and pampered pooches are buried in the park. Many are remembered in heart-rending inscriptions on expensive marble headstones. Others, such as the lovely poodle "Prinzeßchen Sissi", are immortalised in portraits on their memorial stones. Sunday after Sunday, an elderly couple make the pilgrimage from north Berlin to lay fresh flowers on Plot no 1934 where lies their "unforgettable Puppi".

In the ropical House at the Botanical Gardens.

ZEHLENDORF

Zehlendorf, Steglitz's neighbour to the west, enjoys the reputation of being Berlin's most exclusive district. In terms of population it is one of the smallest, having 85,000 inhabitants, yet with an area covering 70 sq. km (27 sq. miles) it's the third largest district after Reinickendorf and Spandau.

Statistics show that the people of Zehlendorf live in the biggest apartments and enjoy the best medical care and have the highest level of education in all Berlin. Here you'll find the most attractive parks in western Berlin: Glienicker Volkspark in the south, the Havel River, Grunewald Forest and a chain of lakes from Nikolassee down to Grunewaldsee.

Exchange on the Havel: One place at the southern tip of the district became internationally famous over the years: the **Glienicker Brücke** (bridge) across the middle of which ran the former border with the GDR. From here in February 1986 pictures were relayed around the world, as hundreds of journalists waited for days in the freezing cold for the arrival of Anatoly Scharansky. After years of imprisonment, the Jewish lawyer from the Soviet Union was finally allowed to emigrate to the West in exchange for Soviet spies.

The Glienick bridge had been used before as a gateway to freedom for top agents from East and West. In 1962 the U2 pilot Francis Gary Powers, who had been shot down over the USSR, was exchanged for the Soviet master spy Ivanovitch Abel.

More than 200 years ago this crossing point already held special significance for Zehlendorf. Prussia's first traffic-carrying paved road, the Potsdamer Strasse, crossed the Havel River here over a wooden bridge. Sleepy Zehlendorf came to life. A travelling speed of up to 10 km (6 miles) an hour was possible on the "Steinbahn". The

coach journey from Berlin to Potsdam took just three hours, and Zehlendorf lay directly between the two.

Barely 50 years after the road was completed, the wind of technological change blew once more through the venerable village, which was officially mentioned for the first time in 1241. The Berlin-Potsdam Railway was built. In 1838 the first train stopped in Zehlendorf. Villa enclaves grew up along the edge of the railway in the second half of the 19th century. They changed Zehlendorf and the surrounding villages into urban suburbs of Berlin.

To the Volksfest via Little America: In the centre of present-day Zehlendorf life is anything but sleepy. At the crossroads of **Potsdamer Strasse**, **Teltower Damm** and **Clayallee** is the district's "City" area, where you'll find assorted shops, the town hall, finance offices and other institutions

Only the small baroque **village church** to the west of the crossroads remains from the olden days, and is at least

somewhat protected from the traffic by an old rural stone wall. On **Potsdamer Chaussee**, which leaves the "City" area and goes eastwards towards Wannsee and Potsdam along the route of the old Reichsstrasse 1, you will find the **Waldfriedhof Zehlendorf** (cemetery). Here are the graves of mayor Ernst Reuter (d. 1953), Erwin Piscator (d. 1966) and other well-known theatre folk and writers.

On Clauerstrasse in **Düppel**, a former manor on the city boundary towards Kleinmachnow, is the **Museum Village** of the same name, a reconstruction of an old Prussian village community from around 1200. It is run by volunteers, who demonstrate medieval handicraft skills on Sundays in the various workshops. In the heart of the western side of the forest, bordering the Havel River, stands the **Grunewald Turm** (Grunewald Tower) which was built at the end of the 19th century as a memorial to Kaiser Wilhelm I. From the tower the visitor can enjoy beautiful views across the lakes.

The Allied High Command also had its headquarters in Zehlendorf, at Kaiserwerther Strasse 16-18. In a discrete villa at Wasserkäfersteig 1, is the **Berlin Document Centre**, where the Americans keep the records of 10.7 million members of the former National Socialist party, as well as the personnel files of other Nazi organisations.

The "Bridge" artists: This section of Zehlendorf, where it crosses into Wilmersdorf at Roseneck, is known as **Dahlem**. Once a country estate, Dahlem is today known as a centre of scientific research, as well as a treasure trove of artworks.

Near Dahlem-Dorf U-Bahn station are the museums of the **Stiftung Preußischer Kulturbesitz** (Prussian Cultural Heritage Foundation), which include the Völkerkundemuseum (Museum of Enthnology), the Gemäldegalerie (Art Gallery) and the Kupferstichkabinett (Collection of Copper-plate Engravings). Not far from here, at Bussardsteig

The spy who came in from the cold: East and West exchange agents on the Glienick Bridge.

9, a low building stands on the edge of the Grunewald – the **Brücke Museum**. This was planned in 1964 on the initiative of the 80-year-old artist Karl Schmidt-Rottlauff and the then Director General of the nation's museums, Leopold Reidemeister. The purpose-built complex was opened in 1967.

Campus in the park: During term-time, tens of thousands of students flock to Dahlem every day. This is the main site of the **Freie Universität** (FU) and its numerous facilities. The university was founded in 1948–49 under difficult conditions. Political pressures at the well-established Humboldt University in the eastern part of the city had become intolerable to some of its students and lecturers. Prompted by these individuals and with the help of the American military governor Clay, the first educational programme began in Dahlem in December 1948.

Before World War I, several scientific research institutes of the Kaiser-Wilhelm Association had already been

established in Dahlem. Here were based the laboratories of famous academics such as Max Planck, Albert Einstein and other Nobel Prize winners. In 1938 at Thielallee 93, the old Chemical Institute, the atomic age was ushered into the world when Otto Hahn and his colleague Fritz Straßmann succeeded in splitting the first uranium atom.

Despite vociferous opposition from anti-nuclear campaigners, a test reactor still operates in the **Hahn-Meitner-Institut** on Glienicker Strasse in Wannsee: an atomic power station in the middle of the city.

Towards the end of the 1960s, the FU went through a turbulent phase when the "non-parliamentary opposition" (APO) and the protest movement against the American war in Vietnam were formed here under the leadership of the Socialist German Students (SDS). Today, the university is western Berlin's largest higher education institute, with about 53,000 students.

Martin Niemöller's presbytery: One memento of the former rural idyll of Dahlem has been preserved in the old section called **Dahlem-Dorf**. The history of this village probably goes back more than 750 years. The simple manor house, with Renaissance traces, opposite the thatched entrance to the U-Bahn station dates from 1679 and is now used partly by the university and partly by the "Friends of Dahlem Desmesne", who are committed to preserving Dahlem's rural heritage.

In the first years of National Socialism, the presbytery of Dahlem parish was used as a base for the "Confessional Church", under Pastor Martin Niemöller, who opposed the pro-Nazi stance of the German Evangelical Church. Niemöller, who spoke out courageously against the Nazi regime in his sermons, was thrown into a concentration camp by the Nazis in 1937. The presbytery is now known as **Martin-Niemöller-Haus** and houses a centre for peace studies.

Not far from here, on the shores of Grunewaldsee (Grunewald Lake),

Physics students at the Free University.

stands a small hunting lodge, built in the mid-16th century in Renaissance style for the Elector Joachim II. **Jagdschloß Grunewald** is now a museum, containing a collection of antique hunting weapons and equipment as well as original paintings by German, Dutch and Flemish masters from the Hohenzollern collection.

Trip to Wannsee spa: In the last 30 years of the 19th century, Berlin acquired a highly modern local transport system, the Schnell (fast) or S-Bahn. The building of the **Wannseebahn** terminus was largely responsible for Zehlendorf's rapid development, once again, as an exclusive place.

The line from Zehlendorf station to Wannsee passes through the prettiest residential districts in western Berlin. The stations have been designed to blend in with their surroundings. Outstanding sights on the route are **Mexicoplatz** station, a perfect example of art nouveau, and **Nikolassee** in the centre of the villa district of that name, which has been preserved in the architectural style of a neo-gothic castle.

From Nikolassee station, a footpath leads to the city's main fresh-water swimming pool. **Strandbad Wannsee** is the largest outdoor pool in all Europe. There has been a fresh-water pool here since the turn of the century, although until 1907 swimming in Berlin's lakes and rivers was officially banned. Between 1927 and 1930, a huge public baths was built to plans by the head of the Berlin city planning department, Martin Wagner, and architect Richard Ermisch. Their aim was to provide recreational facilities for those Berliners "who live in dark, airless tenements and can't afford the luxury of a trip to a spa." Today, Wannsee pool is overcrowded with Berliners on hot summer days. Even the far from clean Havel water doesn't deter people.

Literary workshop: At Sandwerder 5 near Wannsee S-Bahn station is a magnificent villa, no longer used as a family home. Carl Zuckmayer had the oppor-

ummer alace on 'faueninsel, uilt for Minchen ncke", the nistress of riedrich Vilhelm II.

tunity to work in the "Schloß am Wannsee" ("Castle on Wannsee") during the summer of 1925. For over 20 years now this has been the home of the **Literarische Colloquium Berlin** – a studio, meeting place and hostel for writers' conferences and authors from all over the world.

The concept was initiated by the writer and professor of literature Walter Höllerer. He founded the Literary Colloquium in 1964 to demonstrate that literature "occupies the area of tension between science, politics and everyday life." The group's work gives particular emphasis to adapting printed material for other, broadcast media, such as radio, film and television.

Devotees of the poet Heinrich von Kleist regularly makes the pilgrimage to his grave on **Kleiner Wannsee**. In the grounds of Bismarckstrasse 3, you can visit the exact spot on the lakeside where the writer, born in 1777, committed suicide with his married lover Henriette Vogel on 21 November 1811. The reddish stone on Kleist's grave bears a line of verse from his play *Der Prinz von Homburg*: "Now, O Immortality, you are wholly mine."

Königstrasse is the main route through the district of **Wannsee**, a favourite stamping-ground for day trippers and water-sports enthusiasts. Here and in the neighbouring streets, the Rathaus and low-built houses recall Wannsee's rural past. The **Mutter Fourage** gallery has taken over an old farmhouse in Schäferstrasse, with a nursery and pottery, while yacht clubs, sanatoria and private villas line the banks of the **Großen Wannsee**.

Behind Nos. 56–58, just before Heckeshorn hospital, is a half-hidden villa which once belonged to the SS. It was here on 20 January 1942 at the famous Wannsee conference chaired by SA chief Reinhard Heydrich that the decision was made about the "Final Solution to the Jewish Question" – the annihilation of the Jews in occupied Europe. The building was later used by Neukölln Council as a residential centre for problem children. As soon as the necessary funds can be found, **Wannsee Villa** is to be turned into a memorial to the Holocaust.

Castles and gardens: Here in the south of Zehlendorf, on the banks of the Havel, lies one of the loveliest areas of parkland in Berlin. **Volkspark Klein-Glienicke** was reserved for the sole use of royal guests, when Prince Karl lived in the former manor house, rebuilt by Schinkel and his pupils. The Prince, a brother of Friedrich Wilhelm III, not only employed the country's first master architect, but also the leading landscape designer to lay out the beautiful estate.

Over on Königstrasse is **Schloß Glienicke**, with a gentleman's residence and coachhouses. The two round temple-like buildings on the street are the "Large and Small Curiosities": observation turrets which Karl Friedrich had Schinkel build so that the Prince could watch the traffic moving past on the main thoroughfare. In the era of horse-drawn carriage 150 years ago, this may have been a more exciting past-time than it is today!

Set in a park on the opposite side of Königsstrasse is the former royal hunting lodge, rebuilt for Prince Karl in French baroque style by Ferdinand von Arnim. **Jagdschloß Glienicke** is now used as a conference centre.

In the woods south of the avenue, opposite the road to Nikolskoe, you'll find another unusual piece of architecture: the **Loggia Alexandra**. This semicircular building on **Böttcherberg** was built in 1869 as a scenic look-out for the owners of Klein-Glienick castle. Directly opposite the road called Am Böttcherberg, **Nikolskoer Weg** branches off. A winding road through the trees brings you to your destination: an idyllic inn on the hill overlooking the Havel, built in the style of a Russian log cabin. Beside it is an ornate church complete with onion dome.

King Friedrich Wilhelm III had the

Blockhaus Nikolskoe built in six weeks as a gift for his daughter Charlotte, wife of the later Czar Nikolaus I. At that time, relations between Prussia and Russia were dictated by family connections. Just behind the Nikolskoe is the charming church of **St Peter and St Paul** which was designed by August Stüler and whose onion domes continue the Russian theme of the Nikolskoe. It is a favourite for weddings and the Christmas service is also popular, when Nikolskoe looks even prettier under a covering of snow.

Optical illusions: At the end of Nikolskoer Weg is the **Pfaueninsel** (Peacock Island) from where there's a wonderful view over the Havel. One of the most romantic spots in Berlin, this is a favourite lovers' haunt. Friedrich Wilhelm III, the utterly unmilitaristic successor to Frederick the Great, bought the island in 1793 as a refuge for himself and his beloved. He ordered the construction of a steward's house and a dairy farm. The summer palace that looks like a half-ruined castle was intended for his mistress, "Minchen Encke", who later became Countess Liechtenau.

"Superb little place for a summer house, ruined knight's castle springs to mind, will have them build something Gothic straightaway," the pleasure-loving monarch noted in very basic German. Between 1793 and 1797 work continued on the half-timbered building. From a distance the oak panels give the impression of white stone. On the third floor, gaping window frames give the appearance of romantic ruins. The illusion was continued throughout the entire castle, right through to the round turret room.

In 1822 the island was converted into an English-style landscape park by Lenné. Peacocks were brought over from the manor of Sakrow on the opposite bank of the Havel. In time, these brightly-coloured birds took over the whole island and gave it the name by which it is still known today.

"Pack your swimming trunks, grab your little sister and get down to Wannsee".

WILMERSDORF

From the air, Wilmersdorf looks like a topographical cross sitting between the City and Grunewald. The district stretches from the Bundesallee right to the very heart of western Berlin and then westwards to the banks of the Havel. Of its 13 sq. miles (34.3 sq. km), almost half is pine forest. The combination of the city on one side, trees on the other, is what gives Wilmersdorf its charm.

The population of Wilmersdorf, which numbers about 160,000, appreciates its home. It is by and large middle-class and includes an above average proportion of well-educated professional and well-to-do widows. The conservative, bourgeois district has a great bearing on the age pyramid of western Berlin, as a good one-fifth of the population is over 65. Social institutions include no fewer that 49 privately-run homes for the elderly and sheltered housing schemes.

On Bundesallee: The Bundesallee leads from the zoo quarter south to the Bundesplatz. As a former royal boulevard it was among the grandest addresses in western Berlin. What was left standing of the avenue after the air raids was sacrificed to an eight-lane through road in the route planning during the "second destruction of Berlin". Of architectural interest is the former **Joachimstalsches Gymnasium** (high school), a neo-classical brick building with a 50-ft (150-metres) arcade which dates from 1880 and which was inspired by Schinkel. The house is now used by the art college and other institutions, mainly for musical events.

Hidden behind the ancient trees at Schaperstrasse 24 is the **Theater der Freien Volksbühne**. Like the theatre in Wilmersdorf Mendelsohnbahn, this playhouse is devoted mainly to staging works by contemporary authors. Every year in May, the Volksbühne hosts the Berlin Theatre Congress, which attracts attention from far beyond the city. Fritz

Bornemann's cuboid theatre building (1962) blends harmoniously with peaceful **Fasanenplatz**, which is framed by fascinating stucco facades and the trappings of post-modernism. The series of geometric, leafy squares joined by ring roads is typical of this north-eastern corner of Wilmersdorf.

Artists' colony: In the "Golden Twenties", countless tormented artistic souls were drawn to this area, close to the city. Heinrich Mann lived in Uhlandstrasse; Bert Brecht, then working at the Deutsche Theater, had an attic apartment at Spichernstrasse 16, where he wrote *Die Dreigroschen Oper* (*The Threepenny Opera*). At Wittelsbacherstrasse 5, around the same period, Erich Maria Remarque wrote himself to fame with his anti-war novel *Im Westen Nichts Neues* (*All Quiet on the Western Front*). For the refugee from Saxony, Erich Kästner, Berlin was "the only place where there's anything going on". His big-town novel *Fabian* is a furious satire on the decadence of pre-war Berlin, of which he had first-hand experience as a lodger on Prager Platz between 1927 and 1931.

Left-wing writers such as Ernst Busch, Alfred Kantorowicz, Manès Sperber, Arthur Koestler, Erich Mühsam, Walter Hasenclever and Johannes R. Becher lived side by side with 300 artist neighbours in three co-operative blocks on what was then Laubenheimer Platz (now Ludwig-Barnay-Platz). The **Künstlerkolonie** (Artists' Colony) was notorious for miles around as the "red block". On election days the Artists' Colony gained notoriety as "a lonely isle of protest in the middle of a burning sea of swastikas and black and white and red," as the contemporary historian Axel Eggebrecht recorded.

In the evenings, squads of SA used to waylay the "arty bolshies" on their way home. The colony organised its own defence force. Nazi sympathisers were ostracised. Barely had Hitler taken power before the police began to terrorise the "nest of communists" on the

Wilmersdorf widows.

south-eastern edge of Wilmersdorf.

Wilmersdorf prides itself on being a haven of religious tolerance with 32 places of worship, including a Russian-orthodox cathedral and a domed mosque in India mogul style, for most of the different creeds who reside in the district. The **Kirche am Hohenzollernplatz**, a clinker building dubbed "God's Power Station", is a creation of the Bauhaus architect Fritz Hager.

Berlin's biggest office: The **Hohenzollerndamm**, the district's longest arterial road at 5 km (2½ miles), links the inner city with Grunewald and Dahlem. On **Fehrbelliner Platz**, the municipal centre of the district, it crosses an administrative precinct, where 30,000 government officials are employed. The oval nucleus of the precinct is made up of official buildings in the characteristic monumental style of the Nazi era. At one time they were to become part of a "Third Reich Forum". The former Nazi "workfront" is now **Wilmersdorf Rathaus** (town hall). The neighbouring

Kommunale Galerie runs exhibitions of contemporary art and local history.

Old Wilmersdorf: For most of its almost 700-year history, Wilmersdorf was a simple farming community. At its historical heart on Wilhelmsaue the inscription on a granite slab points out that "farmsteads surrounded by fields gave Alt-Wilmersdor its identity in the olden times". A farmhouse on the old village green is the last surviving monument to that rural era. The Schoeler-Schlößchen was built in 1754 and later converted into a little mansion.

West of the city motorway, Wilmersdorf merges with the suburban idyll of Schmargendorf, where at Berkaer Platz you can admire the Rathaus (1902) which is an especially fanciful example of Brandenburg Gothic. Because it is now a register office, its romantic turrets and towers are immortalised in countless wedding albums.

Home of millionaires: At Roseneck, Schmargendorf borders on the Grunewald area, where you'll find Berlin's

Left, Fehrbelliner Platz U-Bahn station. Below, The Russian church on Hohenzollerndamm

most expensive residential area. At the end of 1981, the **Wissenschaftskolleg zu Berlin** (Berlin School of Sciences), modelled on America's Princeton University, opened its doors at Wallotstrasse 19. Top international scientists of all fields pursue their research here as "fellows", free from the usual obligations of university life.

Berlin's upper classes meet in the tennis club "Rotweiß" on Hundekehlensee. Its reputation as Berlin's most feudal tennis club dates back to the early days of the villa community at Grunewald. Conceived in 1890 as the crowning glory of the extended Kurfürstendamm, Grunewald was an ideal choice of home for affluent citizens keen to avoid paying city taxes. Until it became part of Greater Berlin in 1920, the town came under the financial control of Teltow, whose taxes were more lenient.

Grunewald: On a hill on Havelchaussee stands the 55-metres (183-ft) **Grunewaldturm** (tower), a favourite with day trippers from the city. The neo-Gothic building was commissioned by Teltow in 1857 in memory of Emperor Wilhelm I, and designed by Franz Schwechten, who was also responsible for the Gedächtniskirche in Charlottenburg.

The superstructure of a radar station on **Teufelsberg** shimmers in the distance like the holy dome of Sacré-Coeur or some Russian cathedral. The highest point in western Berlin at 115 metres (383 ft), Teufelsberg was piled up after the war from 25 million cubic metres (33 million cubic yards) of rubble. "Prohibited" signs outside a closely guarded installation warn that this is a top-secret area. From the summit Americans and British listened through the ether to what was going on in the former Eastern Block. A lower plateau on Teuffelsseechaussee provides an imitation Alpine setting for western Berlin's amateur sportsmen and women.

Weekend climbers and hang-gliders practise on the slopes of the "rubble mountain", which offers a wonderful panorama at the end of a pleasant walk.

ancy-dress arty at Wilmersdorf e Rink.

The North of Berlin

1600 m/ 1,0 miles

ORANIENBURG

Oranienburger Chaussee

Schönfließer

SCHILDOW - MÖNCHMÜHLE

Schönfließer Str.

SCHILDOW

Zeltinger Str.

Neubrücker Str.   Schönfließer Str.

FROHNAU

Schildower Str.

GLIENICKE

Zeltinger Platz

S2 FROHNAU

Am Eichenhain

Maximiliankorso

Sigismundkorso

Frohnauer Straße

Burgfrau enstr.

Berliner Str.

HERMSDORF

BLANKENFELDE

LÜBARS

BLANKENFELDE

Hauptstr.

Blankenfelder Chaussee

BERLINER FORST

Damm

Damm

Krüger-

Quickborner Str.

Mönchmühler Str.

TEGEL

HERMSDORF

Hermsdorfer

Schulzendrf. Str.

Oraniendamm

Z.

WAIDMANNSLUST

ROSENTHAL

Ruppiner Chaussee

Waidmannsluster Damm

WAIDMANNSLUST

Damm

Hermsdorfer Str.

Oranienburger Str.

Wittenauer Str.

Finsterwalder Str.

Witten. Str.

NORDENI

WITTENAU NORDBAHN

Hauptstraße

Friedrich-

U6 TEGEL

Alt.

Wittenau Str.

Dannenwalder Weg

WILHELMSRUH

Tegel Palace

TEGEL

Gorkistraße

Am RATH. REINICKENDORF im Bau

Nordgraben

Roedernallee

Germanstr.

Engels-

Tegeler

Eichborn-

SCHÖNHOLZ

See

TEGEL

BORSIGWERKE

Karolinenstr.

Berliner Str.

Holzhauser Str.

Wittestraße

EICHBORNSTR.

Eichborn-

KARL BONHOEFFER KLINIK im Bau

WILHELMSRUH

REINICKENDORF

Fischer- Str.

H.-Mann-Platz

Kurt-

Graus straße

Bernauer Str.

HOLZHAUSER STR.

Seidelstr.

WITTENAU Waldstr.

LINDAUER ALLEE im Bau

M.BAU

U8 PARACELSUS-BAD

Lin- dauer Allee

SCHÖNHOLZ

straße

straße

SEIDELSTR.

Antonienstr. Eichborndamm

A.-Victoria-Allee

SCHARNWEBERSTR.

Ollenhauerstr.

Humboldtstr.

Aroser Allee

Resi- denzstr.

RESIDENZSTR.

Berlin-Tegel-Airport

Damm

Scharnweberstr.

Holländer

REINICKENDORF

Emmentaler Str.

FR.-NEUMANN-PL.

Pankower Allee

WOLLANKSTR.

Prinzen allee

Wolla nk.

Schäfersee

K.-SCHUHMACHER-PLATZ

Str.

U9 OSLOER STR.

Osloer Str.

HOHENZOLLERNKANAL

Saatwinkler   Damm

Müller- str.

Afrikan.

REHBERGE

Barfus

WEDDING

Markstr.

Rei-

Str.

PANKSTR.

BORN-HOLMER STR.

VOLKSPARK JUNGFERNHEIDE

K.- Schuhmacher- Damm

Saatwinkler

Seestr.

VOLKSPARK REHBERGE

Str.

SEESTR.

NAUENER PL.

nickendorf Str.

Pankstr.

GESUNDBRUNNI

Heckerdamm

Müller-

WEDDING

HUMBOLDT-HAIN

VOLTAST

SIEMENSSTADT

SIEMENSDAMM

HALEMWEG

J.-KAISER-PL.

Heckerdamm

Damm

Seestr.

PUTLITZSTR.

AMRUMER STR.

LEOPOLDPL.

Amrumer Str.

REINICKEN DORFER STR.

Heidestr.

Husittenstr.

BERNAUER STR.

WERNERWERK

Goerderdamm

BEUSSELSTR.

Siemensstr.

BIRKENSTR.

Lehrter Str.

STADION D. WELTJUGEND

NORDBHF.

SIEMENSSTADT-FÜRSTENBRUNN

Tegeler Weg

JUNGFERNHEIDE

Sickingenstr.

Quitzowstr.

Perleburger Str.

Rathenower Str.

Chaussee

NORDBAHNHOF

Huttenstr.

MOABIT

REINICKENDORF

About four million passengers pass through the hexagonal customs hall at **Tegel airport** every year. Few are aware that they have landed in Reinickendorf, the northernmost of the 12 districts in western Berlin. Since 1975, Tegel Airport has been the terminus for almost all air traffic in and out of West Berlin.

Tegel was already making its mark on the history of aviation at the beginning of the century. In 1909 Count Zeppelin's airship "Z3" landed on what was at that time a rifle practice and exercise ground. In 1931, on the disused military land, 19-year-old Wernher von Braun launched the first liquid-fuel rocket, the predecessor not only of the V2 which was used to bomb London, but also the American space rocket. This makes Tegel one of the birthplaces of world space travel.

The first runway for planes was constructed in 1948–49 during the Berlin Blockade. The 2,400 metres (8,000 ft) was completed in just three months and was at that time the longest in Europe. From then on the four-engine "raisin bombers" droned daily over north Berlin. On 14 April 1949, 362 American airlift planes landed in the space of 24 hours. Tegel has been in use as a civilian airport since 1960. In 1969, when the main airport at Tempelhof could no longer cope with the mounting number of passengers, work began at Tegel on what would become one of the most modern airports in the world, capable of handling even the largest planes. It was completed in 1974.

The "green north": Arriving at Tegel from the air, woods and lakes stretch out beneath you. As in Spandau, they make up a large part of the district. Not for nothing is Reinickendorf known as the "green north": almost one-quarter of it is woodland. But its profile includes fields and meadows and former villages such as Lübars, where some farming is still carried out. Then there are villa communities such as Frohnau and Hermsdorf and, as a contrast, the tower blocks of the Märkisches Viertel, probably German's most famous housing estate from the 1960s.

The city's largest district, covering an area of 90 sq. km (34 sq. miles), Reinickendorf is not only a favourite recreation spot. In the industrial area north of the airport, the old-established Borsig works have been going for 90 years. The Berlin inventor and engineer August Borsig had chased the English competition from the market by the mid-19th century with his steam engines. The **Borsigtor** at the works entrance on Berliner Strasse – an arch embellished with gothic turrets and battlements – bears witness to the company's importance at the turn of the century.

The old village of Tegel, the centre of which lies just a few hundred metres to the north, lost its rural character with the advent of industrialisation. It is now the only place in Berlin where the shopping

BERLIN-TEGEL

AEG-TELEFUNKEN

centre is accessible by steamer. The street Alt-Tegel, which has been a pedestrian zone since 1976, links the shopping centre with the jetties on **Tegeler See** and the **Greenwich Promenade**. The promenade around the 4-metres (13-ft) deep Havelbucht (Havel Bay) is the starting point for some attractive shore walks. But the lake's scenic appearance is deceptive. Even 20 years ago, biologists were raising the alarm when increasing phosphate levels threatened to pollute the lake. A phosphate elimination plant, which is cleverly shaped like a steamer, went into operation in 1985, to improve the quality of the water.

Castles and inns: The gem of Tegeler Forst (forest) is Tegel Castle. Built by the Grand Electors as a hunting lodge, **Schloß Tegel** has been in the possession of the von Humboldt family since 1766. The descendant who now owns it opens the park and family vaults to visitors in the summer months.

Across the lake on the Reiherwerder peninsula, you may catch the facade of a castle-like building shimmering through the trees. Ernst Borsig, the nephew of the locomotive king and owner of the Tegel works, had this palatial residence built in 1911. Villa Borsig, familiar to most Berliners only from a distance or from summer concerts held in the gardens, has been used as a conference centre for the **Deutsche Stiftung für Internationale Entwicklung** (German Foundation for International Development) since 1959.

Not far from the Villa Borsig on the junction of Carolinenstrasse and Heiligenseestrasse, two public houses vie for the title of Berlin's oldest inn. The **Alte Fritz** was still the "Neuer Krug" when the young crown prince Friedrich allegedly changed his horses and drank beer here in the old posting-house on the road to Rheinsberg. Other famous guests of the house were the Humboldt brothers and Goethe, who stopped here in 1778 during his only journey to Berlin. It is said that the innkeeper told him

ghost stories, which he later used in Faust II: "The devil's pack, it pays no heed to rules, we are so clever, and yet in Tegel there are ghouls".

Directly opposite the Alter Fritz, which is currently closed, is the Alte Waldschenke, which only became popular with day trippers from Berlin during this century. Until then it was a workhouse. It is hard to give the simple, half-timbered building an exact date, but it is said to have been erected between 1760 and 1770.

Buddha's temple: Reinickendorf's heritage as part of the Brandenburg March is reflected in its country manor houses. The **Buddhistischer Tempel** (Buddhist Temple) on Edelhofdamm is more recent. This meeting-place of Berlin's 300-odd Buddhist community is not far from the centre of the genteel villa suburb of Frohnau. They are taught and supervised by four monks from Sri Lanka. The temple, which is set in a park on a hillside, was built in the 1920s by the doctor and philologist Dr Paul Dahlke.

Lübars is one of the city's many villages.

He had converted to the Buddhist religion on a journey to Sri Lanka and after his death was buried in the temple gardens.

Fine living: At the turn of the century, as Berlin continued to expand, genteel villa districts grew up in places other than Zehlendorf and Grunewald. The north was and still is popular with the wealthy. **Gartenstadt Frohnau** (Frohnau Garden Suburb) resembles nothing so much as a spa, so tranquil and remote is it from the bustle of the inner city. In former times, the air here was supposed to have been so good that throat specialists recommended that opera singers lived in Frohnau.

Bonnie's Ranch: Reinickendorf, or more accurately the area of **Wittenau**, is also famous for an institution known disparagingly and sometimes discriminatorily as "Bonnie's Ranch". The nickname originated among drug users and refers to the **Karl-Bonhoffer-Nervenklinik** on Oranienburger Chaussee, Berlin's largest psychiatric hospital, which is also involved in treating heroin addicts – of which Berlin has its share.

The clinic was founded in 1880 under the name "Dalldorf City Lunatic Asylum". The farming folk of Dalldorf found it distasteful to be so closely associated with such an institution. So in 1905, approval having been cleared at the highest levels, the town was renamed Wittenau, after its leader Peter Witte. The hospital remained and achieved notoriety in specialist circles for its early attempts to provide its pitiful inmates with therapy as well as sanctuary. During the Third Reich, the clinic's history was less distinguished. Behind these walls, crimes of euthanasia were committed by unscrupulous doctors and wardens.

Brandenburg Quarter: A few kilometres away a 16-storey block in a ghost town towers into the sky, notorious throughout the entire Federal Republic as an architectural disaster. The Märkisches Viertel is a prime example of the dehumanising, purely techno-

avelling by
uble-
cker – a
y
htseeing
r every
e.

cratic building styles of the 1960s. The tallest ugliest building stands on Wilhelmsruher Damm immediately behind the Postbrücke (bridge). The residents' name for it speaks for itself – "Langer Jammer" ("long lament"). The grey tower was designed by the architects Rene Gages and Volker Theissen. The satellite town with space for 50,000 people in 17,000 apartments was built between 1963 and 1974 to rehouse those displaced in the inner-city "redevelopment zone" in "light, air and sun". Progress came in the shape of concrete. Now the authorities are trying to soften the bleak architecture by painting it and making various other improvements.

On Senftberger Ring are two wonders of neo-Brandenburg design. Germany's first adventure playground was built here on the inititiative of local parents and children, who found the recreational facilties here inadequate. At Senftenberger Ring 25 there's also a **children's playhouse**, the first heated house to be built in Europe in the so-called "earthern constuction style" – the work of architect Engelbert Kremser.

Ferry trip to Spandau: A favourite place for daytrippers from the Märkisches Viertel, and from elsewhere too, is the village of Lübars, whose fields reach right up to the high-rise blocks. Seven farmers still live here, farming 140 hectares (346 acres) of corn. In the west of Reinickendorf, wedged between Tegelwald and the Havel, are the villa suburbs of Konradshöhe and Tegelort. This is also where you'll find Berlin's only **car ferry**, which runs from Tegelort across the Havel to the Aalemannufer at Spandau. The service operates throughout summer and winter at reasonable prices, and can carry up to 65 tonnes or 200 people. It carries anything with wheels and riders on horseback are not an uncommon sight.

Right in the north is the sleepy fishing village of **Heiligensee**, one of 30 settlements to have grown up around Berlin in the Middle Ages. The courtyard on the village green on Alt-Heiligensee street betrays traces of the original village character. The artist Hanna Höch (1890–1978), probably the most famous inhabitant of Heiligensee, is buried in the cemetery beside the 16th-century church. Höch is credited with inventing collage. In the 1920s she was the only female member of the "Berlin Dada" school of artists. Denounced as "degenerate" by the Nazis in 1939, she moved to the pergola-like house at An der Wildbahn 33 where she harboured several irreplaceable works by the Dada school until the end of the war.

In 1988 the controversial feeder road to the northern motorway to Hamburg was opened through the Tegel forest. Since then outward-bound traffic has rolled through Reinickendorf on its way north. Residents and conservationists campaigned unsuccessfully against the construction of this motorway. Not only does it cut right through the unique nature reserve of **Tegeler Fließ**, but many precious trees in its path have had to be sacrificed.

Left, last ex to Tegel. Right, a Buddhist monk in the gardens of Frohnau temple.

SPANDAU

In the centre of Spandau there was, and probably still is, a slogan spray-painted on a railway bridge: "It has always been something special to be a Spandauer!"

There is some truth in the saying, which has also been making the rounds as a car-sticker. Spandauers – the inhabitants of the formerly independent town on the Havel – have always been conscious of their origins, especially with regard to their relationship to Berlin. "I have 11 districts and one republic – Spandau," Mayor Reuter once joked about the distinctive local patriotism of the Spandauer smallholders.

They passionately fought absorption into Greater Berlin in 1920. Town councillor Emil Müller anticipated the approaching storm before World War I, when a splendid town hall was built in Spandau for almost 3.5 million gold marks. "May the Emperor's hand pro-tect us from Greater Berlin and administrative union," he stormed in 1911 during the ceremonial laying of the foundation stone. The Emperor departed and Greater Berlin came into being. Spandau became the focal point of the administrative district of the same name. Its 86 sq. km (33 sq. miles) make up almost one-sixth of the total area of the old West Berlin.

Spandau is the only part of Greater Berlin on the west bank of the Havel, and shares a 32-km (20-mile) boundary with Nauen in the old East German district of Potsdam.

Of the historic sights in Berlin, the Zitadelle Spandau with its Juliusturm (tower) ranks at the top of the list. After the war, Spandau's name drew worldwide attention because of its prison for war criminals and the high-ranking Nazis imprisoned there. The German Overseas Development Agency (DED) has its headquarters in Kladow, including a school that prepares 250 aid workers a year for work in the Third World.

Economically and commercially, Spandau plays a major role in the life of Berlin. The largest industrial district in old West Berlin, it's chief claim to fame is that it is the home of Siemens, the Reuter power station and BMW's sleek motorbikes.

Berlin's big sister: Spandau claims to be the oldest community on West Berlin soil. Thanks to its suburban location on the Havel's west bank, it has preserved much of its original rural frontier character. The Old Town was threatened with demolition in the 1960s, but it now has protected status. Its grid of narrow streets and the St Nikolai church are two reminders of Spandau's original autonomy. It is proud to be five years older than Berlin and was first officially mentioned in 1232 when a royal letter awarded the **Civitas Spandowe** market and customs privileges.

Some believe Spandau's union with Berlin was only properly finalised with the advent of the underground. Since 1 October 1984, the extended line 7 has

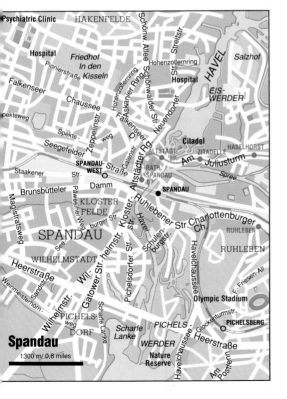

St Nikolai church around the turn of the century.

been transporting people between the city and the heart of Potsdam in 25 minutes.

As if to make up to her big sister for the loss of her independence, the Berlin Board of Works took great care with the decoration of the last three U-Bahn stations. In the terminus by the **Rathaus** (town hall), "Spandau at the gates of Berlin" (as it advertises itself) welcomes visitors with all the trappings of the post-modern age: black marble columns, gleaming brass and old-fashioned light fittings.

On the citadel: Spandau's importance as a trade and fortress town rested on its choice waterside location. The copper-plate engraver Magnus Merian captured this in 1652 in one of the earliest drawings of the city. Directly outside the Old Town, on what is now **Lindenufer**, two navigable rivers meet. The Havel flows from Mecklenburg in the northeast and joins with the Spree on its course to the Elbe. Furthermore, in the Middle Ages the trade route from Magdeburg to Poland also passed through the town. Such a strategically important spot therefore had to be well guarded.

The Brandenburg nobility were quick to recognise this. Documents reveal that Spandau has had a fortress since 1197. In 1557, Elector Joachim II ordered it to be extended into an "impregnable modern stronghold". The master builder Chiaramella de Gandino designed an imposing moated castle in high-renaissance style with four angular bastions. The resulting **Zitadelle Spandau**, the Spandau citadel, is considered to be a masterpiece of "modern Italian fortress construction".

No other European fortress of its like has been so well preserved. As the mighty brick walls come into view through the trees beyond the **Zitadellenbrücke** (Citadel Bridge), they glimmer with a reddish hue. The oldest part of the citadel is the 12-metres (40-ft) wide **Juliusturm** (tower), which dates back to the time of the medieval Spandau castle, the residence of the Brandenburg

princes and nobility. A wooden spiral staircase leads 30 metres (100 ft) to an observation platform, from where you can enjoy a marvellous panoramic view over the diverse Spandau countryside.

The heavily fortified citadel was intended to guard the river-crossing on the road to Berlin. When the Prussian court, including the queen, her sisters-in-law and heir, fled to Spandau in the Seven Years War they took with them the royal finances, silverware and secret documents.

The castle also served as the Prussian state prison, where the rulers had officials and political hot-heads locked up. These included "Turnvater Jahn" (father of modern gymnastics) and 1,495 March revolutionaries from the Berlin uprising of 1848. After the war in 1870–71, the 2.3-metre (8-ft) thick walls of the Juliusturm protected the state war coffers that were filled with French reparation payments: 120 million marks in gold mint packed in 1,200 crates. In 1919, the gold was returned to the new victor as reparation for war damages.

The citadel, which from the air looks like a huge star, was used by the military until 1945. As long ago as 1817 it already housed a secret rocket laboratory. No less recent was the military defence installation where the German army experimented with highly toxic substances. At the end of World War I, these were either simply buried or sunk into wells.

Now life is peaceful in the citadel (open daily except Mondays). In the **Kommandantenhaus** (Commander's House) on the right just after the railway bridge, the **Heimatmuseum Spandau** (local museum) mounts exhibitions such as a series on "Spandau and the History of Europe". Concerts, art exhibitions and poetry readings are held in the former **Palais** (Knights' Hall). In the evenings, visitors can enjoy a medieval banquet to a minstrel serenade in the atmospheric setting of the crypt.

Through the Old Town: The citadel lies on an island outside the town centre.

The bridge **Am Juliusturm** crosses to the right bank of the Havel and the **Old Town**. The oldest part of Spandau, the **Kolk**, stretches to the north, just downstream from the bridge. Time seems to stand still as you stroll along the cobblestones past quaint 18th- and 19th-century dwellings. The names of the three streets recall the old settlements that once stood here. The first, **Bennitz**, already belonged to Spandau in the 13th century.

The Kolk used to be directly linked with the citadel. The house at Behnitz 3 formerly belonged to the military. In the evenings, the castle guards used to make merry in the three village inns. The fishing village **Damm** lay on the edge of the Kolk and, to this day, the allotments still possess royal fishing rights.

At the Kolk, or to be more precise, at the intersection of Möllentordamm and the Behnitz, there is a small "balcony", from where you can observe the **Schleuse Spandau** (lock) in operation. Paddle boats, motorboats, yachts, tugs

and barges, and even the tourist steamer *Moby Dick*, must pass through this needle's eye linking the upper and lower reaches of the Havel. The lock is soon to be enlarged by a second chamber to allow European traffic to reach the industrial zone on the upper Havel. At present more than 35,000 boats use the north-south route every year. West Berlin has a weekend flotilla of about 75,000 yachts and motorboats and about 100 watersports clubs have sprouted on Spandau's shores.

At the Weinmeisterhorn, downstream from the **Frey-Brücke**, is the start of a 2,000 metres (2,200 yd) regatta course. The peak season for weekend sailors is summer when the lock is in operation up to 17 hours a day.

The medieval Old Town which sprawls on the other side of the bridge was built to an oval ground plan in the first half of the 15th century. In the middle rises the church of St Nikolai, one of the oldest Gothic town churches in the Brandenburg March. Rochus,

Count of Lynar, who completed the construction of the citadel in 1594, donated the Renaissance altar. A bronze statue outside the main entrance commemorates Elector Joachim II's conversion to Protestantism is 1539.

The daily life of Spandau has been preserved around **Reformationsplatz**. The Middle Ages are in fact just under the paving. During excavation work for a new building, the foundation walls of a 13th-century Dominican abbey were discovered. The ruins are carefully preserved in an "archaeological basement", and can easily be viewed from the outside through the large glass panes.

Spandau expands: Until the beginning of this century, Spandau led the life of an enclosed fortress town. As early as the 14th century, it had already surrounded itself with a defensive wall, some scenic remains of which are still to be seen in **Kinkelstrasse**. Spandau grew into a military town and the arsenal of Prussia. The first factories were erected for military purposes: in the 18th century the Prussian army set up a carbine factory. Ammunition factories, artillery works and a cannon foundry followed in the 19th century. Products from these are displayed today in the inner courtyard of the citadel. It was only after disarmament in 1903 that Spandau began to grow beyond its old limits and the **Neustadt** (New Town) grew up along the roads leading to the north.

The last prisoner: Until 1987 Spandau's former military prison at Wilhelmstrasse 21–24 was surrounded by high walls and warning signs in a multitude of languages. It was erected in 1878–81 to accommodate up to 600 prisoners. In 1947, the four victorious powers agreed to intern seven of the main defendants in the Nuremburg war crimes trials here, including Rudolf Hess, Hitler's former deputy, who was sentenced to life imprisonment. After 1966 he was the only remaining prisoner in the **Allied Prison**.

Guarded by British, French, Soviet and American troops on a monthly rota, he led an eerie hermit's existence. A

Changing of the Guard at Spandau Allied Prison, since torn down.

pardon would only have been possible by a unanimous decision on the part of the four Allied powers. However, although Hess was over 90 and half-blind, the Soviets blocked his release for 40 years. So the old man's last days were divided between the dark brick building, where he was under heavy guard, and the British military hospital. On the first day of every month there was a ceremonial Changing of the Guard, a rather sorry spectacle which Hess himself finally put an end to through his suicide on 17 August 1987. The building has since been torn down. In its place a shopping centre is to be built here for the families of British soldiers.

Town among fields: A trip to **Gatow** and **Kladow** reveals the delicate charm of the area around the Havel. The BVG ferry line operates a regular passenger service from Wannsee. Both villages in Spandau's deep south were incorporated into the district in 1920. They still lead an independent existence, centred on their historic churches, although more and more villas and bungalows are forcing their way between the last few remaining farmhouses.

About 40 per cent of Spandau is either water or greenery. Two fishermen, the last of their kind, still cast their nets over the Havel in the early morning mist. The district has 69 working farms, cultivating a total of 650 hectares (1,605 acres).

Billowing wheat fields are no strange sight around Kladow in summer, and in Gatow you might get a farmer to sell you milk from his cows or fresh free-range eggs. In the former sewage fields around Gatow, rare ferns and birds have reappeared. The **Gatower Heide** (heath), a 350-hectare (865-acre) nature reserve is a beautiful place to enjoy long walks.

Any description of Spandau would be incomplete without mentioning its industrial counterpart to the east, **Siemensstadt**. In 1899, the rapidly expanding electrical firm of Siemens and Halske opened a cable and dynamo factory on the Nonnendammallee. Land along the Spree then cost seven pfennigs per square yard, but the workers had to contend with a long walk or to commuting by steamer.

By 1906, the factory at the gates of Charlottenburg employed 10,000 people. It was absorbed by Spandau and officially christened "Siemens Town". In the 1920s it developed into a model of a green-field factory town, with its own housing areas which now spread from Siemensdamm to Jungfernheide. The skyline of the "electropolis" is dominated by Hans Hertlein's functional cubic brick architecture.

Its most distinctive feature is the **Siemensturm** (tower) at the Werner-Werk für Messwerktechnik (Werner instrument plant), which is over 70-metres (233-ft) high. About 60,000 people were employed in Siemensstadt during the 1930s. Today, the number has fallen to just 20,000. Siemens has moved its headquarters to Munich but remains the largest employer in Berlin's electrical industry.

pandau
ock.

KÖPENICK

East Berlin's largest district is familiar to the rest of the world only for the pranks of the cobbler Wilhelm Voigt, the "Captain of Köpenick". But Köpenick has more to offer than this tragi-comedy from the days of the German Empire. It is Berlin's greenest district with woods and lakes covering three-quarters of the once-independent district in the southeast of the metropolis, between the river Dahme and the Spree. There is also plenty to see here: the historic old town, the castle island, the regatta course at Grünau, the open-air pools by the lakes and the Müggelberge hills with their numerous inns. In addition, some large businesses, such as the VEB Oberspree cable factory (known as AEG before the war), boatyards, traditional laundries and clothing manufacturers have moved in on the edge of the district.

Like the people of Spandau, the 130,000 residents of Köpenick are proud of their individuality. Both places are notably older than Berlin and still unhappy about having been incorporated into the capital in 1920.

The old town: Köpenick was officially mentioned for the first time in 1209. Archaeological excavations, however, have ascertained that a stronghold stood here as early as the year 800. The town of Köpenick did not receive its charter until around 1300, but there is no record of this. In the middle of the old town centre, where the river Dahme joins the Spree, is the brick **Rathaus** and its red tower. In 1904, barely two years after its completion, the town hall became famous the world over when the unemployed cobbler Voigt marched on it in a borrowed captain's uniform, with an escort of soldiers whom he had commandeered picked up off the streets. Voigt had the mayor arrested and took control of the town coffers, in order to obtain a pass. Voigt was soon caught but

the story swept around the world as a striking example of the Prussian propensity to follow without question anyone in uniform.

The Emperor himself is said to have laughed over the trick. Carl Zuckmayer's farce based on the event, *Der Hauptmann von Köpenick* (*The Captain of Köpenick*), was premiered in Berlin in 1931. Every year during the last week in July, a ceremony takes place outside the Rathaus to mark the start of the "Köpenicker Sommer" festival week.

The actor portraying the captain leads the carnival procession and is handed a box containing the citizens' contributions in response to the cry: "Join in and make our capital beautiful" – a custom that may well have disappeared along with the SED. Hopefully, the custom of duck roasting in the Ratskeller (town hall cellars), famed far beyond Köpenick, will be preserved. Incidentally, it is not inexpensive.

Immediately next to the Rathaus, alongside Luisenhain, the tourist steam-

ers of the Weiße Flotte ("White Fleet") tie up several times daily, although only from May to September. In good weather, it's always worth taking a ride through the sprawling countryside in the direction of Müggelsee, Woltersdorf or Schmöckwitz – coffee and cakes are included in your ticket. Meanwhile, confirmed land-lubbers may like to take a look around the Protestant church next to the neo-Gothic Rathaus, which dates from 1841, and the **Heimatkundliches Kabinett** (local museum), only open on Tuesdays from 9 a.m. to 6 p.m.

These ridiculous opening times are not the only evidence of the Köpenican sense of humour. Among the exhibits are the "Seven Wonders of Köpenick", which include pictures of a teacher called Dumm ("stupid"), a doctor called Todt ("death") and one of an old spinster, who founded the Köpenick Young Men's Brigade at the age of 80. Her motives remain unclear: it's left to your imagination!

From the Rathaus, cross the busy Müggelheimer Strasse to reach the old **Köpenicker Kiez**. The grey single-storey, mostly badly neglected, dwellings which line a cobbled street date in part from the 17th and 18th century. The houses back onto the **Frauentog**, a bay that separates the Schloßinsel from the mainland, where Köpenick's fishermen formerly cast their nets. The Kiez – the word comes from the Slavonic *Chyza*, meaning "hut" – was built in 1260. The baths on the Dahme River behind were closed down after the purity of the water was found to be questionable.

Jaczo de Copanic: A narrow wooden bridge leads over to the **Schloßinsel** (castle island), the site of the **Wendenschloß**, which was built on stilts around AD 825. A few remains of the castle have been uncovered, but sadly they are no longer on display. Around 1100, the castle was run by the legendary Count Jaczo de Copanic. Copanic, from whence comes the name Köpenick, is Slav for "island place". But myth insists on another origin for the name: a magic

Müggelsee fresh-water pool.

giant crab was caught by a fisherman and taken to market, where it is supposed to have kept calling "Kööp nich, kööp nich" ("Don't buy, don't buy"). The fisherman refused to listen and suffered one mishap after another. Jaczo won hegemony in Brandenburg by defeating the Christian army of the Askanian Albrecht the Bear.

In 1157 Albrecht succeeded in ousting Jaczo from Köpenick. After the battle in Groß-Glienicke, he is alleged to have swum the Havel on his horse. He hung his shield and hunting horn on an oak on "Schildhorn" peninsula – in what is now the Grunewald – and was converted to Christianity, which he swore he would do if he was fortunate enough to survive.

The Wendenschloß was pulled down in the mid-16th century. Today, the only reminders of the lost castle are the signposts "Zum Wendenschloß" – "To Wendenschloß". These signs direct you to the villa neighbourhood of the same name and to a fresh-water swimming pool, by the side of which you can obtain refreshments.

In 1558, Elector Joachim II built a splendid moated castle on the same spot, which also didn't last for long. The present baroque pile was built for the Grand Elector Friedrich Wilhelm by the architect Rutger von Langerfeld between 1677 and 1682. There's a particularly fine view of the warm yellow facade from the water. In 1806 the French laid waste to Köpenick on their campaign of conquest towards Moscow, and occupied the castle. From 1830 to 1848, after the war of liberation against Napoleon, it served the Prussians as a prison for young rebels, and was later used as a teaching college and a student hostel.

The castle was restored after World War II. Today three floors of the extravagant rococo interior house the **Kunstgewerbemuseum** (Museum of Arts and Crafts, open Wed–Sun, 10 a.m.–6 p.m.). Here you can marvel at the wood-carved antique furniture, which includes a wonderful Biedermeier

desk with inlaid panels and countless secret drawers, tiled stoves, porcelain, glass, silverware and Empress Griselda's famous jewellery from the 11th century. Against this romantic backdrop, regular weekend chamber concerts are held in the restored chapel throughout July and August, and, on the stage outside, evening serenades are performed under the open skies. You can enjoy a peaceful cup of coffee in the cosy Schloßcafe next to the chapel, which has a lovely view over the Dahme.

Close to the S-Bahn station on the Spree, opposite the island with the tree nursery, is the Platz des 23. April (square) which commemorates the anniversary of Köpenick's "liberation" by the Soviet army, while a stone column 6 metres (20 ft) high recalls the "Köpenicker Blutwoche" ("Bloody Week") in June 1933, when 90 people, mostly communists and Social Democrats, were murdered by Hitler's SA. The monument depicts a symbolically clenched, raised fist. Underneath are scenes from everyday life in the Democratic Republic. Close at hand, you can refresh yourself with sausages, chips or a cold drink at the old-established "Mecklenburgischer Bauernmarket" (farmers' market), right on the banks of the Spree.

In the northwest of Köpenick, on the border with Lichtenberg, is the **Volkspark Wuhlheide**, an idyllic area of woodland where you will find the **Freizeit- und Erholungszentrum** (FEZ), a children's recreational centre. Attractions here include a small lake, a mini-tourist village and a disco to enable Berlin's kids to let off steam. The very young will love the "Pioniereisenbahn", a narrow-gauge railway that runs 7-km (5-mile) circuits of the grounds.

Müggelsee and environs: Three kilometres southeast of Köpenick lies Berlin's largest lake, Müggelsee, which covers an area of 7 sq. metres (8 sq. yds). It is also the city's main supply of drinking water. For years it has been threatened by an acute pollution problem, and motorboats have been banned since 1989. Along the shore, several not particularly cheap restaurants, such as the Müggelseeperle and the Rübezahl, invite weary daytrippers to partake of their hearty fare. By the fresh-water swimming pool on the west beach, the Spree River flows out of the lake.

Friedrichshagen and Rahnsdorf: Located midway between the town of Köpenick and the Müggelsee, Friedrichshagen was founded in 1753 by Friedrich II as a spinners' village. At this time the whole of Köpenick was experiencing a boom as a centre of the textile industry, particularly the silk spinners. The avenue of 200-year-old Chinese mulberry trees on Bölschestrasse, now in a sorry state, is all that remains to remember these affluent days.

Anarchist stronghold: Before the turn of the century, many artists and anarchists moved in to the little village, which at that time couldn't be reached by road. Among them were Erich Mühsam, Frank Wedekind, Arno Holz, Detlow von Liliencron and Gustav

Köpenick old town.

Landauer. The last named published the magazine *Der Sozialist* and is said to have answered the telephone with the words: "This is the revolution – who's that?" Gerhard Hauptmann also lived here for a time. The community was known as the "Friedrichshagener Dichterkreis" (Poets' Circle) but after 1900 it slowly broke up. Nowadays, Friedrichshagen is country-cottage territory, as too is **Rahnsdorf** which lies between the eastern side of Müggelsee and the Müggelspree. From Rahnsdorf S-Bahn station you can take an immaculate, almost 100-year-old tram to **Woltersdorf**, a rather sleepy place on the banks of the Flakensee.

South of the Müggelsee, in the middle of the vast Berliner Stadtwald (city forest), loom the Müggelberge hills, another favourite with daytrippers from Berlin. In winter you can even sledge here – provided there's snow. The hills rise to 110 metres (360 ft) above the mirror of the lake. In Brandenburg terms, that's almost Alpine. On a clear day there's a wonderful view from the **Müggelturm** (tower) all the way from the radio tower at Königswusterhausen to the Rüdersdorf cement works. Köpenick's woodland and its recreational facilities will soon have their tranquility destroyed, as for some time now curious west Berliners have been flocking to the area.

Langer See, Seddinsee, Zeuthener See: These three lakes converge on the old fishing village of **Schmöckwitz**, southeast of Köpenick town which has been settled since pre-historic times. Seddinsee to the east is linked to Müggelsee by the Gosener canal; Langer See to the west flows into the Dahme, with the result that it is possible to make a relaxing circular trip by boat, starting from Köpenick. Every year in June the Grünau international rowing regatta takes place on Langer See. In the other summer months it is possible to hire rowing boats on the lake and just outside the town of Grunau is a somewhat disappointing beach.

Friedrichshagen waterworks, erected in 1893 in English country house gothic.

MARZAHN, HELLERSDORF AND HOHENSCHÖNHAUSEN

*"Wreath, take your place,
on the new house!
The first house of many
on this huge estate.
Where once was marshy ground,
a new town will rise –
part of our great capital,
for it's much in need.
A hundred thousand people
will soon be moving in,
And their lives should be,
spick and span and safe."*

With this topping-out ceremony, the traditional wreath was set above the flats on the new Marzahn estate on 2 September 1977. In the decade that followed, 60,000 apartments which accommodate 160,000 people were built in Marzahn.

The district of Marzahn was founded in 1979, while the neighbouring districts of Hohenschönhausen and Hellersdorf were founded in 1985–86. Today, 400,000 people live in the three districts. Three-quarters of them have moved during the past 15 years and building continues apace. In particular, young families with children have settled in these districts. Hellersdorf currently has the youngest average age in the district with two-thirds of the population being under 26.

"Marxzahn": This satellite town in East Berlin was the heartland of an ambitious housing programme devised by the East German government. By 1990, in the space of less than 20 years, the housing shortage in the GDR was theoretically to have been eliminated. The subsequent expansion of Berlin which would follow the housing programme would serve to emphasise "the growing political and economic strength of the socialist German state of workers and farmers," according to the Central Committee's resolution of 3 February 1976.

Building workers from all over East Germany were assembled to turn the project into reality. The building industry was ordered to concentrate entirely on the construction of new building. As a result of the decline in traditional crafts, houses in older districts and in the provinces had fallen into disrepair, while on the outskirts of Berlin enormous housing complexes sprang up.

There was no time for the niceties of town planning, nor was there the scope or materials for anything other than rows of high-rise blocks across the landscape. Box-like houses, "six-floorers", "10-floorers" and 30-storey "beacons" were pieced together like a jigsaw on the drawing board into entire housing estates, together with the usual shopping centres and hospitals, crèches and schools. What was lacking above all else, and is still lacking today, is local employment. Half of the population commutes into Berlin.

There's a good overall view of the

Left, Marzahn idyll. Right, residents make their own improvements.

new estates from the vantage point of three "rubble mountains" which stand on the border between Marzahn and Hellersdorf: Ahrendsfelder Berg in the north, Hellesdorfer Berg alongside the Berlin Garden Show grounds, and the hill alongside Wuhletal S-Bahn station. The flat, scarred landscape is broken only by the concrete mountains of tightly packed high-rise towers.

First impressions of Marzahn may be totally negative, but they are somewhat relieved the further the visitor ventures into the district. There are spaces between the blocks, thus granting views which it would not be possible to have in the city. Gardens and open spaces are plentiful and varied although it is quite obvious that the trees and shrubs weren't planned on the drawing board, but were planted by the residents themselves. Balconies, too, have been planted with tubs and window boxes.

During its first few years, Marzahn was denounced as "the largest concrete desert in Europe", a political project that had completely failed to take into account the human needs of the residents. Those responsible were accused of "intensively farming" the population, forcing people together like chickens on a battery farm. At that time, the unattractive cubes stood in a sea of sand and mud.

People moved into the flats before the roads were even tarmacked. There was no street lighting, no playgrounds for the children, no trees, grass or even shops. Marzahn was a place to which no one wanted to move, at any cost, even if their old apartment was damp and had no heating.

Nowadays, however, few of them would leave Marzahn. Local facilities have been sorted out, and the locals consider themselves to be Marzahners. They are proud of their district, for they themselves have made it habitable. They planted the trees themselves, tended the flower beds, laid cables for street lighting, and painted the inner courtyards and entrance halls.

Outdoor restaurants in Marzahn.

278

Parents guarded the first playground night after night to keep the children away until the cement had properly set. The new neighbours formed their own housing committees which could deal with problems such as childcare and help for the elderly. Cellars were converted into club rooms, roof terraces began to sprout and barbecues were held out of doors.

In addition, there was a wide range of cultural activities on offer in the **Kreiskulturhaus** (community arts centre) and the youth clubs, which also attracted members from other areas.

As in other satellite towns, there are people who find the uniformity of the new architecture depressing. But it doesn't necessarily have to be completely anonymous: in many blocks, people co-exist like one big family. Old-established Marzahners, who have been helping to build and to plant for 10 years, no longer find their surroundings particularly hostile. Their lives have grown as the district has evolved and a once hostile impersonal neighbourhood has become their friendly home.

The best starting points for a walk through Marzahn are Springpfuhl or Marzahn S-Bahn stations. Here you'll find **Helene-Weigel-Platz** and the **Marzahner Promenade**, the two shopping and recreation centres of the new district where shops, department stores, galleries and cafés abound. On the other side of Leninallee or the Allee der Kosmonauten is **Alt-Marzahn**, the Old Town.

Village idyll: Here, hemmed in by the high-rise blocks, is a wonderful little village built around a village green which was officially mentioned for the first time in the 14th century as Murtzana, Morczane or Mortzan.

Excavations have also uncovered traces of early history, remains of pre-Christian settlements and an 8,000-year-old stag mask. From 1764, during the reign of Frederick the Great, colonists from Pfalz settled on this spot. On the old village street stands August Stüler's

ottages
ake life
weet.

lovely brick church, and approximately 60 old houses and courtyards from the mid-19th century, among them the particularly inviting village inn, the **Marzahner Krug**.

The village of 160 people was painstakingly restored in tandem with the construction of the new estates. Most of the old houses had to be completely demolished and rebuilt stone by stone. In the midst of the peaceful village, it is possible to forget the architectural monstrosity which lies just beyond it. Only now and then does the top of one of the "beacons" loom over the roof of a barn.

A few minutes' walk from Alt-Marzahn, on Otto-Buchwitz-Strasse, is a side entrance to the showgrounds of the **Berliner Gartenschau** (Garden Show). For a minimal entry charge you can visit the show gardens, special displays and water fountains. For the children, there are playgrounds and a children's zoo, where they can stroke the patient goats.

The showground is easily accessible

on foot from the new S-Bahn and U-Bahn station at Wuhetal. Standing on the station platforms it is possible to view the fertile ground and varied vegetation, running alongside the new housing estates at Hellersdorf, half-a-mile (one kilometre) wide.

From the "Wuhlgarten", a thickly wooded park, peer the ruined church tower and neo-Romanesque dome of a castle-like building. This is part of the Institute for the Treatment and Care of Epileptics, now the Central Clinic for Psychiatry and Neurology. Patients live in neat brick villas set among high trees, but the public are free to wander where they like in the grounds and enjoy the soothing effect which the peaceful surroundings have on the nerves.

Alternatively, the visitor can take the opposite direction from Wuhletal station and go towards **Kaulsdorf** and **Mahlsdorf**. Both places belong to the new district of Hellersdorf. As in neighbouring Biesdorf, which also comes under Marzahn, courtyards, villas and houses and gardens from the turn of the century are typical.

In the summer months this is a veritable land of milk and honey: walk past the brimming gardens, and apples and cherries practically fall off the trees into your mouth. The village lies on the main road to Frankfurt and provides views across cornfields to the surrounding countryside.

Here, on the old village street of Kaulsdorf the first packets of sugar made from sugar beet were sold in 1796. This was a discovery of the Kaulsdorf farmer Franz Karl Achard (1753–1821). From being the luxury article that it was at first, sugar developed into a staple food.

Attractions of particular interest include the Gründerzeitmuseum (Museum of Industrial History) in Mahlsdorf and **Schloß Biesdorf**, a small castle which was built in 1868 in late Classical style. This belonged from 1887 until 1927 to the industrialist Werner von Siemens, who conducted the first experiments with wireless telegraphy from the castle tower. The castle now houses Marzahn's arts centre, a library, meeting rooms and a restaurant. In the largely deserted, rather overgrown castle grounds there's also an adventure playground and an open-air stage.

North of Kaulsdorf and Mahlsdorf is the **Hellersdorf Development Zone**. This is still as grim and as horrendous as Marzahn was a few years ago. However, the first bushes have now been planted outside some of the houses, and on a couple of balconies, residents have already had their paintbrushes out.

Hohenschönhausen: The contrast between rural communities and satellite towns common to all three new districts, is less obvious in Hohenschönhausen, because of its proximity to the city centre. The names of its four neighbourhoods – Falkenberg, Hohenschönhausen, Malchow and Wartenberg – come from the original villages, which date back to the Middle Ages.

The most pleasant route from the city centre (from Friedrichstrasse station) is on the No. 70 tram. This goes right up to the north, to the lake at Malchower See, which lies between the new estates at Wartenberg and the old village of Malchow. On the way it touches the prettiest corner of the whole district, the area around **Orankesee**.

The tiny lake and open-air pool with its brightly-coloured basket chairs look like something out of Toytown and you really can fish and swim here. The neighbouring lake, Obersee, is set in the middle of a park.

Somewhat further on you will come upon a jumble of allotments, cemeteries, blocks of flats, 19th-century tenements, factories and shopping streets – a lively street neighbourhood, whose somewhat harsh urban profile is nevertheless toned down by the abundance of surrounding greenery.

In the nature reserve around Faulen See you can listen to the chorus of more than 100 species of birds and, in the background, to the distant rumbling of traffic on the main road.

Left, all set for a nap in the flower beds. *Below*, the industrial museum in Hellersdorf is back in private hands.

POTSDAM

Now that the Wall has come down, Potsdam is once again very close to Berlin. Surrounded by lakes and fields, the town is easily accessible to the population of both eastern and western districts by train and bus. Visitors to Berlin should on no account miss a day trip to Potsdam. Its attractions include not only the famous castles and gardens at Sanssouci, but also a remarkable old town, where the streets and squares reflect a faded charm.

Potsdam is a curious blend of a mighty Prussian garrison town and a royal residence in all its pomp and finery. Admittedly, the splendour is wearing thin in many places, but that too reflects a part of its varied history. For centuries, Potsdam's fate was closely bound with the rise and decline of Prussia. Last but not least, the devastation of World War II and the misjudged building schemes of the socialist era have left their mark.

History: In October 1990, Potsdam once again became the capital of the newly re-formed "Land" or county of Brandenburg. Until then, for almost 40 years, it had been the capital of the East German district of Potsdam. In 1993, the town will celebrate its 1,000th anniversary. This date refers to records from the year 993, in which the placename "Poztupimi" (generally interpreted as Potsdam) is mentioned for the first time. Little is known of the origins of the Slavonic settlement of Poztupimi. German feudal lords conquered the area in the 12th century.

The first official records mentioning Potsdam by name date from the 14th century. Its inhabitants lived on fish they caught, and off the land. The town lay off the main travel routes and was not strategically important.

The situation changed dramatically in the second half of the 17th century, when Elector Friedrich Wilhelm elevated Potsdam to the status of royal

Preceding pages: Potsdam's main attraction: "carefree" Sanssouci; *Flute Concert at Sanssouci*, a painting by Adolf Menzel (Frederick the Great is in the middle). Below, the Big Three at the Potsdam Conference.

seat of the house of Brandenburg-Prussia. Why he should have chosen this little town in particular we can only guess. Certainly, the surrounding countryside with its extensive woodland played a part: the Hohenzollerns were keen hunters. Another factor may have been the town's lack of economic and political significance. There was no self-important bourgeoisie who might have opposed the Elector's absolutist rule. As a result, Potsdam's architecture was almost exclusively moulded by the court and royal taste and its economy developed according to the needs of the court and its garrisons.

The earliest example of Electoral architecture, the **Potsdamer Stadtschloß** (town castle) on Alter Markt, which dated from 1660, no longer stands. It was badly damaged in April 1945 in the great air raid on the city. The ruins were removed in 1961, a decision that is still a subject of argument today. Since summer 1990, however, the possibility has been discussed of pulling down the der-

elict new theatre which now occupies the site and rebuilding the original facade of the Stadtschloß around a modern hotel.

The two other buildings that dominate the Alter Markt, the old town hall and the church of St Nikolai, were rebuilt in the 1960s and 1970s. The **Alte Rathaus** was built during the reign of King Friedrich II to resemble an Italian *palazzo*. Its tower, on top of which a gilded Atlas supports a globe, is one of the town's main landmarks and can be seen from a distance. In the process of reconstruction, the architects linked the building to the neighbouring Knobelsdorffhaus. Together, they serve the town as an arts centre.

The **Nikolaikirche** must be one of the most important achievements of the neoclassical era. The stately central building and dome were erected in the mid-19th century according to plans of Friedrich Schinkel. The church is now used for concerts and recitals.

A couple of hundred yards to the west

ne victorious
owers
etermined
ermany's
ture at
ecilienhof
astle.

are the former royal stables which were originally built as an orangery towards the end of the 18th century. Today the **Marstall** houses a **Film Museum**. For Potsdam is, last but not least, a film town. The giant DEFA (called UFA until 1945) studios are situated in Babelsberg on the Havel, not far from the Alter Markt.

Socialist building crimes: On Lange Brücke (Long Bridge) towers one of the ugliest, most ill-conceived examples of modern architecture: the Potsdam Interhotel, a boring concrete box completed in 1969 and "a witness to the socialist reconstruction of Potsdam," as an old East German travel guide proudly notes. That such monstrosities can destroy the architectural harmony of a town only filtered through to the official consciousness of the GDR planning authorities in the 1980s. Their pride in concrete tower blocks, insensitively set down side by side with existing buildings, is attributable to a belief in progress, a belief that has left its sorry marks in the

West, too. But in this instance, another factor comes into play, namely the inconsistent attitude of the East Germans towards Prussian tradition, of which Potsdam is essentially a symbol. Quite correctly, these traditions were regarded are being the embodiment of militarism, servility and power politics. But instead of taking a critical stance towards this aspect of the nation's past, it remained repressed until the 1980s.

An example is the fate of the Potsdam **Hof- und Garnisonskirche** (Court and Garrison Church), which formerly stood on Wilhelm-Külz-Strasse along from Lange Brücke. The church was built in the 1830s by architect Philipp Gerlach and, with its renowned carillon, represented a remarkable architectural achievement. It achieved regrettable notoriety on 21 March 1933 – "Potsdam Day" – when Hitler and Hindenburg agreed to the symbolic alliance between fascism and Prussian militarism within its walls. In 1945 the church was gutted by fire after an air raid. Only the tower

Musical instrument maker Martin Schmidt in Potsdam.

remained in one piece. In 1968, in the face of considerable local protest, it was knocked down and a computer centre erected in its place. Those who campaigned for it to be preserved were reprimanded. The official line was that the demons of fascism and militarism were being destroyed along with the tower, as though these demons weren't more likely to have lived in men's heads than in the sacred stones.

The **Kommandantenhaus** (Commander's House) in Otto-Nuschke-Strasse, a side street off Wilhelm-Külz-Strasse, has another story to tell. The Dutch-style brick construction dates from the first half of the 18th century, when it served as the residence of the commander of the guards regiment. Later, the district court moved into the building. During the years of the fascist regime, resistance campaigners were interned in the cell block behind the courts. Injustice and violence sadly persisted when the Soviet Secret Service moved in to the Kommandantenhaus in

1945 and in 1952 the State Security Force took over the building. The Potsdam population remembers with fear the trials and detentions that took place here, often over trivialities. The demonstrations in autumn 1989 unlocked the cell doors. Popular campaign groups and political parties set up offices in the Kommandantenhaus. The intention is to turn the cell wing into a memorial to the victims of fascist and Stalinist violence.

The Kommandantenhaus lies in the middle of the town's "second baroque development", an historic quarter bordered by Wilhelm-Pieck-Strasse, Schopenhauerstrasse, Hegelallee and Hebbelstrasse. Work on the area began in 1734 during the reign of King Friedrich Wilhelm I. The soldier king needed space for his royal guard, known as the "Tall Boys", and other troops, which he wanted to moved to Potsdam from various towns around Brandenburg. He ordered the building of two and three-storey baroque houses. Crafts-

ll over
urope,
olish
raftsmen are
estoring
lassical art.

men and tradesmen moved in and soldiers were stationed in the fitted gabled houses.

The main shopping street is Brandenburger Strasse, which runs from the Brandenburg Gate to St Paul's church. In the late 1970s, when there was a change of building policy in the GDR, the street was carefully restored and turned into a pedestrian zone. At that time it was still called Klement-Gottwald-Strasse, which name it once more bears today. But walk a few yards down one of the side streets, and with every step you'll notice signs of decay and despair. Although the whole "development" is protected by a preservation order, there is only enough money for the main show-case street.

The Dutch Quarter: It was only after protests at home and abroad that work hesitantly started on saving the unique Holländisches Viertel (Dutch quarter) between Friedrich-Ebert-Strasse and Hebbelstrasse, whose 134 red-brick houses formed a district of their own. The rest of the area, however, is falling into ruin, and more and more houses have been pulled down in recent years. On Gutenbergstrasse and Hermann-Elflein-Strasse the gaps have been filled by modern timber constructions, which although following the old style vaguely in terms of height and design look plain and stark. Only after the recent political changes was the local campaign group Argus able to halt the demolition in the town centre. For many houses it was already too late. Of the 389 baroque houses still intact in 1945, fewer than 300 survived. As late as August 1989, Theodor Sturm Haus on Dorfaustrasse was ripped down, in spite of considerable public protest and although it was in no way unsafe.

Sanssouci: The vast grounds of Sanssouci offer wonderful walks at any time of year. You can wander for hours among the castles and historic buildings, along avenues and walkways, exploring little side turnings, discovering another new view over the summer houses, sculptures and follies. The park's special attraction lies in the total harmony of landscape and architecture, which is at the same time incredibly varied.

Sans souci ("without cares") is the name that Friedrich II gave to the summer palace, built for him by Knobelsdorff between 1745 and 1747 which, in turn, gives its name to the entire estate. Friedrich did not intend the palace as somewhere to entertain official guests, but as a rural retreat, where he could enjoy life, occupy himself with the arts, and enjoy intellectually stimulating conversation with fellow philosophers. The most famous of these was Voltaire who was Friedrich's guest from 1750 to 1753. However, the two did not get along and Voltaire wrote of Sanssouci: "There are an extraordinary number of bayonets but very few books". The Emperor, possibly as a riposte, said: "When you have sucked an orange, you throw away the peel" and said that "Voltaire had the slyness and the ill will of an ape".

The Palace, a single storey building with a massive green central dome, radiates the serene ease of the rococo, an impression amplified by the vineyard in which it sits, the sweeping flights of steps between six terraces, the carefully shaped hedges, pergolas and goldfish ponds. On the garden front the palace cornice is supported by 35 massive caryatides and on the dome the name *Sanssouci* is inscribed in gold letters. At the foot of the terrace is the Parterre, an ornamental basin surrounded by white marble statues, some of which have suffered from atmospheric pollution, with a jeté in the middle. The rococo interior of the palace (some rooms open to the public: conducted tours only) reflects Frederick's personal taste and reveals that this was not a family residence but a hideaway to satisfy the whims of the king.

The main one-mile long avenue from the large fountain to the **Neues Palais** (New Palais) takes you past the

Chinesisches Teehaus (Chinese tea house), its golden figures glimmering through the trees and bushes. The little round pavilion is an example of the Chinese fashion which was affected at European courts in the 18th century. Among the golden animal figures adorning the eaves is a large monkey with Voltaire's features. The pleasure gardens, which were largely the work of Knobelsdorff, end with the geometrically clipped hedges. The adjacent parkland was laid out by Peter Josef Lenné in the first half of the 19th century. The spacious lawns, groves and coppices and the little stream give the appearance of being natural, rather than artificially devised. Around the buildings, Lenné created individual gardens to complement their respective architectural styles.

Work on the **Neues Palais** began immediately after the Prussian victory in the Seven Years' War, the second most elegant building in the park. Friedrich II, whose epithet "the Great" originates from this time, is said to have described the palace as a "fanfaronnade", a showing-off. The palace was intended to demonstrate to the world that, despite the burdens of the war, Prussia's strength was in no way diminished. Built by Carl von Gontard in 1765–69 it is even more imposing than Schloß Sanssouci having two storeys and a dome topped by a statue of the Three Graces holding aloft Frederick's crown. The rooms, some of which can be visited, were furnished in corresponding splendour.

Behind the Neues Palais is the **Commun**, also the work of Gontard, domestic buildings which housed the royal household and servants.

Other buildings that arose at Sanssouci in the 19th century are closely associated with Karl Friedrich Schinkel and his pupils. Particularly outstanding are the Charlottenhof, a classical palace, the Roman baths, built to resemble an Italian villa, and the Friedenskirche (Peace Church), based on a Roman basilica. Most monumental of them all is the **Neue Orangerie** (New Orangery).

Carl Haider, pastrycook and chef of his own café.

Only one of the enormous plant rooms still houses palms and orange trees. The main part of the building is used by the Potsdam State Archives. This department, idyllically located in the solitude of the park, was a much sought-after place of exile by discredited SED functionaries, who could here live out their remaining years until retirement.

Cecilienhof: Cecilienhof in the Neues Garten is the only castle in Potsdam to have remained in the possession of the imperial family after 1918. It was confiscated in 1945. The Neues Garten is the town's second main park, lying between the lakes of Heilige See and Jungfernsee. The castle was built for Crown Prince Wilhelm just before World War I. While people in the country starved and soldiers died at the front, the royal heir who never came to the throne, treated himself to this luxury.

Cecilienhof entered the world history books in 1945 when the heads of state of the three victorious powers convened there to decide the future of conquered Germany in the *Potsdamer Abkommen* (Potsdam Agreement). The crown prince and his family had fled the castle shortly before the Soviet troops marched in, taking all the furnishings with them. It was hastily refurbished to enable the delegation to carry out their task. You can visit the original conference room with the famous round table, as well as the studies of Stalin, Churchill and Truman's, which are unchanged.

According to the Allies, the stipulations of the Potsdam Agreement were to provide the foundations for the democratic development of a united Germany. Until winter 1989, anyone on a tour of this historic house needed only to look out of the window of the Blue Salon to see evidence of a divided German before their very eyes – the Berlin Wall, something that did not feature on the agenda of the foreign leaders. For almost 30 years, the border with West Berlin prevented access to the lake and a part of the park.

Two attractions worth visiting in this area are the **Meierei** (dairy farm) and the **Muschelgrotte** (mussel grotto). The farm occupies a renovated 19th-century inn, in the style of a Norman castle. It suffered in terms of war damage and decades of neglect, as did the Muschelgrotte, particularly after the Wall came down and souvenir-hunters began to dismantle the mussels and crystals at the entrance. Barriers have therefore had to be put up.

"Soft" tourism: Potsdam makes a pleasant excursion for tourists. Art historians and nature-lovers will find plenty here to interest them. And it will remain for a while, until the "tourist infrastructure" – as it is so euphemistically put – reaches western standards. There's a shortage of hotel accommodation and a shortage of restaurants with a decent cuisine. The roads are in a bad condition and there aren't enough car parks to cope with demand. Potsdam's tourist experts would prefer to come to terms with the traffic problem by offering alternatives. "Soft" tourism is to be promoted – walking or cycling.

Below, The Royal Stables now house a film museum Right, Russian soldiers in front of the Neues Palais

292

THE PEOPLE'S OWN DREAM FACTORY

The DEFA production being filmed on the set of the cinema city at Potsdam-Babelsberg, the largest in Europe, is called *The Adventures of a Peace-Lover*. A lady in period costume with tightly laced stays is preparing her entrance. The script, set in the Napoleonic era, was officially banned for 12 years. Now, as a result of the bloodless revolution, it can be produced.

In 1912, when German film-making was in its infancy, the film company Bioscop opened its first atelier in Babelsberg. A little later the German general staff attributed the disastrous course of World War I to poor propaganda. In order to avoid repetitions of the problem in future, the UFA (Universum Film AG) was set up under the auspices of the Deutsche Bank. From 1921 the company transformed Babelsberg into its central film factory and

continued to produce films until Soviet multiple rocket launchers rolled onto the site. The old management of UFA had its headquarters quietly moved across to West Berlin.

A "film work team" took over what was left in the Eastern sector. One of those involved was Kurt Maetzig, who under the Nazis was only allowed to work as cameraman in a small company which made cartoons – despite a higher degree and production experience – because his mother was of Jewish extraction. The "work team" formed the core of the DEFA (Deutsche Film AG), which received its official licence to make films from the Soviet authorities on 17 May 1946. At a ceremony in a Babelsberg studio a communist party official said: "Films should no longer serve as the opium of the masses, but should give our people strength, courage, determination and pleasure."

Film production had already begun before the celebrations. The news outside broadcast team and its leader, Kurt Maetzig, travelled around in a van with a wooden carburettor, and often arrived too late: Mrs Roosevelt's press conference was already over when they appeared. It is hardly surprising that the weekly news programme sometimes appeared only once a month.

On 4 May 1946 the clapboard fell in Babelsberg for the first post-war German feature film. *The Killers Amongst Us* is about war criminals who returned to their civilian jobs as if nothing had happened. The producer, Wolfgang Staudte, was refused permission to film in the Western sector. The DEFA thus gained a head start which was recognised in international circles. A number of other highly-regarded films followed and by June 1947 Babelsberg had 1,500 employees.

By now the Cold War was heating up, and the newly created German Democratic Republic firmly controlled the DEFA. The political film was succeeded by the party political feature, and critical realism gave way to social realism.

Left, on set, preparing for the next shoot.

Solutions and justice were no longer sought after; everyone knew what it was all about. Men like Maetzig still longed for the occasional "artistic experiment", but were forced to toe the political line. From 1955 Staudte worked in the West.

In East and West the film industry was faced with a crisis as a result of the arrival of mass television. In the GDR the problem was exacerbated by the monotony of the dogma and the eternally positive heroes. This made no difference to the size of Babelsberg which now produced 40 to 80 films annually. An article published during the 1950s in the East German *Film Review* advised visitors to the studios, covering half a million square metres, that they would do well to take a "map and compass".

Meanwhile, following the construction of the Wall, the DEFA artists hoped that in the resulting "closed" society they would be permitted to speak and film more openly. "With you I would even go to see a DEFA film", remarked Manfred Krug in 1966 in *Spur der Steine* ("The Trace of the Stones"). A week later the film had disappeared from the cinemas. A further dozen films suffered the same fate. And yet these films, dating from the "thaw" in the GDR, are not really searching for new ways – a middle path between capitalism and a single-party state – but rather suggest possible improvements within the party machine.

After November 1989 banned films suddenly appeared from the archives. *Spur der Steine* was finally a success in both East and West. The attempt to produce better films under production conditions free from market constraints has temporarily failed. Instead of the market, the State exerted the pressure and the artists were unable to assert themselves.

The market economy is now the order of the day, and redundancies frequent. Babelsberg may still be the largest dream factory, but it is also a studio like any other. What remains are the traces of the stones – and the ruined film sets.

THE COUNTRYSIDE

Berlin's coming back to life. West Berliners in particular are being smitten with the travel bug. For almost 30 years East Germany was *terra incognita*, cut off by the Wall. Now Berliners are mobilising, getting behind the wheels of their cars, yachts or mobile vans and sounding out the previously uncharted territory on the other side of the Wall.

In the past a "short break" for many Berliners meant either shutting yourself away for a while, making the obligatory weekend trip to Wannsee via the traffic jams on Havelchaussee, or indulging in an exhausting *tour de force* to West Germany, to border areas such as the Lüneberg Heath, Fichtel mountains or to the western Harz. Who'd chose to make the gruelling journey from your own front door to a foreign country when hindered by the minimum currency exchange and the need for authorisation from the East German authorities? However, now thanks to the democratic revolution in the GDR, the back of beyond is once again within easy reach, real, genuine and there to be experienced.

Like dunces, we read up on our local history, find our bearings on the tourist and walking maps – often pure invention on the part of East German cartographers. We've already dutifully looked at Sanssouci Palace and perhaps taken a punt out in Spreewald. But the blossom in Werder we only know from tales our grandparents have told, and we may have confused the East Berlin idiom KW (for Königswusterhausen) with the "show-case of the West", the KaDeWe. And what about Uckermark, Schorfheide, Barnim? Until now they've only been white splodges on the map and in our minds.

Draw a circle around Berlin to take in everywhere within a 100 km (60 mile) radius. This area is the "Brandenburg Marsch". The "Marsch" is more than just the sandpit it's often described as; it's an area of infinite variety. Alongside wide tracts of sandy land are vast forests of pine and beech and oak, more than 3,000 lakes, clear and not so clear, in which to bathe, as well as little towns and villages, many of which have churches dating back to the 12th and 13th centuries, their medieval brick Gothic facades still beautifully preserved.

West of Berlin, near Potsdam, is the region known as **Havelland**, through which the Havel River winds its way via a series of straggling lakes. This was the largest fruit-growing area in the former GDR. Here is **Brandenburg**, renowned for its charming, medieval architecture, much of which survived wartime bombing. (The joys here are diminished by the knowledge that this was the site of the Nazis' first concentration camp.)

To the north, are the extensive forests of **Ruppiner Schweiz** and the **Schorfheide** heath. The latter was the favourite playground for the SED elite

whose hunting lodges still dot the area. They had inherited the region from the Nazi hierarchy but, long before that, generations of Prussian noblesse had used the heath as their personal *Jagdgebiet* (hunting district).

To the east is the **Märkische Schweiz**, a wooded and hilly conservation area of gorges and deep-carved lakes, and the Oderbuch, a fertile agricultural valley known as "Berlin's fruit-basket" whose several villages look as if they have been preserved in aspic.

To the south lies the **Spreewald**, a unique beautiful forest and lagoon region which can be divided into the **Unterspreewald** and **Oberspreewald**. The latter, to the south of the town **Lubben**, is known as the *Fließe*, because of its more than 300 stretches of water which are fed by the Spree River. Punts (motorised craft are *Verboten*) ferry visitors around the region whose Sorbish street signs are indicative of the fact that most of the population consists of Slavic Sorbs. "What a place!" rever-

entially exclaimed Theodore Fontane's coachman Moll on seeing the countryside which Fontane also described as "Venice as it might have been 1,500 years ago".

Everything a weekend holidaymaker could wish for can be found in the region around Greater Berlin. For example, the 700-year-old **Zisterzienser-Kloster Chorin** (Chorin Cistercian Abbey), in the south of Uckermark, is a unique example of north German Gothic. Every year, tourists armed with folding chairs and picnic baskets attend the concerts of the "Choriner Summer of Music" series, held in the seductive atmosphere of the church cloisters. Or for something entirely different, there's the **Schiffshebewerk Niederfinow** (Niederfinow Ship Elevator), which is a masterpiece of technology. The largest ship lift in central Europe was constructed to negotiate the 36-metres (118-ft) drop between the Oder and Oder-Havel canals. It heaves the barges up in less than five minutes.

There's always time for a natter.

Or there's Buckow, in a charming location on the lake at Scharmützelsee in Märkische Schweiz. Buckow is an old holiday resort for Berliners. Here, in his lakeside home Bert Brecht recovered from his exhausting theatre work. From the top of the **Bollersdorfer Höhe** (heights) and the inn of the same name, there's a lovely panoramic view over Scharmützelsee 129 metres (423 ft) down below.

Only from such comparisons do we discover the shortcomings of our western countryside. "Over there", in what used to be East Germany, there is still unspoilt scenery and rivers like the Müggelsee aren't restrained but allowed to follow their natural course. Avenues and streets still haven't been relieved of all their excess bends and curves, but twist tree-lined to left and to right through fields, as they do around Stausberg. The main roads through the villages of the Marsch haven't been ironed out flat; in the centre the cobblestones have been preserved and provide a natural speed

restriction. An oversight on behalf of the transport department – or environmental foresight? How long will this unspoilt countryside be able to evade technological innovation and modernisation?

Where else can you find the perfect idyll, where time seems to stand still, other than on an expedition through the countryside around Berlin? Sheep and shepherds at the roadside, storks' nests in the church towers and stone barns, reeds on the lake shores where ospreys nest, geese and ducks paddling on the pond on the village green. Relics of unspoilt nature which were able to survive in the shadow of the Wall? Soon to be lost for ever?

As with all idylls, there's no room for over-romanticising. Plaster is crumbling from the facades, and not only from those of the many houses that have been left to the ravages of time. The environment, too, has long since shown its cracks: a good 50 percent of the trees are diseased and one-quarter of the lakes

Concert in
Chorin Abbey.

and rivers are dirty to the point of contamination.

Chance for "soft" tourism: Many of the people who live outside Berlin are worried that their lovely countryside could slip into bad ways. Already, many of the attractions of the Brandenburg Marsch are extremely popular with day-trippers in search of recreation. Many environmentalists and naturalists see the currently poor tourist infrastructure, the dismal provision of restaurants and hotels, as the ideal opportunity to introduce a "soft" form of tourism to the area: in other words an environmentally sound, socially responsible form of tourism, which takes into account both the countryside and its resident population. What is called for is not arbitrary building in the fields, but touristic development, aimed at conserving the natural and social environment. Necessary though the construction of a flourishing road network from the outside may be, the experts argue, equally imperative is a heightened awareness of its ecological

effects. They are fighting to have nature reserves like the former hunting-ground of Schorfheide, and Spreewald – which attracts 1.8 million tourists every year – recognised by UNESCO as biosphere reservations, to protect them from becoming commercialised and built up.

Tourism and sport in their voracious, self-destructive search for unspoilt, untouched land, provide the greatest threat to the countryside. There is no shortage of examples. In the face of massive protest, a world power boat tournament took place on the already abused Schwielowsee south of Potsdam. An estate dealer in Grünefeld near Nauen trod roughshod over a building ban and chopped down trees in the middle of a nature reserve to put up houses, an airfield and campsite with 500 spaces. Berlin golf clubs are moving in, claiming territory for their sport, where previously they have had to be content with a nine-hole course in Wannsee.

The same dilemma faces many local authorities. They are in a weak position

Bert Brecht, too, enjoyed the idyllic surroundings of Buckow or Scharmützels

because agriculture is in dire straits. They grasp at tourism as the last straw and want to convert farming land and make capital from its attractive position. Building contractors and investors sniff the air, knowing that lucrative businesses with tidy returns will be lured by the tourist projects. But controversial areas such as catering and accommodation can not be solved overnight, and environmentalists and builders are likely to be at loggerheads for a long time to come. The pressure on politicians must be intensified, lest joy at the opening of the border should be eclipsed by caterwauling over the destruction of nature. "Biesenthal has only one tourist option," claim community leaders.

But there are lots of Biesenthals. Almost every week another report on a major tourist project hits the press. For example, a safari park and two golf courses in Michendorf or a 5,500 hectare (13,500 acre) leisure park near Tempitz.

How fortunate that the countryside around Berlin is still comparatively "unsuitable" for traffic. Why should it be? When Berlin has an excellent public transport system (buses and S-Bahn), which will have to be modernised and in some places extended.

It's already possible to transport bicycles on the S-Bahn to end-stations at Erkner, Strausberg-Nord or Königswusterhausen and from there get to know the district. Or in four or six hours, longer if you allow for detours and stopping off on the way, to travel right round the outside of Berlin, on a combination of S-Bahn and the legendary double-decker "Sputnik train". Or to take a party on a Weiße Flotte steamer, from Potsdam to Brandenburg for example, or do the seven-hour round trip by boat from Berlin-Grünau via numerous canals and lakes to Bad-Saarow-Pieskow on Scharmützelsee, coming back by bus. Or just to wander on one of the many marked trails around Liepnitzsee, with a detour to the former enclave of the SED party elite at Wandlitz, or to the marshy Briese valley in north Berlin.

Marsch trail: There are no secret trips to be shared. Everyone will find their own enchanted village, own deserted lake shore with bed of reeds or stretch of lonely woodland on their own tour, and piece together Berlin's surrounding countryside for themselves.

"Whether you should travel, you ask, travel in the Brandenburg Marsch? Try it, by all means, and you won't regret it. You will discover plenty along the way, for wherever you go you will be entering into what is, from a traveller's point of view, 'virgin territory'. You will encounter abbey ruins, which are known at most only as far as the next town, and then only slightly; in old village churches… you will find vast wall paintings or in vaults without steps rich copper caskets with crucifixes and gold-encrusted shields; you will cross battlefields, Wendish churchyards, graves on the heath long forgotten by men." (Theodor Fontane, 1864, from his *Walks in the Brandenburg Marsch*).

ght, the
hip Elevator

ederfinow.
llowing
ges: the
eues Palais
Sanssouci.

TRAVEL TIPS

GETTING THERE

BY AIR

Most western visitors to Berlin will arrive at Tegel airport, in former West Berlin. Schoenefeld airport in former East Berlin is continuing to serve countries to the east of Germany. Between them, the two airports have links to much of the world. Principal carriers into Berlin are still those airlines from the Allied countries on the winning side in World War II: the UK, France, US and Soviet Union. Lufthansa, the German national airline, has international routes and operates a domestic service.

From Tegel airport there is a regular bus service to the city centre, from where regular trains run into what used to be East Berlin.

BY SEA

There are ferry connections from northern Germany (Hamburg and Rotterdam) with Scandinavia and the UK (Scandinavian Seaways sailings on the Harwich-Hamburg route). The former East German port of Warnemünde has sailings to Trelleborg in Sweden.

BY TRAIN

From northern Europe, the best train connections to Berlin are from Ostend in Belgium and Hook of Holland in the Netherlands. Daily trains leave in the evening to arrive in Berlin early the following morning.

TRAVEL ESSENTIALS

VISAS & PASSPORTS

Visitors flying into Berlin generally have the easiest time of it; as is the case everywhere else in Germany, only direct flights arriving from foreign countries are subject to passport control. German citizens are required to be in possession of a valid personal identity card, although in accordance with international laws, this ruling may be altered in the future.

CUSTOMS

Customs regulations adhere to the usual European Community guidelines.

GETTING ACQUAINTED

GEOGRAPHY

Berlin is situated in the very heart of Europe. On a map you'll find it located at approximately the same latitude as London and the same longitude as Naples. Before its division in 1945, this flourishing city was both the national capital and geographical middle point of the German Empire, established in 1871. Since the dramatic reunification of the two German countries in 1990, Berlin has reclaimed its status as the national capital.

Berlin is the largest city in all of Germany. It encompasses a total land area of 883 sq. km. From north to south the city measures about 38 km (24 miles), and the city limits in the east and west lie approximately 45 km (28 miles) apart. The two highest points in the vicinity are Große Müggelberg, (115 metres/385 ft), which is located in the east, and Teufelsberg, (120 metres/400 ft) situated in the west. The latter is made from the rubble of houses and buildings bombed during the war. Berlin lies at an average of about 34 metres (115 ft) above sea level. Two-thirds of its total surface area is composed of water, woods and meadows. If you took all the paths running along the banks of various rivers and lakes in Berlin and strung them all together, their total length would measure 324 km (203 miles)!

CONSTITUTION & HISTORY

Berlin can be simultaneously considered both a country and a city. It is situated in the middle of the German state called Brandenburg, of which Potsdam is the capital. Even before the German reunification took place on 3 October 1990, the two half-cities of East and West Berlin – including their respective administrations – had been gradually growing closer together.

The Municipal Authorities (Magistrat) in the East and the Senate (Senat) in the West, (commonly referred to as the Magi-Senat), work together to a large degree unimpeded by political differences. There are plans for a common, unified government to be established following local elections in the wake of reunification. At the present time there are approximately 3.2 million people living in Berlin. It is predicted that by the year 2000, this number will have increased to 5 million.

The city of Berlin is divided into 23 administrative districts, or boroughs, each of which is responsible for making local decisions and carrying out a wide variety of tasks. District authorities and mayors must answer to local district representative assemblies.

For 41 years Berlin made headlines as a divided city and turn-table between the East and West. The city's political split began in 1948 with the commencement of the Cold War and blockade. Ever since this time, there have been two city governments and two different monetary currencies in Berlin. At that time, in 1961, the division of the old empire's capital was sealed with the building of The Wall. However in 1971 at least this period of acute East-West confrontation

in and around Berlin came to a close with the signing of the new four-power agreement. With the falling of The Wall on 9 November 1989, the divided city of Berlin was finally joined together again.

The festivities in the jubilee year 1987 – at that time still celebrated separately – were based on a document dating from 28 October 1237. In this official document, the neighbouring merchant settlement Cölln, situated on the left bank of the Spree, was mentioned for the first time. But both Berlin and Cölln, which were joined together under a common administration in the year 1307 and in 1432 united to form the double-city Berlin-Cölln, had actively existed long before the written records show. Archaeological sites excavated in the past decade indicate that they had already been established as far back as the last third of the 12th century.

A brief glimpse of the 750-year history of Berlin succeeding its unification with Cölln reads as follows:

1470: Residency of the Electors of the Brandenburg Marches.

1709: Royal-Prussian capital.

1740: Friedrich II (Frederick the Great) takes office; as the capital of Prussia, Berlin is awarded European rank.

1871: Capital of the German Empire.

1920: Formation of the unified community "Gross-Berlin", composed of 20 districts.

1933: Seizure of power by the National Socialists.

1944: The London Protocol calls for the division of Germany into occupied zones as well as for a special Berlin area.

1945: Signing of the unconditional capitulation in Berlin-Karlshorst. The founding of the Allied Command and Allied Control Council.

1948: The Soviets withdraw from the Allied Control Council. Beginning of the 11-month long blockade.

1961: The city split by force with the erection of The Wall.

1971: Signing of the Berlin Agreement.

1987: Lavish 750-year jubilee celebration in both parts of the city including prominent guests from the East and West.

1989: The Wall is breached.

1990: The official reunification of both the former half-cities of East and West Berlin. Election of a common government.

TIME ZONES

During the winter months, standard time in Berlin corresponds to Central European Time (MEZ), and from April until September to Central European Summer Time (MESZ). When it is 12 noon (MEZ) in Berlin (or in Paris, Rotterdam, Madrid or Rome, for that matter), it is:

11 a.m. in London
8 a.m. in Buenos Aires and Sao Paulo
6 a.m. in New York and Montreal
4 a.m. in Denver
1 a.m. in Honolulu and Anchorage
12 midnight on the Midway Islands
1 p.m. in Athens
2 p.m. in Moscow
4 p.m. in Karachi
9 p.m. in Sydney

CLIMATE

The climate in Berlin is characterised by a mixture of ocean winds from the Atlantic and continental air. During the winter it is seldom very cold and in the summer months extremely high temperatures are also rare. Nevertheless it is not unusual in January or February for temperatures occasionally to drop to minus 20°C. The weather frequently remains quite cool until April. During the height of summer temperatures may climb at times to about 30°C and sometimes, even higher! The cooler temperatures of autumn come at the latest in the middle of October.

Unfortunately, the proverbial invigorating air of Berlin is nowhere to be found any more. In the winter there are frequently inverted weather conditions: cold air up above keeps the warm air down low. This gives rise to a variety of problems as the city's industry and vehicle traffic, as well as the brown coal power stations in the surrounding areas, produce a high amount of sulphur dioxide. The result of this is smog, which at times may be so bad that when a smog alarm is announced, cars without catalytic converters are forbidden to travel on the streets.

BUSINESS HOURS

In Berlin, most post offices are usually open from 8 a.m.–6 p.m. Monday to Friday, on Thursdays until 8.30 p.m., and on Saturdays from 8 a.m.–noon. The post offices located in the railway station on Friedrichstrasse and at the Palast der Republik both maintain hours from 10 a.m.–10 p.m., and the post office situated in Bahnhof Zoo remains open around the clock. The post office located in Tegel Airport is open from 6.30 a.m.–9 p.m. Monday to Friday, the one in the International Congress Centre from 9 a.m.–1 p.m. and from 1.45 p.m.–4 p.m. Monday to Friday.

The dialling code for Berlin from outside the city is **030**, for East Berlin **0372**. This will remain the case until telecommunications for both places have been standardised.

If you should need to exchange money or cash in Euro or traveller's cheques outside of regular business hours, the following banks are at your disposal: **Exchange Office** at **Bahnhof Zoo** (8 a.m.–9 p.m. Monday to Saturday, 10 a.m.–6 p.m. Sunday), the **Exchange Office** at **Joachimstaler Str. 1** at Bahnhof Zoo (7.30 a.m.–9.30 p.m. Monday to Friday, 7.30 a.m.–6 p.m. Saturday) and **Tegel Airport** (8 a.m.–10 p.m. Monday to Sunday). Outside their normal business hours, the following banks also maintain additional hours: the **Bank of Trade and Industry**, Kurfürstendamm 26a (10 a.m.–1 p.m. Saturday), the **Berlin Bank of Commerce,** located in the Wertheim Department Store, Kurfürstendamm 231 (10 a.m.–1 p.m. Saturday and on extended Saturdays until 6 p.m.) and the **Bank of Trade and Industry** in KaDeWe at Wittenbergplatz (8 a.m.–2 p.m. Saturday and on extended Saturdays until 6 p.m.). You'll find cash machines at regular and savings bank branches all over the city.

WHAT TO WEAR

What people wear in Berlin depends first and foremost on the time of year and the current weather conditions. It is absolutely necessary to take along warm clothing when travelling during the months between October and April. In the summer you'll also be happy to have brought along a sweater or jacket. A lightweight raincoat will also stand you in good stead. With respect to the latest styles, just about everything and anything goes in Berlin; whether or not you attend the theatre dressed in an evening gown or jeans is entirely a matter of personal preference. At discos especially, you can't be dressed outrageously enough!

The majority of the people living in Berlin are members of the Protestant Church. Catholics are somewhat of a minority here, making up just 12 percent of the total population. The many churches situated all over the city are for the most part closed outside regular service hours. However, the Protestant Kaiser-Wilhelm Commemorative Church, located on Kurfürstendamm, is open throughout the entire day.

In the eastern part of the city several churches have been converted into museums and exhibition rooms, for example Nikolai Church, which is in the city centre and contains archaeological finds from Berlin's past history, or Friedrichwerdesche Church where the Schinkel Museum is presently housed. In any case the people of Berlin were never particularly pious church-goers; many churches remain unused and empty.

Just about all Christian churches and world religions have congregations and places of worship in Berlin. The Jewish congregation here is composed of nearly 6,200 members and has several synagogues, which have been rebuilt following the destruction caused by the Nazis and the war. The large synagogue located in Oranienburger Strasse is also to be partially renovated and will ultimately serve as a museum. There are two Russian-Orthodox churches, dozens of mosques and even a Buddhist monastery (addresses can be found in the telephone book).

COMMUNICATIONS

NEWSPAPERS

In the middle of the 19th century, Berlin developed into a significant media centre. Up until 1929, this city with its 147 political newspapers had become the largest newspaper-metropolis in the world! At the end of World War II, the powers occupying Berlin issued special newspaper licences and in 1967 there were only 10 papers with a total circulation of around 1.1 million. Thanks to increased competitiveness in the advertisement market, the number of papers has since decreased further.

Today, the daily press including the right-wing conservative *Berliner Morgenpost* and both the popular papers *BZ* and *Bild*, published by Axel Springer, dominate the market. As competition there are only the *Tagesspiegel* and the liberal left-wing Volksblatt Berlin. The alternative paper *taz* offers a change from the usual political monotony. This newspaper was the first to issue its own East German edition following the momentous changes in 1990 and published an all-German, nationwide paper just prior to reunification.

Since 1990 newspapers in what used to be East Germany have also achieved a new image: The *Neues Deutschland*, formerly the compulsory paper of the masses, appears today in serious garb, the *Junge Welt* presents itself as critical and rebellious, and the traditional paper *Berliner Zeitung* has evolved into a popular daily tabloid. It is expected that even more new newspapers will be started up in the future; Berlin has once again become an interesting market for advertising and along with this, a trade centre for all printed media.

CITY MAGAZINES

The two city magazines, *tip* and *zitty*, are published monthly (every 14 days you can get hold of the latest edition of either one or the other) and play an independent role in the Berlin media scene. In addition to these, the magazine *Prinz* has also been available since 1990.

Along with an editorial section which is primarily focused on local politics and cultural events, all three publications offer quite an extensive "What's on" service; all the important, public events in Berlin from daily television and radio broadcasts to theatre productions, concerts, films, art exhibits and panel discussions are listed here. In addition to all this, you'll find an index of addresses and an abundance of interesting announcements including many under the headings "Spirits" and "Lonely Hearts".

RADIO & TELEVISION

Under favourable circumstances, it is possible to receive 24 different radio channels in the city, provided that you live in a household with a cable connection. If you don't live in a house with cable, there are still plenty of channels to choose from: Sender Freies Berlin (SFB) transmits four different channels and RIAS (Rundfunk im Amerikanischen Sektor), established in 1946 by Americans as a German language station, has two channels. With its four medium wave bands, one short wave and four ultrashort wave bands this is one of the most powerful stations in all of Europe. News reports are broadcast around the clock every half hour; on SFB you can tune into newscasts every hour on the hour. In Berlin you can keep yourself up to date with the latest events by turning on the radio every half hour. For young people, there are the two programmes transmitted by Radio 100 (which is similar to the *taz* newspaper in that the focus is on the more alternative scene) and the former East German Jugendradio DT-64 (which is expected to continue broadcasting).

All three of the Western Allies transmit their own radio programmes, the Americans over AFN and the British over BFBS (in addition to this you can also tune into the BBC on UKW in both the German and English languages). If you prefer listening to French, listen in with the north of Berlin to the Parisian programme from FFB over UKW. There are also four channels broadcast from former East Germany, whose union with the SFB is still being discussed. And as if all these stations weren't enough, you can also tune into several privately run stations from the western part of Germany!

There is also quite a large selection of television channels to choose from. The regional "Berliner Abendschau" programme, on the air at 7.22 p.m., has the largest viewing audience in the city.

DIPLOMATIC REPRESENTATIVES

In the western part of the city the missions and cultural centres of the victorious World War II powers – the United States, Great Britain and France – are well represented. In addition to these you'll also find numerous military missions, consulate generals, consulates and delegations from other countries, some of which are also represented through German honorary consuls. Many countries still also maintain additional representatives in what used to be East Germany, stemming from the time when East Berlin was the capital of the GDR. In the light of the future development of Berlin into the capital of a unified Germany, these doubled representations will prove to be superfluous. It is expected that in the future many additional embassies will be established in the city, thus creating a completely new "diplomatic landscape". The Commission of the European Community is represented through a press and information office. (For addresses, look under *Useful Addresses*.)

EMERGENCIES

SECURITY & CRIME

Before The Wall was erected, Berlin enjoyed the reputation of being one of the safest cities in Europe. Like everywhere else, things have changed somewhat here and nowadays, particularly in crowds or while making use of public transport, it pays to keep a look out for pickpockets who prefer operating in big cities. Following the dismantling of The Wall, the number of assaults – which not infrequently are violent – occurring during the night has also been on the rise. If you find yourself at night in a relatively unpopulated area, the wisest thing to do is call a taxi.

EMERGENCY NUMBERS

Nearly all the bigger hospitals maintain ambulances specifically for accidents as well as emergency rooms. There are emergency phones (free of charge) in telephone booths located in front of larger post offices and in other places too; emergency telephone posts are commonly located in suburbs. The following is a list of the emergency telephone numbers:

Police, tel: 110
Fire Brigade and Ambulance, tel: 112
Emergency Rescue (East), tel: 115
DRK Rescue Service, tel: 8585
Emergency Medical Service, tel: 310031
Emergency Medical Service (East), tel: 1259
Emergency Chemist's Service, tel: 1141
Emergency Dental Service, tel: 1141
Poison Advisory Service, tel: 3023033
Emergency Drug Service, tel: 247033
AIDS Hotline, tel: 3026031
Crisis Intervention Hotline, tel: 11101
Women's Crisis Hotline, tel: 654243
Emergency Service for Young People, tel: 344026
Emergency Service for Children, tel: 610 063333
Children's Protective Services Agency, tel: 4556070
Emergency Veterinary Service, tel: 6819799/1141
Lankwitz Animal Shelter (Emergency Service), tel: 7721064
(Other important telephone numbers can be found in *Useful Addresses* section.)

GETTING AROUND

INFORMATION CENTRES

Information of all kinds is available at the Berlin Tourist Information Centre and Berlin-Information. Both agencies will provide help for travel preparations and upon request will send brochures, hotel and shopping guides, the calendar of events preview "Berlin tut gut", as well as a variety of other informative publications. You can also book hotel rooms through them by sending a written, detailed account of what you would like and mailing it off at least four weeks in advance. Waiting until the last minute to find

a room is only successful if you're quite lucky!

The Tourist Information Centre can be contacted at D-100 Berlin 30, Europa-Center. Telex: 1-83356.

The main information office, located at the entrance to Budapester Strasse, is open daily from 7.30 a.m.–10.30 p.m. and can be reached at tel: 2626031 or 2626033.

The (ex-East) Berlin-Information maintains its visitor centre in the converted television tower (Panoramastrasse 1), and is open 1 p.m.–6 p.m. Monday, 8 a.m.–6 p.m. Tuesday–Friday and 10 a.m.–6 p.m. Saturday and Sunday.

There are other information centres located in the main halls of the Bahnhof Zoo (a railway station), and Tegel Airport, as well as in the high-rise travel agency on Alexanderplatz. Information and literature concerning the political situation in Berlin are available at the Informationszentrum Berlin, located not far from Bahnhof Zoo at Hardenbergstrasse 20. (Hours: 8 a.m.–7 p.m. Monday–Friday, 8 a.m.–4 p.m. Saturday. Tel: 310040.)

PUBLIC TRANSPORT

In Berlin the public transportation system is so well-developed that you can safely forget your car. The Berlin transportation services (BVG and BVB) operate underground trains (U-Bahn), fast-trains (S-Bahn), bus lines, tramlines in the eastern part of the city, a well-organised network of buses running throughout the night as well as boat connections crossing the Havel River between Wannsee and Kladow. The quickest and most ecologically sound way of getting around the city is on the underground system's 10 different lines.

This system (which is, moreover, the largest in all of Germany) is augmented by an excellent and extensive fast-train network. By taking advantage of the underground, the commuter transportation network on the Ringbahn and smaller, connecting fast-trains you can travel beyond the city limits and into the countryside surrounding Berlin. For example on an inner-city fast-train you can get to Potsdam, Werder, Nauen, Oranienburg, Bernau, Strausberg, Erkner, Fürstenwalde and Königswusterhausen. It's a good idea to spend DM 2.00 on the map which shows all the BVG transport routes and relevant schedule information. If needed, you can also purchase a booklet containing information regarding public transport at night.

Fare prices increase from time to time, generally on 1 May, however, there are still plenty of opportunities to save a few pfennigs in the form of multi-journey and tourist tickets.

In the city you can travel between Wittenbergplatz and Rathenauplatz on the number A 19 and A 29 buses with a Kurfürstendamm ticket for the bargain price of just DM 1.00. Single and multi-journey tickets are available at the machines in all underground stations. Special tourist tickets can be obtained, among other places, at the BVG-Information in ICC, the BVG kiosk at Bahnhof Zoo, at the BVG Customer Service Office (located in the train station at Alexanderplatz, on the corner of Potsdamer and Grunewalder Streets), as well as at various underground stations where regular season-tickets are sold, at the ZOB Bus Station and at the KaDeWe box office. Further information is available around the clock by calling BVG Customer Services on tel: 2165088.

BY CAR

Driving Tips: There are currently over 1.2 million registered cars cruising the streets of Berlin and since the opening of the border, this number has been increasing rapidly. The adac (the German automobile association) has predicted that by the year 2000, the current number of motorised vehicles will have doubled – a veritable vision of ecological horror for the city.

Things are already so hairy in Berlin at the present time that the city is threatened with a complete traffic collapse. It's not only the cars driven by city dwellers, or by daily commuters which cause all the congestion; more and more visitors coming in by car from other German states are contributing to the difficulties too. Berlin's broad boulevards, lengthy arterials and generous network of urban motorways which were once quite able to manage all the traffic coursing through the city, have long been unable to keep things moving. And as if conditions weren't horrendous enough during the already catastrophic rush hours, frequent traffic jams and other obstructions occur at just about any time at all during the day.

Finding a parking place in the city has become a real challenge; it's no rare occurrence that even in relatively quiet residential areas, chances are good you'll have to drive around for half an hour until you discover a spot to ease into! Meanwhile, cars tend to speed through the streets at a breakneck pace, especially through many of the well-travelled areas in the city where additional lanes designated for buses only have been established. By racing along in these supposedly restricted lanes, you're sure to reach your ultimate goal more quickly.

If, in spite of this sobering description of traffic conditions in Berlin, you still think you want to drive into the city, the best thing to do is to park your vehicle at one of the Park-and-Ride lots and hop on a bus or underground from there.

Throughout the city no-parking and no-stopping zones are patrolled with an eagle eye. The only cars tolerated along the roadsides and the Kurfürstendamm median are those parked for no longer than two hours (a parking disk must be set and placed on the dashboard so it is visible) between 9 a.m.–2 p.m. Stubborn parking sinners can expect – among other unpleasant things – to pay about DM 200 to retrieve their car should it be towed away. If this should happen to you, contact either the nearest police station, for example the one at the Bahnhof Zoo, or call the main radio headquarters at 110. There are no less than three automobile associations which will come to the tourist's rescue with both word and deed if necessary.

There are a few traffic regulations in East Berlin and in what was formerly known as the GDR which differ from those in the West: the legal blood-alcohol content limit will remain at 0.0 until the end of 1992. This means that you are permitted to have absolutely no alcohol in your bloodstream while driving. (In what used to be called West Germany, this limit is 0.8). In built-up areas the speed limit is 50 kph (30 mph). The maximum speed-limit on motorways is set at 100 kph (60 mph) until 1 January 1992, after which it will be raised to 130 kph (80 mph). As of 1991, the speed limit for heavy lorries is 60 kph (a little less than 40 mph). The number of filling stations selling unleaded petrol has been growing by leaps and bounds in what used to be the GDR.

The following is a list of useful telephone numbers:
ADAC City Breakdown Service, tel: 19211
AVD City Breakdown Service, tel: 4622070
ACE City Breakdown Service, tel: 2112255

You can dial the preceding telephone numbers from the former GDR, however it may prove to be more efficient to use the following local numbers:
Towing Service (day and night), tel: 5592500
The Central Kfz Rescue Service, tel: 116
Auto-Aid (from 6 a.m.–10 p.m.), tel: 524 3565
(For additional addresses and telephone numbers, as well as for car rental agencies, look under the heading *Useful Addresses*.)

TOURS

For a mere DM 1.00 (transfer prohibited) you can hop on one of the Butterfly Lines – marked by a triangle – and end up in some of the greener, more natural places of Berlin, or at the waterside. One of these routes is in operation from May until the end of August and runs along the Havel, by Schildhorn and the Grunewald Tower. Points of departure for these trips are the underground station (U-Bahn) at Theodor-Heuss-Platz (U1), or the fast-train station (S-Bahn) Wannsee (S1/S3). In addition to these, there is another special line that commences at the fast-train station Wannsee and goes to Pfaueninsel (Peacock Island), also in operation between May and October. Two other train lines travel between the S-Bahn station Nikolassee to Strandbad Wannsee (Wannsee Beach), and from the U-Bahn station Tegel (U6) to Strandbad Tegel.

During the season, excursion steamboats belonging to the White Fleet depart from the harbour near the S-Bahn station at Treptower Park. You can get further information and book tickets in advance at the tourist agency high-rise on Alexanderplatz (tel: 2123375), the Treptow office (tel: 2712326), as well as at the White Fleet Passenger Information Desk (tel: 2728741).

Several businesses offer various city sightseeing tours. These include the Berliner Bären Stadtrundfahrt (BBS), tel: 8836002, Berolina, tel: 8833131, Bus-Verkehr-Berlin (BVB), tel: 8822063 and Kultur-Kontor, tel: 310888. (The latter company chiefly organises cultural-historical tours.) For more information regarding these and other tours, contact the Tourist Information Centre or Berlin-Information.

Without much ado at all, you can get a good glimpse of a fairly large portion of the city from the seat of a double-decker bus. The Number 19 runs from Kottbusser Tor in Kreuzberg over Kurfürstendamm to Grunewald (in the west); the Number 70 tram (in the east) completes this little tour.

TAXIS

There are about 5,000 taxis in West Berlin and in addition to all these, numerous cabs from East Berlin. You can hail one where they wait, either at special taxi parking zones or by placing a call to one of the taxi telephone posts located throughout the city. Taxis can also be ordered through the four different radio dispatch services by calling one of the following numbers:
Tel: 6902
Tel: 261026
Tel: 216060
Tel: 240202

In East Berlin the numbers to call are:
Tel: 3646
Tel: 5646
Tel: 3654176

Currently, the base rate for any journey is DM 3.40; each additional kilometre costs DM 1.58 on workdays between 6 a.m.–midnight, and DM 1.60 at night, weekends or during holidays.

WHERE TO STAY

Hotels in Berlin enjoy a long and illustrious tradition. The classy hotels in this former capital city of the empire are located cheek by jowl in the heart of the city; nevertheless, it has always been possible to find more reasonably-priced accommodation in the city centre as well.

These days, guests visiting West Berlin will find approximately 26,000 beds in about 350 hotels and pensions to choose from. As yet, the number of beds available in East Berlin is not quite as high and there is a decided dearth of smaller hotels and pensions. However, these conditions should be rectified within the course of the 1990s. As a rule during the main tourist seasons, just about every bed in the city is booked solid. Less-demanding travellers may want to take advantage of the opportunity to lodge in privately-run establishments. Through the Mitwohnzentralen (housing agencies that arrange private accommodation) it may be possible to rent an entire apartment which has been temporarily vacated by its usual inhabitants.

The following list includes only a small selection of hotels available in Berlin. Although telephone numbers are given, it may prove easier to make a room reservation through the Tourist Information Centre.

LUXURY HOTELS

Prices for one night range from DM 160–700.
Avantgarde, Kurfürstendamm 14/15. Tel: 8831330
Berlin Excelsior Hotel, Hardenbergstr. 14. Tel: 31993
Grand-Hotel, Friedrichstrasse 158–164. Tel: East Berlin 20920
Grand-Hotel Esplanade, Lützowufer 15. Tel: 261011
Inter-Continental, Budapester Str. 2. Tel: 26020

Kempinski Bristol, Kurfürstendamm 27. Tel: 881091
Metropol, Friedrichstr. 150. Tel: East Berlin 22040
Palasthotel, Karl-Liebknecht-Str. 5. Tel: East Berlin 2410
Schloßhotel Gehrhus, Brahmsstr. 4–10. Tel: 8262081
Schweizerhof, Budapester Str. 21–31. Tel: 26961
Steigenberger, Rankestr. 30. Tel: 21080

MODERATE HOTELS

Prices for one night are between DM 80 and DM 180.
Artemisia (first women-only hotel in Europe), Brandenburgische Str. 18. Tel: 878905
Domus, Uhlandstr. 49. Tel: 882041
Frühling am Zoo, Kurfürstendamm 17. Tel: 8818083
Plaza, Knesebeckstr. 63. Tel: 88413-0
Stadt Berlin, Alexanderplatz. Tel: East Berlin 2190
Unter den Linden, Unter den Linden 14. Tel: East Berlin 2200311

PENSIONS

Prices for one night are from DM 40–130.
Atlas, Lietzenburger Str. 78. Tel: 8834746
Domino, Neue Kantstr. 14. Tel: 3216906
Savoy, Meinekestr. 4. Tel: 8813700
Terminus, Fasanenstr. 48. Tel: 8814909
Transit, Hagelberger Str. 53/54. Tel: 7855051

PRIVATE ACCOMMODATION OFFICES

Mitwohnzentrale am Kudamm-Eck, Kurfürstendamm 227. Tel: 8826694/95
Frauenmitwohnzentrale (a housing agency run by women for women only), Kurfürstendamm 227. Tel: 8826284
Mitwohnzentrale Kreuzberg, Mehringdamm 72. Tel: 7862003/2270

CAMPING GROUNDS

Information regarding all camping grounds located in Berlin is available through the Tourist Information Centre or the Deutscher Camping-Club, Geisbergstr. 11. Tel: 246071/72.

FOR YOUNG PEOPLE

Young people visiting Berlin should have no trouble finding suitable accommodation. Travel groups are best off getting in touch with the Informationszentrum Berlin, Hardenbergstrasse 20, Berlin 12. Tel: 31004172.

At the centre you'll find a brochure entitled *Berlin für junge Leute* (Berlin for Young People), which contains a wealth of interesting tips and addresses. The Informationszentrum also has a list of the addresses of numerous guest houses for young people in West Berlin.

The Fürst-Donnersmarck Institution runs a guest house especially set up for accommodating young handicapped visitors. The address is Wildkanzelweg 28, Berlin 28. Tel: 402021.

The Berlin Regional Chapter of the German Youth Hostel Association (Bayernallee 35, Berlin 19. Tel: 3053055) maintains a list of all youth hostels located in the city.

There is also a list of all German youth hostels and a clearly laid-out map (both free of charge), including an introduction written by the president, available from the Deutschen Jugendherbergswerk, Postfach 220, 4930 Detmold, tel: 05231/7401-1. If you happen to find yourself on the doorstep of one of these youth hostels without a valid international youth hostel card, don't worry; you can become a member on the spot. Membership fees are DM 17 for junior and DM 26 for senior citizens. Drinking alcohol and smoking on the premises are frowned upon. Guests can either bring their own bedding with them, or rent it from the establishment.

FOOD DIGEST

WHAT TO EAT

It can't really be said that Berlin has cultivated a particularly indigenous cuisine. However, this doesn't mean that there aren't a number of true Berlin specialities. Over the course of the past decades, the restaurants where you can have an authentic Berlin meal have been getting harder and harder to find. They tend to be easier to locate in the eastern part of the city, but even here it seems like the number of dining establishments specialising in foreign foods are taking over.

The true restaurateur from Berlin – wherever you may come across him – is especially happy to dish his customers up a plate of "Aal grün", otherwise known as Havel eel in an herb sauce. Various types of freshwater fish including *Hecht* (sturgeon), *Barsch* (perch), and *Welse* (catfish) are also caught in local waters and eventually find their way onto some diner's plate, usually at a waterside restaurant. It's not a bad idea to ask your waiter just where the fish you're contemplating ordering came from. Since the lakes and rivers in Berlin cannot exactly be considered as clean, it may well be that you won't want to eat any fish caught locally.

Generally speaking, freshwater fish are imported from other areas in Germany, or have been bred for culinary purposes. As is fitting, guests can order a roasted joint of wild pork from the Forsthausrestaurant, situated not too far from the hunting grounds in Grunewald.

These days nobody feels uncomfortable any more about having an "Alt-berliner Buffet" arranged for parties, even if they're going to be quite large. Guests will stand in line for *Schusterjungs mit Schmalz* (rye rolls with dripping), *Kartoffelpuffern mit Apfelmus* (a kind of potato pancake served with applesauce), *Bouletten mit Mostrich* (a type of croquette made from meat and served with mustard), *Pfannkuchen* (the special pancakes referred to outside of the city simply as "Berliners"), *Rollmops* (herring marinated in vinegar), and *saueren Gurken* (pickled gherkins). Various cafés throughout the city will sometimes offer what's called a "Katerfrühstück" (hangover breakfast), which always includes herring prepared in some way or another. It's practically considered a culinary offence not to serve *Matjeshering* (young herring) with apples, onions and gherkins in cream. Another herring speciality which is frequently initially regarded with scepticism, but nearly always raved about after being tasted, is *Matjeshering* served with green beans and potatoes boiled in their jackets; the *Matjes* fillets are nestled between ice cubes and accompanied by butter.

There are still a few places left in Berlin (and among these are sometimes even classy restaurants), where the Berlin speciality *Eisbein* (pork knuckles) is prepared. Traditionally, this dish was also served at topping-out ceremonies. Nowadays, many people are becoming more and more conscious of their fat intake and often would rather eat *schnitzel* (veal or pork cutlets) instead. *Eisbein*, served with *sauerkraut* and green pea purée, is quite popular especially during the winter in Berlin, though younger people in particular tend to prefer eating lighter meals. It's said that true Eisbein experts just lay the fat aside anyway and go directly to the lean, inner meat. The dish is usually accompanied by beer and ice-cold *Schnaps*.

Finding a good *Kartoffelsalat* (potato salad) or *Berliner Bouletten* is really a matter of luck. In bad restaurants, ready-made *Kartoffelsalat* is just slapped onto a plate out of a plastic bucket and the *Bouletten* often have too much bread dough in them. Because of this, they're often mockingly referred to as "verzauberte Schrippen" (bewitched buns). Probably the best place to try these two items is at a meal prepared by friends, or perhaps at what's called a "Berliner Party".

Another dish you may want to try in Berlin is *Kasseler*, or cured spare ribs, chops, or belly of pork. It also comes prepared as a "Rolle", which is made of pressed meat rolled up. By the way, this dish is not named after the German city Kassel, but after the expert butcher from Berlin called Kassel. Freshly roasted and accompanied by a tasty sauce, this dish is the real solution to what to serve at a family party. It's also quite delicious eaten cold, cut in slices and served with Berliner *Kartoffelsalat* prepared with either mayonnaise, or oil and vinegar. Either way, plenty of finely chopped onions are absolutely crucial to its success.

You'll find *Königsberger Klops* appearing regularly both on restaurant menus and on dinner tables in private houses. They contain about the same quantity of meat as *Bouletten*, but are boiled rather than baked; the optimal mixture of meat is one part ground beef to one part minced meat. A light-coloured caper sauce is then made out of the broth. Potato soup, prepared with pieces of fried bacon or sausage and fresh parsley, is frequently served at family dinners on Sunday evenings.

Boiled potatoes accompanied by *Quark* (a kind of soft curd cheese) with Spreewälder linseed oil is apparently a dish that in order to get down, you have to have been born and raised in Berlin. A fine hollow is made in the quark and filled with oil. Strangers to Berlin will most likely never be able to understand, let alone appreciate, this particular dish.

Beer is the most typical of all beverages served in Berlin. Around the turn of the century, over 100 breweries were producing approximately 5 million hectolitres of beer! Since that time, breweries have merged with one another or disappeared until today, there are only four well-known brands: *Schultheiss*, *Engelhardt*, *Berliner Kindl* and *Hochschul-Brauerei*. *Berliner Weisse* (a type of light, fizzy beer made using top-fermentation yeast) is referred to as the "champagne of the North" and can be traced back all the way to the Huguenots. As the local beers were too bitter for their taste, the Huguenots began at about the end of the 17th century to brew the very first top-fermented *Weißbier*. The special flavour is the result of a shot of raspberry or woodruff syrup, which lends the beer its singular taste and red or greenish colour.

WHERE TO EAT

There are literally countless restaurants in Berlin. Culinary offerings run the gamut from speciality restaurants serving dishes from all four corners of the world, to simple inns, and from sophisticated dining establishments right down to numerous snack bars and sausage stands, (the most famous of which is located at the Dimitroffstrasse underground station).

If you include pubs, beer taverns and bars, the total number of businesses in the city involved with serving food comes to a whopping 6,000! Every hungry visitor is sure to find something to satisfy his or her palette, be it "New German Cuisine", or an international speciality (choices range from delicacies served in Copenhagen to those served in Bombay), to good old home cooking, or a juicy *currywurst* (curried sausage). If you feel more than a little overwhelmed by the culinary variety, it may not be a bad idea to pick up a copy of the Gastronomic Guide at one of the tourist information centres. This is an up-to-date listing of most restaurants and eateries in the city which does not, however, include quality ratings.

For those who'd prefer to have a little better idea regarding what they're getting their stomachs into, consult the *Michelin Guide*, or the special magazine issue *Essen, Trinken* und *Tanzen*, recently published by *zitty*. In the guides *Berlin Billiger* (Berlin on a Budget) and *Berlin Zwischen Sekt und Selters* (Berlin from Champagne to Seltzer) you'll find a list of the more reasonably priced eating establishments in the city. (The latter includes addresses of bars and discos.)

WEST BERLIN

The following is just a very limited selection of the restaurants Berlin has to offer: at the present **Rockendorf's**, located way out in the northern reaches of the city at Düsterhaupstr. 1, is the place for fine dining. At least that's the opinion of the gourmets and French cuisine fans who do not let themselves be put off for a moment by the long trip out to Waidmannslust in the Reinickendorf district. Be sure to call for a reservation in advance, as your chances of getting a table are slim if you don't (tel: 4023099).

Another excellent restaurant situated right across the city and much favoured by gourmets, is the **An der Rehwiese**, Matterhornstr. 101, in Nikolassee (tel: 8032720).

If you're looking for something to eat somewhere a bit more centrally located, try the **Alt Luxemburg** at Pestalozzistr. 7a, in Charlottenburg (tel: 3238730). Or, if you mouth is positively watering for fish or

shellfish, go to **Le Poisson**, Westfälische Str. 41, in Wilmersdorf (tel: 8925691).

If you'd like to get a good look at a few famous characters from Berlin's cultural milieu while enjoying a delicious meal, stop in at **Florian**, Grolmannstrasse 52, in Charlottenburg, or at the **Paris-Bar**, Kantstrasse 152.

There are also quite a few excellent restaurants housed in international hotels, for example **Kempinski** in the Bristol-Kempinski, **Steigenberger** in the Steigenberger, **La Reserve** in the Palace and **Hugenotten** in the Inter-Continental. Experts swear by the food and service in the **Berliner-Grill**, located in the Hotel Berlin and the **Conti-Fischstuben** in the Hotel Ambassador on Bayreuther Strasse also enjoys a glowing reputation. The **Pullman** restaurant in the ICC, though perhaps not as well-known as the dining establishments already mentioned, is very highly regarded. It has been renovated and decorated in the old style, and the view alone is actually enough to make it popular: the restaurant is housed in the radio tower, where diners can gaze out over city rooftops while they eat.

The biggest stuffed cabbage rolls are without a doubt to be found at **Heinz Holl**, Damaschkestrasse 26, in Charlottenburg (tel: 3231404). During the day-time, visitors wanting to partake in one or another of Berlin's culinary specialities, for instance *Bouletten* (a type of croquettes made of ground meat), *Schusterjungs* (rye rolls), *Rollmöpse* (herring marinated in vinegar) and *Rote Grütze* (a kind of jelly made from red fruits) can drop into the Berlin Museum's **Weißbierstube**, Lindenstrasse 14, in Kreuzberg; at night the place to go is the **Alt-Berliner-Buffet**, Georg-Wilhelm-Str. 20, Halensee. The best *Eisbein* (pork knuckles) to be had in Berlin are served beginning at 10 p.m. in the rustic ambience of **Hardtke**, Meinekestr. 27 (tel: 8819827). Hungry souls needing to keep an eye on their budgets can eat reasonably priced meals in the youthful, swinging atmosphere of **Max and Moritz**, Oranienstrasse 162, in Kreuzberg.

In the restaurant-café **Josef Diekmann** (Meinekestrasse 7), you can not only enjoy a delicious nouvelle cuisine meal, but also actually shop until midnight! The restaurant is furnished with items for sale from the period of rapid industrial expansion in Germany, beginning in about the year 1871. In addition to refreshments and colonial articles, there are also changing exhibits of works done by young local artists.

If you're hankering for some good, original cooking, try the **Tafelrunde**, Nachodstr. 21, in Wilmersdorf. Here you can indulge in a filling, seven-course medieval meal, eat with your fingers and pass around the horn brimming with mead.

The Europa-Center is the place for those who'd like to eat their way around the world, but without having to go to all the expense and trouble of actually doing so. There are so many different restaurants packed together in this one building that even if you spent an entire week trying, you still probably wouldn't manage to test them all! The Japanese **Daitokai** is especially exotic, the **i-Punkt**, located on the 20th floor, offers a wonderful view of the city and there's an excellent salad-bar as well as delicious ice-cream at **Mövenpick**.

You'll find Italian, Greek, Yugoslavian and Asian restaurants throughout the city, many of which are decidedly mediocre. At the moment, the best Italian restaurant – graced by one of those coveted Michelin Stars – is the **Ponte Vecchio**, Spielhagenstr. 3, in Charlottenburg (tel: 3421999). Connoisseurs of fine Italian cooking also recommend **La Savoia**, Windscheidstr. 31, in Charlottenburg (tel: 3241807), and **Don Camillo**, Schloß Str. 7-8, in Charlottenburg as well (tel: 3223572). The **Bar Centrale**, Yorkstrasse 82, in Kreuzberg is also outstanding. You can either go ahead and eat a really first-class Italian meal here, or just order a leisurely beer while sitting at one of the bistro tables.

There are loads of Turkish restaurants located in Kreuzberg. One of the best in the whole city is **Istanbul**, Knesebeckstr. 77 (tel: 8832777). During the summertime, the **Bagdad**, Schlesischen Strasse 2 is especially worth a visit. In the wonderfully tacky little garden you'll rub elbows with people in the hip Kreuzberg scene and on the weekends there's usually a belly dancer weaving her way among the tables to the beat of a Turkish band.

The best Indian food in town is at the **Calcutta**, Bleibtreustr. 17 (tel: 8836293). **Hakuin**, Martin-Luther-Str. 1 (at the corner of Kleisstr.), operated by a Buddhist collec-

tive, is sure to delight all vegetarian cuisine fans. When the weather is good, guests can dine out of doors (except on Thursdays) in the centre garden, listening to the fountain splash and keeping an eye on the fish in the pond (tel: 242027).

There are a number of restaurants worth mentioning located somewhat further from the centre of things, alongside various lakes or in the greener areas of Berlin. The **Alte Dorfkrug** (in Lubars), the **Alte Fischerhütte** (on Schlachtensee) and the **Forsthaus Paulsborn** (in the middle of Grunewald) all serve exceptionally fine examples of German cooking. The **Bistro-Café am Kalenderplatz**, situated along Massiner Weg on the grounds where the National Garden Show once took place, is also worth a trip, not only because the biggest sundial of the entire world is located right there.

Berlin is "open" 24 hours a day. That doesn't mean, of course, that all eateries are open around the clock, but it does mean that you can always find something to eat or drink somewhere at just about any time of the day or night. For instance in **çava**, Pariser Strasse 56, you can order a hot meal at 3 o'clock in the morning and in the **Schwarzen Café**, Kantstrasse 148, predominantly hip young people on the Berlin scene meet at just about any time you could imagine (except on Tuesdays) for breakfast.

EAST BERLIN

Restaurants in East Berlin are less varied than in the West and often do not reach or maintain such high standards. However, this situation is gradually changing. Even prior to the recent and dramatic turning point in Berlin's history, the restaurant serving the most delicious food was (and still is) in the **Grand Hotel**, Friedrichstrasse 158. The ambience in the "Grand Restaurant Silhouette" is stylishly elegant. The food is excellent here and rather expensive. In the "Brecht-Keller", Chausseestrasse 125, you can order dishes allegedly made from recipes taken out of Helene Weigel's cookbook! Call in advance to make a reservation if you want to be sure of getting a seat (tel: 2823843). The restaurant is located in the cellar of the house where Bertolt Brecht once lived and the author's numerous family photographs decorate the vaulted walls. Brecht's favourite dishes are served here, referred to on the menu as he himself referred to them in his plays: as "attempts". For example Attempt No. 8 is bean soup with smoked meat.

Two outstanding restaurants are the **Französische Hof**, Otto-Nuschke-Strasse 56, and the **Fondue**, located in the Ephraim Palace at Poststrasse 16. The **Aphrodite**, Schönhauser Allee 61 (tel: 4481707) is another restaurant with high standards, as is the **Ratskeller** in the Roten Rathaus (the Red City Hall) and **Restauration 1900**, Husemannstrasse 1. The staff at the **Alt-Cöllner Schankstube**, Friedrichsgracht 50, are exceptionally friendly; they've even been known on occasion to write a little ditty in honour of a favourite guest or two.

At **Zur letzten Instanz**, Waisenstrasse 14/16, you get a good deal on a decent meal, but the place is always overcrowded. It's considered to be the oldest pub in Berlin, mentioned for the first time in the year 1621 as the **Brandweinstube**. Its present name is the result of the fact that the pub is situated right next-door to the former Berlin City Courthouse! At the bar there's a 200-year-old majolica stove and the walls are covered with pictures of the city. In **Ermeler-Haus**, Märkisches Ufer 10, guests can lean back and allow themselves to be thoroughly spoiled in the Rose, Diana or Flora rooms by waiters wearing tail coats and serving delicacies.

There are lovely old hand-painted tiles, pale coloured-glass windows and ceramic plates at the **Altberliner Bierstube**, Saarbrückerstr. 17, in Prenzlauer Berg. They serve a selection of oddly named dishes, for instance, an *Ofenrohr* (stove-pipe), which actually refers to beef roulade, *Plumpse* (a tumble), which is fresh blood sausage, or *Droschkenkutscher* (cab driver), a drink that is composed of beer and schnapps mixed together.

Restaurants serving foreign specialities in East Berlin mainly emphasize the cuisine from Eastern European countries. Two dining establishments well worth mentioning are the **Moskau**, Karl-Marx-Allee 34, where you can get an excellent Ukrainian meal, and the **Haus Budapest**, Karl-Marx-Allee 90 which serves good and filling food. At **La Habana**, located in the Hotel Metropol, Friedrichstrasse 150, you can sit back and enjoy an exotic meal while listening to Caribbean music. At the **Jade**, in the Palast Hotel,

Karl-Liebknecht-Strasse 5 and in the **Peking**, Friedrichstrasse 58, guests are served exquisitely prepared and wonderfully presented Asian food of the highest quality.

In view of the current culinary changes and developments now taking place in East Berlin, probably the best things to do is just set off on your own and follow your nose. However, if you'd rather play it safe, drop by or call the **Gaststättenservice** (Restaurant Service) located at Alextreff on Rathausstrasse (tel: 2124293).

BARS

Most city inhabitants still prefer to meet with friends and take their guests to the traditional neighbourhood bar. These don't necessarily have to be located right around the corner, but they do have to possess a familiar, cosy atmosphere.

It's usual for people of a particular age group to gather together in the same bar. (This tendency doesn't apply to establishments that attract an expressively tourist clientele.) For the most part, young people hang out mainly in the places which are current hot spots in the Berlin social scene. These venues have for the most part evolved away from the Kreuzberger bohemian style so prevalent in the 1970s and are managed now as music cafés, highly stylized New-Wave and cocktail bars.

There are others who prefer the cosy Berlin beer bars which are decorated with a variety of junk, where you can boost your spirits and energy with *Soleiern* (hard-boiled eggs marinated in salt-water), *Bouletten* and *Bratkartoffeln* (roasted potatoes). No matter where you end up going, Berlin's bars are the social gathering places outside private homes, where the name of the game is to see and be seen. Customers become regulars, get to know the bartenders by their first names and every once in a while (if need be) drink a beer on credit.

Folks searching for an especially original Berlin bar eventually end up sooner or later at Leydicke, located at Mansteinstrasse 4 (a side street heading off from Yorkstrasse). This venerable, 100-plus year old establishment with self-service at the counter is as well known for its antique furnishings as it it for its colourful, mixed clientele and the unpredictable effect of its home-made fruit wines and liquors. Two bars situated right in the city centre amidst a veritable labyrinth of drinking establishments are the **Ku'dorf**, Joachimstaler Strasse 15 and the **Sperlingsgasse**, Lietzenburger Strasse 82–84. The bars in this area are primarily frequented by tour groups and tourists; Berlin natives are seldom spotted here.

In today, out tomorrow is a phenomenon that applies to a whole slew of bars and garden cafés that suddenly, somehow become the most popular places around to be seen in. The question as to what catapults a specific establishment into the position of being one of the most popular rendezvous points for prominent and "in" guests – as well as for a whole host of curious "normal" people – is usually in retrospect a complete mystery.

The **Paris Bar**, Kantstr. 152, has managed to remain on this particular list for the past three years due to the fact it is consistently frequented by a number of prominent members from the literary and art scenes. **Fofi's**, Fasanenstrasse 70, has the reputation of being the meeting place for the especially stylish segment of the population. The clientele at the **Ax**, Liebnitzstr. 34 and **Exil**, Paul-Lincke-Ufer 44, in Kreuzberg, is made up in part from people in the film and entertainment industries. Both places possess a rather Austrian air, no doubt due to their founder Ossi Wiener. (You don't have to rush to get here in the evening as things don't really get going until 11 p.m.)

During the day-time the **Café Einstein**, Kurfürstenstrasse 58, is a popular hang-out for members of the **Culture Mafia**. It's run in the style of a traditional Viennese coffee house; in the summer guests can take a leisurely breakfast outside under the trees. Make sure you try a piece of their *Apfelstrudel*; it's out of this world!

The **Galerie Bremer**, located on Fasanenplatz, is actually an art gallery, but which also houses a pub, open in the evenings. Rudi von Laak, a friendly old-timer in the Berlin night scene, personally supervises his numerous guests.

Around Nollendorfplatz and further along in the direction of Kreuzberg, pubs and other popular meeting places tend to become more off-the-wall and shrill. There are a number of underground cafés on Goltzstrasse; **Slumberland**, located on Winterfeldplatz,

Swing, on Nollendorfplatz and **Oranienbar**, at Oranienstrasse 168 in Kreuzberg all belong to this particular genre of establishments. Keep in mind that the few names mentioned here stand for absolutely dozens of others located all over the city. The best thing to do is prick up your ears and don't forget that what was referred to yesterday as an "in" place, may well already be "out" by the time you get there tomorrow.

Listing bars chiefly frequented by the homosexual community would make a chapter by itself. If you haven't already picked up a few addresses by just keeping your eyes and ears open, all you have to do is take a stroll through the side streets between Wittenbergplatz and Nollendorfplatz. The **Vagabund**, Knesebeckstrasse 77, is a traditional meeting place for gay people. Young homosexuals tend to congregate at **SchwuZ**, located in the gay people's centre at Hasenheide 54.

For more tips and addresses, consult the *Siegessäule*, a monthly publication put out by the Berlin gay community. There are also some pubs located around Eisenacherstrasse and Motzstrasse which are frequented by lesbians. They're not too difficult to recognise, thanks to names such as **Pour Elle** and **Lipstick**.

NIGHTLIFE

Because Berlin is pretty much open 24 hours a day, going from a drink at a bar or two right into the thick of city nightlife is a relatively effortless manoeuvre; it's no problem to decide at the last minute whether to go to a disco or cabaret, to be topped off with a late dinner at a restaurant. However, it must be said here that Berlin's nightclubs and shows are not of the world-class calibre they used to be; they seem to still be living from the nearly mythical reputation they earned in the roaring 1920s. About the only place to occasionally find a show of international repute is at the Friedrichstadt Palace.

The **Quartier**, located in Potsdamer Strasse and reopened in September 1990 after months of extensive renovations, seems to be quite promising. With its bar, café, cinema and performance hall built to fulfil a variety of purposes, the centre is patterned after the grand establishments of the 1920s like the famous "Haus Vaterland". In any case, in both its aspirations and orientation the Quartier is an undertaking certainly worthy of the thriving metropolis that Berlin has once again become.

When a Berlin native is looking for somewhere special to take his or her guests, chances are that they'll end up on the basement floor of the Europa-Centre (tel: 2614795) for a visit to the **Stachelschweine** (literally, the Porcupines). This cabaret group has pretty much become an institution in Berlin humour. Wolfgang Gruner is the longstanding star of the show.

The cabaret **Die Wühlmäuse**, Nürnberger Strasse 33 (tel: 2137047), is named after a theatre group which is actually no longer in existence. The programme itself is quite varied with solo artists in this literary and satirical cabaret giving guest performances. From time to time quick-change artists and other entertainers are also on stage. Another possible way of spending a very entertaining evening is to take in the show at the **La vie en rose**, an international revue with transvestite performance artists, located at the Europa-Centre (tel: 3236006).

If striptease joints are more what you're looking for, you'll get your money's worth from the erotic dancing girls in the dimly-lit **New Eden**, Kurfürstendamm 71 (tel: 3235849). A speciality of the Berlin nightlife scene are the transvestite cabarets along Martin-Luther-Strasse.

Probably the most risqué show you'll come across in the city takes place in **Chez Nous**, Marburger Strasse 14, where your chances of getting a table are about nil if you don't have the foresight to call and reserve one in advance (tel: 2131810). A few street corners away from here there's another good transvestite cabaret, spiced with plenty of satire and parody in **Dollywood**, Welserstr. 24 (tel: 248950); in **Crazy Theater Dreamboy's Lachbühne**, located in the Excelsior highrise, Anhalter Str. 1, Straps-Harry entertains audiences with a decidedly burlesque-flavoured show. The **Lützower Lampe**,

Witzlebenstrasse 38, in Charlottenburg (tel: 32120) specializes in the same type of entertainment. You should expect to pay about DM 50 (including entrance fee and drinks) on weekday evenings; on the weekends, the price is correspondingly higher.

Although there isn't an international super-disco comparable to New York's Palladium, the choice of places to go dancing in Berlin is extensive enough to ensure that no matter how old you are or what your taste in music is, you're certain to find something that appeals to you.

Despite the fact that the laser-disco **Metropol**, Nollendorfplatz, is actually quite large, on the weekends it's full to overflowing. Live concerts often take place here too. The **Tango Bar**, decorated in the style of the 1920s, is located in the same building and open for business on Friday and Sunday nights only. Compared to these two places, the **Cha Cha**, Nürnberger Strasse is tiny, though this doesn't seem to have any influence on the number of visitors it attracts. Just a few metres away is the **Dschungel**. This disco has been extremely popular for years; anyone who considers himself or herself to be the least bit "in" or "cool" comes here to shake a leg.

A bright star amongst the top discos is the **First**, Joachimstaler Str. 26. **Far Out**, Lehniner Platz, is run by Bhagwan disciples and is also well-frequented. At **Abraxas**, located on Kantstrasse, you can jam to the sounds of funk and soul. A good tip for dancers around the age of 30 is the **Blue Note**, Courbièrestr. 13. The stylish Ku'damm crowd lets it all hang loose in **Coupe 77**, Kufürstendamm 177, as well as in the **Ciro-Bar**, Rankestrasse 32. Enthusiastic dancers of all ages turn out on the rooftop garden of the Hotel Inter-Continental.

The name of the disco on the top floor of the Europa-Center is **VIP**. Prices here aren't exactly what you'd call cheap, but you'll get a great view of Kurfürstendamm at night and if you're single, a big-city romance is almost guaranteed.

For years, the "in" disco in Prenzlauer Berg has been the **Café Nord**. Located at Schönhauser Allee 83, it opens from 9 p.m.– 5 a.m. Tuesday to Friday, 8 p.m.–4 a.m. on Saturday and 6 p.m.–midnight on Sunday. In contrast, things are a bit classier at the **Yucca** (open from 8 p.m.–3 a.m.), at the corner of

Neumannstrasse and Wisbyer Strasse. The place is said to have been paid for by the Stasi (former East German secret police) for the pleasure of diplomats and playgirls. You can get something to eat in the restaurant here when everywhere else in East Berlin has already closed up for the night.

If you're someone who enjoys being a part of a huge crowd, head on over to **Alex-Treff**, Alexanderplatz, where the enormous hall and energetic atmosphere attract masses of dancers. People from the red-light district tend to congregate in **Lolott**, Schönhauser Allee 56. Models, musicians, painters and idlers from the former GDR rendezvous collect at a little, cosy club with a mini dance floor called the **Sophienclub**, Sophienstrasse 6 (open from 8 p.m.–4 a.m.). The **Knaak-Club**, Greifswaldstrasse 89, offers live music to as many as 400 people at a time. Independent music fans from both parts of Berlin meet here at this former factory to listen to punk, clash and German new-wave music. (Hours are from 7 p.m.–midnight and on Saturday until 2 p.m.)

As a rule, things are somewhat more exclusive in the nightclubs housed in the big hotels. For older people, the **Sinus-Bar** in the Palast-Hotel is said to be the most beautiful bar in the whole city where you can also dance. The disco **Operncafé**, Unter den Linden 5, has the reputation of being more or less a meat market and if you're looking for companionship, chances are excellent that you'll find someone in the **Lotos-Bar**, Schönhauser Allee 46. In **Lindencorso** on Unter den Linden, a fair amount of importance is attached to conventional clothing.

At **Café Keese**, Bismarckstrasse 108, it's customary for ladies to invite – or not to invite, as the case may be – gentlemen out on to the dance floor. Rumour has it that this particular establishment has frequently played a decisive role in the welding of not a few solid marriages. (Open every day except Monday.) A more mature clientele gathers to scout out potential partners in the **Tanz-Café Huthmacher**, Hardenbergstrasse 29; another popular spot for aged singles is the **Clärchens Ballhaus**, Auguststrasse 24, where a dance band plays old ballroom tunes.

You'll find an overview of what Berlin has to offer in the way of discos and other amusements in the *Berlin-Programm* and in the special *zitty* entertainment publication. The brochure *Berlin für junge Leute* (available free of charge at the Informationszentrum Berlin) contains a list of the names and addresses of discos oriented towards a younger clientele.

There are a large number of what are referred to as private clubs, film bars and other related establishments which offer a variety of live shows, private rooms, FKK social gatherings (FKK is the name of a popular nudist society), saunas and similar amusements, mainly for the benefit of big-spending businessmen who are travelling alone. Put plainly, these all have to do with commercial sex. For an overview of what Berlin has to offer in this regard, as well as for more exact details and prices, pick up a copy of the city plan for men (available at just about every kiosk throughout Berlin).

CULTURE PLUS

INFORMATION

The best way to get a feel for what is going on in Berlin at any given moment is to take a look in either of the two city magazines *tip* or *zitty*. You'll find current events and performances listed under the headings Theatre, Dance, Music, Film, Cabaret, Fine Arts, etc. The Berlin brochure *Zu Gast in Berlin* and the weekly calendar which appears in the Wednesday edition of the *Tagesspiegel* both serve as trusty guides in helping you to decide where to go and what to do.

There is also an announcement service you can call to find out what's happening in the city and last but not least, the big, round free-standing pillars pasted over with posters and situated throughout city are another good source of information. In the special programme section in the Friday edition of the daily paper *taz* you'll find a general summary of everything that will be going on over the weekend.

The box offices of most larger theatres are open in the mornings and it is possible to call in to reserve tickets. (A selection of telephone numbers and addresses can be found under the heading *Useful Addresses*).

Information, tickets, books, posters and brochures for various festival events and performances are available at the Information Shop, located in the Europa-Center, Budapester Str. 48. The shop is open daily from 14 March to 22 November between 10 a.m.–7 p.m.; during the rest of the year hours are from noon–6 p.m. daily, except for Mondays (tel: 25489250). Otherwise, further information can be obtained by writing to the Kartenbüro der Berliner Festspiele (the ticket office), 1000 Berlin 30, Budapester Str. 50, or by calling them at 030/25489100 between 10 a.m.–4 p.m., Monday to Friday.

BERLIN PHILHARMONIC ORCHESTRA

It is only possible to reserve tickets in advance for orchestra performances by mail. The annual programme is released each year at the end of April; if you'd like a copy, send a stamped, self-addressed envelope to their press department. All enquiries concerning the orchestra itself should be addressed to the Philharmonie, Matthäikirchstr. 1, D-1000 Berlin 30, tel: 25488-0; if you have any general questions, call 2614383. Box office hours for buying tickets in advance are from 3.30 p.m.–6 p.m. Monday to Friday, and from 11 a.m.–2 p.m. on Saturday, Sunday and holidays. There are also a number of theatre ticket outlets which accept ticket reservations from out-of-town visitors. For a selection of these, look under *Useful Addresses.*

MUSEUMS

The museums in Charlottenburg, Dahlem and Tiergarten, all owned and operated by the Stiftung Preussischer Kulturbesitz (the Institute of Prussian Cultural Possessions), constitute the largest number of museums and permanent exhibits in West Berlin. In addition to these establishments, the Kunstbibliothek (Art Library) in Charlottenburg and the Preussische Geheime Staatsarchiv (Secret Prussian State Archives) in Dahlem both belong to the institute. Further enquiries pertaining to other state-owned museums may be addressed to Stauffenbergstr. 41, Berlin 30, tel: 030/2666. (For more information, consult the chapter *On Museums in Berlin*, or the list under *Useful Addresses*.)

CINEMA

Berlin always was and still is a fantastic city for filmgoers, and not only during the annual film festivals in February, which for the first time in a long time where held again in both parts of the city in 1990. Numerous film production studios have their headquarters here and much of the up-and-coming talent of the future is cultivated at the Deutschen Film und Fernsehakademie Berlin (DFFB) (the German Film and Television Academy in Berlin), Berlin 19, Pommernallee 1 (tel: 3036-1). In addition to these, the huge DEFA production studios (formerly called the UFA), are located in Babelsberg, near Potsdam.

The biggest cinemas right in the heart of the city are pretty much all concentrated in the area between the Europa-Center and Uhlandstrasse. They frequently have five or six different films running at a time! In addition to these monsters, there are many smaller, more eccentric cinemas which emphasize a selection of avant-garde, political, experimental, classical and exotic films. Especially worth mentioning here is the **Arsenal**, located right behind Wittenbergplatz at Welserstrasse 25 (tel: 246848). The **Freunde der Kinemathek** cinema offers a programme of retrospective movies dealing with specific, historical film topics. Consult their very instructive monthly calendar for more information.

At the **Odeon**, Schöneberger Hauptstrasse 116 (tel: 7815667), English-language films are shown exclusively in the original. Other foreign language films in the original are also occasionally played at the Amerika Haus, the British Centre, the Institut Francais and in the Sowjetischen Kulturzentrum on Karl-Marx-Allee.

The private **Berliner Kinomuseum** in Kreuzberg, Grossbeerenstrasse 57, scarcely larger than a living-room, is devoted to caring for and preserving old films and projectors. There are presentations on Wednesday, Friday and Saturday at 8.30 p.m. and 10.30 p.m., with an additional show on Saturdays at 6 p.m. The former grand hotel **Esplanade**,

Bellevue-Strasse 16 (at the Tiergarten) has been in the process of being converted into the Filmhaus Berlin.

MUSIC SCENE

Although the jazz, rock and pop music scene in Berlin is constantly in motion, there are a few places where people have been going for years to hear good live music. In addition to the Jazz Festival in November and "Jazz in the Garden", which takes place each year during the summer in the sculpture garden of the National Gallery, jazz fans will definitely want to drop into **Flöz**, Nassauischen Strasse 37 (tel: 8611000). Flöz is run by Franz de Byl, himself a master of jazz guitar. For the most part, internationally known free-jazz musicians perform here, though occasionally de Byl will bring other types of performance arts to the stage, for instance Horst Buchholz's cabaret show.

At **Quasimodo**, Kantstrasse 12a (tel: 3128086) you can hear famous jazz as well as rock and blues musicians at work. The **Quartier**, Potsdamer Strasse 96 (tel: 2613707), housed in what was once a cinema and later a music hall, has taken on a new life as an multi-purpose culture and amusement temple. In addition to rock, pop and blues concerts, you can also see non-mainstream theatre productions here. The **Loft**, Nollendorfplatz 5 (tel: 2161020) offers a mixed bag of concerts, including the most promising discoveries fresh out of Berlin basements, the British independent charts and the psychedelic and rockabilly underground scene in the US. The **K.O.B.**, Potsdamer Strasse 157 (tel: 2165296) is another spot where post-punk fans gather.

Reggae and funk lovers can jam to their favourite tunes live in the **Ecstasy** disco, Hauptstrasse 30 (tel: 7848565), and the **Go In**, Bleibtreustrasse 17 (tel: 8817218) is still the place to go for folk music fans, even if it is pretty much oriented towards tourists. You can sip the first beer of the day while hearing live music in the little York castle, Yorkstrasse 15, in Kreuzberg, where there is a live band playing every Sunday beginning at 2 p.m.

Music fans can pick up a free copy of *Music Scene Berlin* in most pubs, cinemas and theatre box offices. This publication is issued monthly and contains a list of ad-dresses pertaining to the music scene in Berlin. You'll also find tips appearing regularly in the *tip*, *zitty* and *taz* magazines.

LITERARY BERLIN

The era of the **Romanische Café**, which is located just across from the memorial church in the Ku'damm, has long since passed. But despite the fact that literary Berlin has taken on another face, the focal meeting point remains predominantly in Charlottenburg. In May 1986 the Literaturhaus, housed in a tastefully renovated city villa at Fasanenstrasse 23, was opened as a centre for all manner of events and performances having to do with books. The centre includes three lecture rooms, a café with garden, the Tucholsky Memorial and a book store in the basement. A calendar of events is available; for further information tel: 8826552.

Other places and institutions where people interested in literature tend to congregate are at Akademie der Künste (Hanseatenweg 10, tel: 3911031), the Literarische Colloquium Berlin in Wannsee (Am Sandwerder 5, tel: 8035681) and the Neue Gesellschaft für Literatur E.V. (Bismarckstr. 17, tel: 3422059). There is also a forum of unknown authors who meet at Akazienstr. 19 (tel: 7844583), in Schöneberger and the Literatur-café, Winterfeldstr. 36.

A hefty percentage of Berlin's bookstores can be found in the Charlottenburg district, especially in the vicinity of Savignyplatz along Knesebeckstrasse and Carmerstrasse, as well as around Alexanderplatz. On Tuesdays bookworms gather together in the cosy reading room at the Autorenbuchhandlung (this bookshop is run by authors), Carmerstr. 10 (tel: 3101151).

Among all Berlin's numerous bookshops, you'll find a real curiosity located at Motzstrasse 30, in Schöneberg. Richard Schikowski's new and used bookstore has an especially extensive assortment of volumes pertaining to esoteric, occult, astrological and para-psychological topics. (Hours: 2 p.m.–6 p.m. every day except Wednesday, 9 a.m.–1 p.m. Saturdays.) The German philosopher Rudolph Steiner once worked in this very same building. A bit further along the Winterfeldstrasse book lovers will be delighted to find no fewer than six second-hand bookshops in a row.

The "alternative" scene has taken root in Berlin as nowhere else in Germany, or even Europe. Evidence of this can be seen in the existence of numerous alternative centres and institutions. You can tap into this scene by hanging out in various pubs, but the real way to get to know the city's alternative sub-culture is by visiting the centres themselves.

The largest collection of projects is to be found in the **Mehringhof**, Gneisenaustrasse 2; over 30 groups have made this building their headquarters.

On the basis of its sheer size and infra-structure, the **Ufa factory** for culture, sports and craft workshops, Viktoriastr. 10–18, is practically a village in itself. The **Kunsthaus Tacheles**, Oranienburger Str. 54 is also quite enormous. A lively, varied programme including concerts and films, as well as a café (Café Zapata) are offered in the ruins of what was once the Friedrichstadt Passage.

A popular place for women to meet is in the neighbourhood culture centre **Begine**, Potsdamer Str. 129, or in the **Schoko-Fabrik**, Naunystr. 72, in Kreuzberg.

For those interested in elevating body, mind and spirit, drop into **Pan Paradise Now**, Uhlandstr. 68, or the **Zeitlos-Zentrum**, Akazienstr. 27.

You'll find more addresses pertaining to the sub-culture scene in Berlin in the city magazines *tip*, *zitty* and *taz*.

SHOPPING

As is usual in Germany, shops are generally open from 8 or 9 a.m. until 6 p.m. Monday to Friday. On Thursdays, most tend to remain open for business until 8.30 p.m., though this decision is left entirely up to the shopkeepers themselves. As a rule, grocery stores close at 6 p.m. on Thursdays. Within the city where many shops don't open much before 10 or even 11 a.m., closing hours are generally at 6.30 p.m. On Saturdays most stores are open from 9 a.m.–1 p.m; the larger department stores don't close before 2 p.m. Shopping hours are extended on the first Saturday of each month and on the four Saturdays in Advent until 4 p.m. During the summer months, the laws regulating closing hours in the city, (mainly around Ku'damm), tend to become pretty liberal; many smaller businesses and boutiques often remain open until 9 p.m.

At a pinch it is possible to purchase (at slightly higher prices!) food, wine, liquor, etc. after regular business hours at the Metro stands in the underground stations at Kurfürstendamm (5–11 p.m., Saturday until midnight), Fehrbelliner Platz (until 10.30 p.m.) and at Schloß Str. (3–10 p.m., 1–10 p.m. Saturday).

International newspapers, magazines, city maps, etc. can be purchased after regular business hours from various stands at the train stations Zoo and Friedrichstrasse, at the Ku'damm square and in the Europa-Center (until 11 p.m.). Fresh flowers are also available in the evenings at Bahnhof Zoo and near the train station on Friedrichstrasse.

There's only one rule that applies to shopping in Berlin: there's nothing that you can't buy. The KaDeWe (the biggest department store on the entire continent!), located at Wittenbergplatz, is an absolute shopping "must". Here you'll find seven floors positively stuffed with an enormous selection of chic fashions, home furnishings and international specialities from all over the world. The store has become even more elegant since the ground floor was transformed into a mini-mall.

Small boutiques bearing big names, like Fendi (for leather items), Davidoff (for tobacco products) and Charles Jourdan (for shoes) are grouped around the giant cosmetic department and counters displaying jewellery and watches. The high-fashion centre of the KaDeWe is located on the second floor; here ladies can try on the finest Haute Couture styles direct from Paris and men will find everything from Boss and Burberry to Daniel Hechter. The food department on the 6th floor brims with a nearly overwhelming selection of items and diverse stands offering a wide variety of samples. This is not only a place to purchase things, but a veritable tourist attraction in its own right!

Ku'damm-Eck (the corner of Kurfürstendamm and Joachimsthaler Strasse), Ku'dammer Platz (near Uhland Strasse) and the previously mentioned Europa-Center are all wonderful places to indulge in a shopping spree, especially if the weather's nasty. At any time of the year you can stroll from shop to shop with dry feet and without a coat! There are large, multi-storey car parks close by which, however, are often completely full during peak business hours.

It is said that, in Berlin, styles are both set and created. This saying is easily substantiated by taking a look around at all the boutiques located on Kurfürstendamm. But Ku'damm certainly isn't the only street worth mentioning in this respect; the numerous little side streets in its vicinity also offer a wide selection of shops and boutiques.

You will find fashionable clothes for young people on Bleibtreustrasse and the shops along Uhlandstrasse are equally interesting. The boutiques in Fasanenstrasse are especially elegant and in Nürnberger Strasse at Tauentzien there is one chic shop after another. For eccentric imported and designer items at relatively reasonable prices, pay a visit to one of the two Chrome stores, located on Kantstrasse and Motz Strasse. If second-hand clothing is more your style, drop by the Garage on Ahornstrasse at Nollendorfplatz. They stock a huge assortment of original clothes that you can purchase by the kilo. If you're in pursuit of more unusual apparel, take a look in Maria Makkaroni and in Kaufhaus Schrill, both located on Bleibtreustrasse.

Berlin is real paradise for antique lovers of all classes and price ranges. There is a high concentration of good – and extremely expensive – antique shops along Keithstrasse and in that general area, on and between Eisenacher and Motz Strasse, as well as on Fasanenstrasse and Kurfürstendamm. Another place you may want to start out antique hunting is Suarezstrasse in Charlottenburg.

The junk shops in Nollendorfstrasse, in Kreuzberg around Bergmannstrasse and in Neuköllner Flughafenstrasse may not be as exclusive as the aforementioned shops, but they are without a doubt much cheaper. In addition to all these, there are four flea markets (Flohmarkt) worth mentioning: the flea market located in the street-level train station at the underground station Nollendorfplatz is open daily (except for Tuesdays) from 1 p.m.–7 p.m. On Saturdays and Sundays from 8 a.m.–3.30 p.m. both the flea market on the Strasse des 17 Juni and the Kreuzberger Krempelmarkt at Reichpietschufer are open for business. The flea market located at Askonaplatz in Prenzlauer Berg is open from 8 a.m.–4 p.m. on Saturdays and Sundays. Shoppers looking for the very latest in fashion may want to check out the selection of avant-garde clothing designs at Allerleirauh in East Berlin, tel: 4722512, or at Larifari, tel: 2828552.

Arts and crafts can be purchased all over the city, but the area around the pedestrian zone in Wilmersdorfer Strasse is especially worth recommending for these items. Experts will no doubt be interested in the Berlin Pewter Figure Gallery, whose reputation extends quite far beyond the city limits on account of its own manufactured, hand-painted pewter figures. For reasonably priced photography equipment and supplies, you may want to pay a visit to the shopping centre located on Augsburger Strasse, just behind Kurfürstendamm. Wegert's main store (Berlin's largest shop specialising in film and photos), is located on the corner of Potsdamer and Kurfürsten Strasse.

Berlin is literally bulging with dozens of bookstores. At Schropp's (Potsdamer Strasse 100) you'll find a good selection of maps and travel guides, try Richard Schikowski's (Motzstr. 30) for books on the occult and esoteric subjects, Marga Schoeller's stocks a good assortment of English literature and if you're looking for something in the field of Romance Languages, drop by the Romance Languages Bookstore (Knesebeckstr. 18).

If you happen to have some spare money burning a hole in your pocket and are searching for something extra-special, how about paying a visit to some of Berlin's jewellery shops? You're sure to find something you can't live without at Hülse (Kurfürstendamm), for instance, or Krischke (Schlüterstrasse), (they specialise in art deco objects, jewellery and silver from old Russia), or at the world-famous Cartier jewellery shop (there's a branch on Fasanenstrasse).

In the eastern part of Berlin the shopping culture has not yet quite evolved to be on par with Western standards. However, there are still quite a few interesting shops to discover in various areas. Unter den Linden is well on its way to becoming the elegant shopping street it once was, and has already upped its prices in anticipation. During the former days of the GDR, the largest Meissen Porcelain shop was to be found here.

There are a variety of folkloric objects for sale in various cultural centres – for example, Hungarian items at Karl-Liebknecht Str. 5, Polish items at Karl-Liebknecht Str. 9 and Russian goods at Natascha in Hans-Beimler Strasse.

Another street fit for shoppers is the Karl-Marx-Allee with its large – sometimes even too large – shops; in any case the Karl-Marx Bookstore (Karl-Marx Allee 78–84) is well worth taking a peek into. Other bookstores you may want to check out include Internationales Buch (Spandauer Strasse 2), where you'll find two floors filled with books, Das gute Buch (Alexanderplatz 2), whose popularity is unfortunately confirmed by the long lines at the cashier, the University Bookstore (Unter den Linden 69), the Kunstsalon Berlin (Unter den Linden 37), the Modernes Antiquariat (Schönhauser Allee 126, tel: 4497853), where you'll find literature pertaining to art and a selection of prints, and the Zentrales Antiquariat (Rungestrasse 20, tel: 2792195).

There are more and more little stores cropping up along Friedrichstrasse which look inviting enough to warrant at least some leisurely window shopping. Souvenirs made to imitate old Berlin objects can be found in the Nikolai Quarter. Around Alexanderplatz there are plenty of places to shop conveniently interspersed with cafés to sit down in and relax for a few moments. Here you'll also come across a number of booths and market stalls, where you can all too frequently find an assortment of not particularly lovely or even very interesting items.

The free guide *Shopping in Berlin* is available from the Tourist Information Centre.

Sports

The city itself keeps visitors pretty active, but for those who still have the energy and desire after all the sightseeing, shopping and whatnot to partake in a little physical exercise, Berlin offers a wide range of opportunities. If a brisk run (or a slow trot) is what you need to keep you on your toes, head out for a jog around Grunewald Lake, where you're certain to meet a number of people who all have the same idea. Or how about a game of tennis on one of the many outdoor courts, or going for a swim in a public indoor or outdoor pool, depending on the time of year? (International hotels all have their own swimming pools.)

The Neoköllner "Blub", is one of the biggest and best swimming and recreational areas in all of Europe and the recently opened Kreuzberger Wellenbad (a swimming pool with artificially induced waves) on Spreewaldplatz is also quite popular. While swimming in the lakes and rivers in Berlin is not classified as life-threatening, it is not exactly advisable because of the high percentage of water pollution.

During the winter, skaters flock to the ice-rinks in Lakwitz, Neukölln, Wedding, Weissensee and Wilmersdorf, as well as to the Berlin Skating Club on Glockenturmstrasse and to the ice sports stadium on Jaffestrasse. And when the weather gets really cold, skaters come out in droves to glide across Berlin's lakes. In the summer it is possible to go sailing on some of these larger lakes. The use of motor-boats is considerably limited and on Müggelsee it is absolutely forbidden. This is not just because these boats are noisy, but because of their not inconsequential contribution to both water and air pollution.

You'll find fitness paths in nearly all larger forested areas as well as skiing and sledding slopes in the city. But as snowfall is no sure thing in Berlin, you can't really count on the city to be consistently suitable for winter sports. For further information about sports opportunities in Berlin, contact the Landessportbund Berlin e.V., Jesse-Owens-Allee 1/2, Berlin 19, tel: 300020.

The Berlin Marathon is another event that has gained recognition both in and beyond the city limits. Each year in September over 10,000 participants don their track shoes to run the more than 42 km (26-plus miles). In addition to this gruelling event, in May there's another lengthy, 25-km run, (more than 15 miles), organised as a joint effort by the Berlin Track and Field Association and the French garrison. Both events are open to anyone who thinks they can survive the exertion. If spectator sports are a little more to your liking, the International Indoor Soccer Tournament takes place in the beginning of January and the All-City Water Polo Competition at the end of the same month. About the end of February you can watch the International Ice-Speedway Races; in the middle of May the International Women's Tennis Championships and the Avus Race, sponsored by the ADAC, take place in the city. In August there's the International Stadium Sporting Events Festival ISTAF, in October the legendary Six-Day Race is held in the Deutschlandhalle, and in November you can get tickets to watch the International Horse Riding and Jumping Competitions.

It is not yet clear as to whether or not Berlin will be chosen to host the Olympics in the year 2000. Despite this uncertainty, planners have been at work since 1988, evaluating how Berlin could be transformed into an Olympic village. Prior to the reunification in 1990, both West and East Berlin each had their respective well-developed athletic facilities and grounds. However, these would not be sufficient to meet with Olympic requirements.

If Berlin was indeed chosen to host the 2000 Olympic Games, it would be the second time in its history. The first time was in the year 1936 and unfortunately, left a bad impression in the minds of most people; the National Socialists abused the games as an arena in which to mount a propaganda exercise extolling their own virtues.

SPECIAL INFORMATION

TRADE FAIRS & CONGRESSES

Berlin is a city that has an international reputation for its trade fair and congress facilities. The Internationale Congress Centrum (ICC) and its associated exhibition and trade fair hall (all located by the radio tower), are optimally situated with respect to traffic and transport. In addition to the many local and regional events, there are a number of big, international trade fairs and exhibitions held annually or biennially which draw throngs of visitors into the city each year.

The "season" starts rolling at the end of January/beginning of February with the traditional agricultural fair **Grüne Woche**. In March, the travel department of the **Internationalen Tourismusbörse** (ITB) organises its world-wide congress. There's a large pharmaceutical and medical technological exhibition which takes place in conjunction with the **Congress für ärtzliche Fortbildung** (Congress for Further Medical Education) in May/June.

Every two years (falling in those with odd numbers), the huge **Internationale Funkausstellung** (International Radio Exhibition) is held in Berlin in August/September, drawing visitors from all four corners of the world. This is followed in September/October by the **Partner des Fortschritts**, an exhibition with overseas importing as its theme. Further information is available from the Berlin Tourist Information Centre or the Berlin Ausstellungs-Messe-Kongress-GmbH (AMK), D-1000 Berlin 19, Messedamm 22, tel: 303 8-1.

CHILDREN

There are playgrounds for children all over Berlin. At the 40 adventure playgrounds kids are even allowed to build, saw and hammer! The Lübars Recreational Park, located on Quickborner Street in Berlin Reinikendorf, offers numerous opportunities for various kinds of play and sports activities. They also manage a young people's farm, where visitors can view the handmade items formerly produced and used in the countryside.

The following is a list of farms – complete with resident animals – designed for children in inner-city districts where both large and small visitors are welcome: the Weddinger Kinderfarm, Luxemburger Strasse 25, Berlin 65, the Kinderbauernhof Görlitzer Park, Wiener Strasse 59, Berlin 36, the Kinderbauernhof Mauerplatz, at the corner of Adalbertstrasse and Leuschnerdamm, Berlin 36, and the Kinderbauernhof located in the UFA factory, Viktoriastrasse 13–18, Berlin-Tempelhof. One of Berlin's most well-known self-help projects has been developed here on the grounds of the former UFA factory. Amongst other events offered, there are regularly scheduled theatre, music and circus performances especially for children. There's also a children's circus where the kids themselves have a chance to participate as artists, located at the "Tempodrom", in the Congress Hall at the zoo. In the park for kids only, situated in what used to be the Pioneer Park in Wuhlheide, children can participate in a variety of organised activities or just play by themselves.

There are several performance stages in Berlin which cater specifically to children. Perhaps the best known productions are those put on by the "Grips" theatre, located in Altonaer Strasse 22, Berlin-Tiergarten. "Klecks", Schinkelstrasse 80, Berlin-Neukölln and the Berlin Figure Theatre, Yorkstrasse 59 in Kreuzberger, Berlin 61, both offer programmes that are suitable for younger children.

There are also plenty of exciting things for children to explore in Berlin's museums. Especially interesting are the Museum of Ethnology, Lansstrasse 8, Berlin 33, the Transport and Technology Museum, Trebbiner Strasse 9, Berlin 61, and the German Folklore Museum, Im Winkel 6/8, Berlin 33. In the Düppel Museum Village (Clauertstrasse in Berlin-Zehlendorf) visitors can view the reconstructed layout of a village from around the 12th century and even take a ride in a cart drawn by oxen! Children of all ages will be sure to enjoy the grounds where the National Garden Show was held in 1985 (Massiner Weg in Neukölln). And, of course, there are the aquarium and two zoos in Berlin. The main zoo on Budapester Strasse has plenty of outdoor enclosures, a tropical and nocturnal house, pony and carriage rides, as well as a section where you can stroke and pet all the animals.

During the summer holidays the City of Berlin offers a holiday pass which enables children to participate in a number of events. The brochure *Berlin – für die ganze Familie*, put out by the Tourist Information Centre, contains a veritable wealth of information. The city magazines *tip* and *zitty* both print a special page devoted to children's news. Here you can read the latest tips on any guest circuses in town and on children's films being shown in various cinemas.

In addition to these two magazines, there are two other publications. One is an illustrated city guide of Berlin for children, which includes a rendition of the 750-year-old story *Raus in die Stadt!* (published by the Elephanten Press), and the other is the Berlin guide for mothers, fathers and children called *Was machen wir heute* (Nicolai). A good way for kids to get to know the city is through the colouring book *Ausmalbuch Berlin*, by Beate Nowak (also published by Nicolai).

For parents who'd rather sightsee without their offspring: the Free University's "Heinzelmännchen" (tel: 8316071) and the Technical University's TUSMA (tel: 3134054) will both arrange baby-sitters. The hourly rate is about DM 13.

USEFUL ADDRESSES

GENERAL INFORMATION

Police, tel: 110
Fire Brigade, tel: 112
Medical Emergency Service, tel: 310031

Taxi, tel: 6902/240202 or 216060
National Telephone Information, tel: 1188
International Telephone Information, tel: 00118
Telegram Sending Service, tel: 1131
Wake-up Service, tel: 1141
Weather Report, tel: 1164
Road Conditions, tel: 1169
Time, tel: 1191
Berlin Tourist Information Office, tel: 2626031/33

Police Stations in:
  Wilmersdorf, tel: 8914086
  Charlottenburg, tel: 111398-1
  Wache, tel: 39871242
  Bahnhofswache Zoo, tel: 3136041
BVG Lost and Found: Potsdamer Str.188, tel: 2161413
Police Lost and Found: Platz der Luftbrücke 6, tel: 699-1
National German Railways Lost and Found: Friedrichstrasse, tel: 0372/4922340
Central Lost and Found (East): Wilhelm-Pieck-Str. 164, tel: 2826135, 2823472/73
National German Railways Lost and Found (East): S-Bahnhof Marx-Engels-Platz, tel: 49216
Post Office 11 Lost and Found: Möckernstr. 135–141, Berlin 61, tel: 2682653

AIRLINES

Aeroflot (SU): Budapester Strasse 50, Berlin 30. Tel: 2618250/51
Air Berlin (AB): Berlin Tegel Airport, Berlin 51. Tel: 41012781
Air France (AF): Berlin Tegel Airport, Berlin 51. Tel: 25025
ALIA Royal Jordanian Airlines (RJ): Budapester Strasse 14a, Berlin 30. Tel: 2617057/58
Alitalia (AZ): Tauentzienstrasse 16, Berlin 30. Tel: 2110129/95
Austrian Airlines (OS): Tauentzienstrasse 16, Berlin 30. Tel: 245024
AVIANCA Columbian Airlines (AV): Kurfürstendamm 178, Berlin 15. Tel: 8826276/77
British Airways: Berlin Tegel Airport, Berlin 51. Tel: 691021
Finnair (AY): Budapester Strasse 26a, Berlin 30. Tel: 2618055/56
Iberia (IB) Lineas Aereas de España: Reservations Tel: 2617001

Japan Air Lines (JL): Budapesterstrasse 18 a, Berlin 30. Tel: 2611374/75
Yugoslav Airlines (JU): Kurfürstendamm 50a, Berlin 15. Tel: 8836522
KLM Royal Dutch Airlines (KL): Kurfürstendamm 17, Berlin 30. Tel: 8811081
LOT Polish Airlines (LO): Budapester Strasse 18, Berlin 30. Tel: 2611505
Lufthansa (LH): Kurfürstendamm 220, Berlin 15. Reservations and information Tel: 88755; Berlin Tegel Airport, Ticket office Tel: 88758
Malev Hungarian Airlines (MA): Budapester Strasse 14a, Berlin 30. Tel: 2614867, 2615155
Pan Am: Berlin Tegel Airport, Tel: 881011
Sabena – Belgian Airlines (SN): Kurfürstendamm 209 (Ku'damm Karree), Berlin 15. Tel: 8817011
Singapore Airlines (SQ): Tel: 3243056, Reservations Tel: (069) 7240204
Swissair (SR): Kurfürstendamm 209 (Kudamm Karree), Berlin 15. Tel: 8839001
Turkish Airlines (TK): Berlin Management, Budapester Strasse 18b, Berlin 30. Tel: 2624033/34
VIASA Venezuela International Airways: Ku'damm 179, Berlin 15. Tel: 8827807

INTERNATIONAL TRAVEL AGENTS

Deutsches Reisebüro (DER)
Kurfürstendamm 17, Berlin 15. Tel: 8821094
Theodor-Heuss-Platz 2, Berlin 19. Tel: 3025001
Augsburger Strasse 27, Berlin 20. Tel: 240121
Teltower Damm 22–24, Berlin 37. Tel: 8016091
Albrechtstr. 3, Berlin 41. Tel: 7912011

Hansa Reise und Verkehr
Platz der Luftbrücke, Berlin 42. Tel: 78000810
Berlin Tegel Airport, Berlin 51. Tel: 41013365/66
Tempelhofer Damm 152, Berlin 42. Tel: 7526058
Kurfürstendamm 56, Berlin 15. Tel: 3237041/43

Hapag-Lloyd Reisebüro
Kurfürstendamm 199, Berlin 15, Tel: 8827124
Rheinstr. 11, Berlin 41.Tel: 8522096

Berlin Tegel Airport, Haupthalle. Tel: 4135061, 41013360

Reisebüro Globus
Uhlandstraße 121, Berlin 31. Tel: 873660, 874660

Wagon-Lits
Kurfürstendamm 42, Berlin 15. Tel: 8816683, 8818039

Berlin-Service
Alexanderplatz 5. Tel: 2123375

CITY SIGHTSEEING TOURS

Bärenrundfahrt (BBS): Rankestrasse 35, Berlin 30. Tel: 2134077. Departure point: corner Rankestr./Kurfürstendamm opposite the memorial church.
Berolina Stadtrundfahrten: Berlin 15, Meinekestrasse 3. Tel: 8833131. Departure point: corner Meinekestr.1/Kurfürstendamm.
Busverkehr Berlin (BVB): Kurfürstendamm 225, Berlin 15. Tel: 8822063. Departure point: Kurfürstendamm 225, opposite Café Kranzler.
Holiday Sightseeing (HRI) **Bus tours**: Fasanenstrasse 67, Berlin 15. Tel: 88420711. Departure point: Hardenbergstrasse, directly outside Zoopalast.
Severin und Kühn Berliner Stadtrundfahrten: Kurfürstendamm 216, Berlin 15. Tel: 8831015. Departure point: corner Fasanenstr./Kurfürstendamm.

All the aforementioned enterprises organise tours daily; tickets can be purchased directly on the bus.

FOR DRIVERS

24hr Filling Stations
West Berlin
Shell (Kant-Garages): Kantstrasse 126, Berlin 12. Tel: 3134496
Shell (Uhland Garages): Uhlandstrasse 187, Berlin 12. Tel: 8834378
Shell: Hohenzollerndamm 41/42, Berlin 31. Tel: 871774
Shell: Tiergarten, Reichpietschufer 16/18, Berlin 390. Tel: 2613780
BAB Petrol Station Dreilinden: Dreilinden Westseite, Berlin 39. Tel: 8034030

East Berlin
Adlershof, Adlergestell 118 (Köpenick). Tel: 6762768
Holzmarkstr. 36–42. Tel: 2793777
S-Bahn station Pankow-Heinersdorf. Tel: 4813346
Alt-Mahlsdorf, on the corner of Landsberger Str. Tel: 5277297

Breakdown Service
Heinz Fischbach: Antwerpener Str. 47; Berlin 65. Tel: 4536156 (day and night).
City Autodienst: Seesener Str. 8, Berlin 31. Tel: 8924088. Tel: 8531025 (weekends).

Repairs
Kurth Aral Petrol Station: Potsdamer Chaussee 6, Berlin 37. Tel: 8027007
Horstmann Emergency Tire Service: Sachsendamm 68–70 Berlin 62. Tel: 7814406
Katens & Warnke Breakdown Aid: Koloniestr. 8, Berlin 65. Tel: 4942598. From 10 p.m.. Tel: 4329342

Official Authorities
Police Headquarters: Platz der Luftbrücke 6, Berlin 42. Tel: 699-1
Confiscated Vehicles: Belziger Str. 52–58, Berlin 62. Tel: 781071.

Car Rental Agencies
Avis International: Budapester Str. 43, Berlin 3. Tel: 2611881. Berlin Tegel Airport Tel: 41013148
Europa Service Car Rentals Arnim: Kurfürstendamm 65, Berlin 15. Tel: 8835013, 8838958
European Car Rental: Kurfürstenstrasse 101–104, Berlin 30. Tel: 2137097/98
Guse Car Rental: Kantstrasse 155, Berlin 12. Tel: 3139009
Hertz Autovermietung: Budapester Str. 39, Berlin 30. Tel: 2611053. Berlin Tegel Airport, Tel: 41013315
Inter Rent: Xantener Str. 14, Berlin 15. Tel: 882 79 80. Berlin Tegel Airport, Tel: 41013368

American Express International
Kurfürstendamm II, Berlin 15. Tel: 8827575

OFFICIAL AUTHORITIES & ASSOCIATIONS

Industrie und Handelskammer (Chamber of Commerce): Hardenbergstr. 16, Berlin 12. Tel: 3180-1

Handwerkskammer Berlin (Berlin Trade Corporation): Blücherstr. 68/ Mehringdamm 15, Berlin 61. Tel: 2510931

Informations- und Beratungsdienst für zuwandernde Arbeitnehmer (information and counselling service for immigrant workers): An der Urania 4–10, Berlin 30. Tel: 21222441/42

Auskunfts- und Beratungs-Center (abc) Informationsdienst für "Neu-Berliner" (information and counselling service for newcomers to Berlin): Hohenzollerndamm 125, Berlin 33. Tel: 82008260/61

Verbraucherzentrale Berlin (Berlin Consumer Association headquarters): Bayreuther Str. 40, Berlin 30. Tel: 219070

CONSULATES & MISSIONS

European Community Commission: Press and information office, Kurfürstendamm 102, Berlin 31. Tel: 8924028

American Consulate General: Clayallee 170, Berlin 33. Tel: 8324087, 8197450

British Consulate General: Uhlandstr. 7/8, Berlin 12. Tel: 3024350

French Consulate General: Kurfürstendamm 211, Berlin 15. Tel: 8818028/29

Austrian Embassy: Otto-Grotewohl-Str. 5, Berlin-Mitte. Tel: 2291031

RELIGIOUS COMMUNITIES

Evangelisches Konsistorium (Protestant consistory): Bachstr. 1–2, Berlin 21. Tel: 39091-399

Bischöfliches Ordinariat Berlin (Diocesan authorities): Wundtstr. 48/50, Berlin 19. Tel: 32006-118

Jüdische Gemeinde zu Berlin (Berlin Jewish Community): Fasanenstr. 79/80, Berlin 12. Tel: 88420332/34

THEATRE & CULTURE

IN WEST BERLIN

Deutsche Oper Berlin (Berlin German Opera Company): Bismarckstrasse 35. Tel: 3414449

Schiller-Theater: Bismarckstr. 110. Tel: 3195236

Schloß-Theater: Schloßstr. 48. Tel: 7911213

Theater der Freien Volksbühne (Free People's Theatre): Schaperstr. 24. Tel: 8842080

Komödie (comedy theatre): Kurfürstendamm 206, Tel : 8827893

Renaissance-Theater: Knesebeckstr. 100. Tel: 3122053/54

Tribüne: Otto-Suhr-Allee 18–20. Tel: 3412600

Hansa-Theater: Alt-Moabit 48. Tel: 3914460

Berliner Kammerspiele (intimate theatre): Alt-Moabit 99. Tel: 3916531, 3915543

Kleines Theater im Südwestkorso: Südwestkorso 64. Tel: 8212021

Junges Theater (Youth Theatre): Friesenstr. 14. Tel: 6928735

Theatermanufaktur am Halleschen Ufer: Hallesches Ufer 32. Tel: 2510941

Freie Theateranstalt: Klausenerplatz 19. Tel: 3215889

Grips Theater: Altonaer Str. 22. Tel: 3914004

Rote Grütze: Mehringdamm 52. Tel: 6926618

Theater zum Westlichen Stadthirschen: Kreuzbergstr. 37. Tel: 7861009

Theater am Kurfürstendamm: Kurfürstendamm 206. Tel: 8823789

Schaubühne am Lehniner Platz: Kurfürstendamm 153. Tel: 890023

Mehringhoftheater: Gneisenaustrasse 2. Tel: 6918021

Tanzfabrik: Möckernstr. 68. Tel: 7865861

Transformtheater: Hasenheide 54, Tel: 6923239

Theater 36: Muskaner Str. 43. Tel: 6126294

Vaganten-Bühne: Kantstr. 12. Tel: 3124529

IN EAST BERLIN

Berliner Ensemble: Bertolt-Brecht-Platz. Tel: 2823160

Deutsche Staatsoper (German State Opera): Unter den Linden 7. Tel: 2054556

Deutsches Theater und Kammerspiele: Schumannstr. 13a. Tel: 2871225/26

Komische Oper (Comic Opera): Behrenstr. 55–57. Tel: 2292555

Maxim-Gorki-Theater: Am Festungs-

graben 2. Tel: 2071790
Metropol-Theater: Friedrichstr. 100–102.
Tel: 2071739
Puppentheater (Puppet Theatre):
Greifswalder Str. 81/84. Tel: 4361343
Schauspielhaus Berlin: (only used as a
concert hall) Platz der Akademie. Tel:
2272129
Theater der Freundschaft: H.-Rodenberg-
Platz/Parkaue 25. Tel: 5570306
Theater im Palast: Marx-Engels-Platz. Tel:
23823/54
Volksbühne (People's Theatre Organisa-
tion): Rosa-Luxemburg-Platz. Tel: 2829607
Friedrichstadt-Palast: Friedrichstr. 107.
Tel: 2836474
Die Distel: (Berlin Cabaret) Friedrichstr. 101.
Tel: 2071291; Degenerstr. 9. Tel: 3875174

THEATRE BOX OFFICES
Centrum: Meineckestr. 25, Berlin 15. Tel:
8827611
Concert Concept: Hauptstr. 83, Berlin 41.
Tel: 8524080
Europa Center box office: Tauentzienstr.
9, Berlin 30. Tel: 2617051
KaDeWe: Tauentzienstr. 21, Berlin 15. Tel:
248036
Ottfried Laur: Hardenbergstr. 7, Berlin 12.
Tel: 3137007
Sasse: Kurfürstendamm 24, Berlin 15. Tel:
8827360
Wertheim: Kurfürstendamm 231, Berlin 15.
Tel: 8822500
Wildbad Kiosk: Rankestr. 1, Berlin 30. Tel:
8814507
Theatre box office in Zehlendorf: Teltower
Damm 22, Berlin 37. Tel: 8011652

FOREIGN CULTURE CENTRES

IN WEST BERLIN

Amerika Haus Berlin: Hardenbergstr. 22/
24, Berlin 12. Tel: 8197661
Aspen Institut Berlin: Inselstr. 10, Berlin
38. Tel: 8039041
**The British Council – The British Centre
Berlin**: Hardenbergstr. 20, Berlin 12. Tel:
310176.
Institut Français de Berlin: Kurfürstendamm 211, Berlin 15. Tel: 8818702,
8817620.

IN EAST BERLIN

**Bulgarisches Kultur- und Information-
szentrum** (Bulgarian culture and information centre): Unter den Linden 10. Tel:
2000261, 2071505
Haus der Ungarischen Kultur (House of
Hungarian Culture): Karl-Liebknecht-Str. 9.
Tel: 2109146
**Kultur- und Informationszentrum der
CSFR** (Czechoslovakian culture and infor-
mation centre): Leipziger Str. 60. Tel:
2000231
**Polnisches Informations- und Kultur-
zentrum** (Polish culture and information
centre): Karl-Liebknecht-Str. 7. Tel: 2123268
Französisches Kulturzentrum (French
culture and information centre): Unter den
Linden 37. Tel: 2291020
**Haus der Deutsch-Sowjetischen Freund-
schaft** (German-Soviet Friendship Society):
Am Festungsgraben 1. Tel: 20010
**Haus der Sowjetischen Wissenschaft und
Kultur** (Centre of Soviet Science and Culture): Friedrichstr. 176–179. Tel: 2217320

VENUES

Akademie der Künste (Academy of Arts):
Hanseatenweg 10, Berlin 21. Tel: 3911031
Alte TU-Mensa (Technical University Re-
fectory): Hardenbergstr. 34, Berlin 12. Tel:
3112233
Audimax FU (Free University Auditorium):
Garystr./Ecke Boltzmannstr., Berlin 33.
Deutschlandhalle: Messedamm 26, Berlin
19. Tel: 30381
Eissporthalle (Ice-sport stadium): Jafféstr.,
Berlin 19. Tel: 30381
Hebbeltheater: Stresemannstr. 29, Berlin
61. Tel: 2512773
Hochschule der Künste (School of Art):
small concert hall and theatre: Fasanenstr. 1,
Berlin 12. Concert hall: Hardenbergstr. 33,
Berlin 12. Tel: 31850/31852374
ICC (International Congress Centre):
Messedamm, Berlin 15. Tel: 8813538
Jüdisches Gemeindehaus (Jewish Com-
munity Centre): Fasanenstr. 79–80, Berlin
12. Tel: 8813558
Bundesallee Concert Hall: Bundesallee 1–
12, Berlin 15. Tel: 310331
Kreuzberg Markt: Kreuzbergstr. 37/38,
Berlin 61. Tel: 7861009
Künstlerhaus Bethanien: Mariannenplatz

2, Berlin 36. Tel: 6148010
Literaturhaus (House of Literature): Fasanenstr. 23, Berlin 12. Tel: 4656604
Messehallen (Trade Fair): Am Funkturm, Berlin 19. Tel: 30381
Metropol: Nollendorfplatz 5, Berlin 30. Tel: 2164122
Olympic Stadium: Berlin 19. Tel: 3047472
Philharmonia: Matthäikirchstr. 1, Berlin 30. Tel: 254 88-0
State Library: Potsdamer Str. 33, Berlin 30. Tel: 2661
Tempodrom: An der Kongreßhalle, In den Zelten, Berlin 21. Tel: 3944045
Ufa factory for culture: Viktoriastr. 13, Berlin 42. Tel: 7528085
Urania: Kleiststr. 13–14, Berlin 30. Tel: 2490/91

MUSEUMS

IN WEST BERLIN

Anti-Kriegs-Museum (Anti-War Museum): Genter Str. 9, Berlin 65. Tel: 4617837
Ägyptisches Museum (The Egyptian Museum): Schloßstr. 70, Berlin 19. Tel: 32011
Antikenmuseum (Museum of Antiquity): Schloßstr. 1, Berlin 19
Berlin-Museum (Berlin Museum): Lindenstr. 14, Berlin 61. Tel: 2514015
Berlinische Galerie (Berlin Gallery): Stresemannstr. 110, Berlin 61 . Tel: 2586-0
Bauhaus-Archiv (Bauhaus Museum): Klingelhöferstr. 13–14, Berlin Tel: 2611618
Botanisches Museum (Botanical Museum): Königin-Luise-Str. 6–8, Berlin 33
Bröhan-Museum (Bröhan Collection): Schloßstr. 1a, Berlin 19. Tel: 3214029
Brücke-Museum: Bussardsteig 9, Berlin 33. Tel: 8312029
Deutsches Rundfunkmuseum (German Radio Museum): Hammarskjöldplatz 1, Berlin 19. Tel: 3028186
Friedensmuseum (Museum of Peace): Stresemannstr. 27, Berlin 61. Tel: 2510186
Gemäldegalerie (Painting Gallery): Arnimallee 23/27, Berlin 33. Tel: 418301-248
Georg-Kolbe-Museum: Sensburger Allee 25, Berlin 19. Tel: 3042144
Gipsformerei (plaster casts): Sophie-Charlotten-Str. 17–18, Berlin 19. Tel: 3222367
Große Orangerie (Large Orangery): Schloß Charlottenburg; Berlin 19. Tel: 3201253
Hamburger Bahnhof: Invalidenstr. 50, Berlin 21
Kleine Orangerie (Little Orangery): Schloß Charlottenburg; Berlin 19. Tel: 3005388
Kunstgewerbemuseum (Museum of Decorative Arts): Tiergartenstr. 6, Berlin 30. Tel: 2662902/03
Museums in Dahlem: Lansstr. 8, Berlin 33. Tel: 8301-438
Museumsdorf Düppel (Düppel Museum Village): Clauertstr. 11, Berlin 37. Tel: 8026671
Museum für Deutsche Volkskunde (Museum of German Folklore): Im Winkel 6/8 Berlin 33. Tel: 832031
Museum für Verkehr und Technik (Transport and Technical Museum): Trebbiner Str. 9, Berlin 61. Tel: 25484-0
Museum für Vor- und Frühgeschichte (The Museum of Pre- and Early History): Schloß Charlottenburg, Langhansbau, Berlin 19. Tel: 32011
Musikinstrumentenmuseum (Musical Instruments Museum): Entlastungsstr. 1, Berlin 30. Tel: 25481-0
Nationalgalerie (The National Gallery): Potsdamer Str. 50, Berlin 30. Tel: 2662662
Post- und Fernmeldemuseum (Museum of Postal and Telecommunication): An der Urania 15, Berlin 30. Tel: 2128201
Staatliche Kunsthalle (National Art Gallery): Budapester Str. 42, Berlin 30. Tel: 2617067

IN EAST BERLIN

Ausstellungszentrum am Fernsehturm (TV Tower Exhibition Centre): Am Alex. Tel: 2103293
The State Museums of Berlin (Museum Island): Bodestr. 1–3. Tel: 2200381
Märkisches Museum (Brandenburg Marches Museum): Am Köllnischen Park 5. Tel: 2 754902/24
Museum für Naturkunde (Museum of Natural History): Invalidenstr. 43. Tel: 28970
Museum für Deutsche Geschichte (Museum of German History): Unter den Linden 2. Tel: 2000591
Neuer Marstall: Marx-Engels-Platz 7. Tel: 2383287/2383311
Otto-Nagel-Haus: Märkisches Ufer 16–18. Tel: 2791402
Hugenotten-Museum (Huguenot Mu-

seum): (in the French Cathedral), Platz der Akademie, entrance Charlottenstr., Tel: 2291760

Kunstgewerbemuseum (Arts and Crafts Museum): (in Köpenick Palace), Schloßinsel. Tel: 6572651, 6571504

Deutsche Staatsbibliothek (German State Library): Unter den Linden 8. Tel: 20780

ART/PHOTO CREDITS

INDEX

Q & R

S

Y & Z